John Fiske, Grover Flint

Marching with Gomez

A War Correspondent's Field Notebook, Kept During Four Months....

John Fiske, Grover Flint

Marching with Gomez

A War Correspondent's Field Notebook, Kept During Four Months....

ISBN/EAN: 9783337165895

Printed in Europe, USA, Canada, Australia, Japan

Cover: Foto ©ninafisch / pixelio.de

More available books at **www.hansebooks.com**

Marching with Gomez

A War Correspondent's Field Note-Book
kept during Four Months with
the Cuban Army

By GROVER FLINT

Illustrated by the Author

With an Historical Introduction
By JOHN FISKE

Lamson, Wolffe and Company

Boston, New York, and London   MDCCCXCVIII

To A. S. F.

who in her lifetime
treasured his unskilled writings
and careless sketches
THE AUTHOR DEDICATES
this book

Contents

		Page
Introduction	. . . .	xi

Searching for Gomez

Chapter
I.	A Pacifico Household	3
II.	Savanas Nuevas	12
III.	Singeing the King's Beard	28
IV.	A Skirmish with the "Gringos" . .	34
V.	"Pacified Matanzas"	43
VI.	With Lacret and his Staff	55
VII.	The Prefectura Pedrosa	72
VIII.	Marto's Men	79
IX.	The Zone of Cienfuegos	89
X.	Typical Atrocities — The Olayita Massacre .	98
XI.	Crossing the Line	110

Marching with Gomez

I.	The Man under the Hub	119
II.	Gomez' Staff	129
III.	Manajanabo	139
IV.	Our Last Skirmish in Las Villas . .	147

Chapter		Page
V.	Into Camaguey	159
VI.	Gomez' Moral Campaign in Camaguey	174
VII.	Gomez and Hernandez	186
VIII.	The Battle of Saratoga	198
IX.	Echoes of Saratoga	214
X.	The Itinerant Government	222
XI.	Cuba Libre	237
XII.	The Sub-prefectura Yatal	254
Appendix A		271
Appendix B		276
Appendix C		280
Appendix D		282

Introduction

THE first glimpse that we get of Cuba, after its discovery by Columbus, reveals to us with startling vividness the impression already entertained in the island with regard to Spaniards. It was not until 1511 that they began to occupy Cuba. The wrecking of Columbus' best ship on the coast of Hispaniola (Hayti) led to the founding of the first settlements upon that coast, and the discovery of gold in 1496 began bringing Spaniards by hundreds to the New World. How they behaved themselves in beautiful Hispaniola was long ago described for us by the good Las Casas, in his famous book, "The Destruction of the Indies." The story makes one of the most hideous chapters in the history of mankind. Rumors of what was going on from time to time reached the ears of a certain important chieftain in the neighboring island of Cuba, and he sent spies over to Hispaniola, who more than confirmed the worst things that had been reported. One day this chieftain, whose name was Hatuey, found a large ingot of gold and forthwith called together his tribal council. " Know ye, my brethren," said he, " that this yellow thing is the god of the Spaniards; wherefore let us propitiate it with songs and dances, and pray it to turn the mind of those people away from coming to Cuba."

So the Indians danced around the ingot until they grew weary, when their chief further observed, "Let not this deity remain above ground and visible, lest if the Spaniards come peradventure he may prompt them to wickedness." So the yellow idol was picked up and thrown into the river. Thus did these cunning red men seek at once to cajole and to baffle the enemy. But it was in vain. In the year 1511 came Diego Velasquez, and it was not long before poor Hatuey was tied to a stake and fagots piled about him. While the flames were licking the flesh from his bones, a black-robed priest held up the crucifix and begged him to repent of his sins and secure a place in heaven. "Where is heaven?" cried Hatuey; "are there any Spaniards there?" "Yea, many," quoth the priest. "Then," said the writhing victim, "pray let me go somewhere else."

The dismal reputation thus won by the Spaniards, when they first took possession of the island of Cuba, has been maintained by them to the present day, when they are clearly fast losing their hold upon it. Here, as in other parts of America, the Spanish conquest created a situation which must sooner or later become unendurable. Under varying circumstances the rule of the Spaniard has nearly always been odious, not only to the aboriginal races but to the Creoles of his own blood. Not that the coming of Spaniards to the New World was everywhere an unmixed evil. There were quarters where they introduced a better state of things than they found. In Mexico, for example, there can be no doubt that the change from the hideous priests of Huitzilopochtli to the noble followers of St. Francis and St. Dominic was as welcome as it was salutary. Even in Peru, where aboriginal America appears on the whole at its best, the rule of the Spanish viceroys proved in some respects less oppressive than that of the Incas. It should further be remembered that among the Spaniards who for three centuries made up the governing classes in the tropical and southern portions of America, not all were tyrants. Among them were reckless adventurers, with whom all considerations of policy or humanity were lost in the ravening thirst for pelf. But there were others eminent for virtue and ability, such as the illustrious Marquis de Cañete, who governed Peru so admirably in the sixteenth century; or Don José de Vertiz, the enlightened ruler of Buenos Ayres in the eighteenth.

On the whole, however, after making all due qualifications, the Spanish system of government in America was so thoroughly bad that even in the hands of saints it could not have succeeded. It was based upon two bad things, commercial monopoly and political despotism. As regards the first of these, the original purpose of all European states in founding colonies beyond sea was to obtain a commercial monopoly. This was well illustrated in the English Navigation Act of 1651. In order that merchants in England might buy Virginia tobacco very cheap, the demand for it was restricted by cutting off the export to foreign markets. In order that they might sell their goods to Virginia at exorbitant prices, the Virginians were prohibited from buying elsewhere. Similar restrictions were placed upon the trade of the other English colonies, and the shameless rapacity of the merchants was such as might have been expected under such fostering circumstances. The effects of this unjust legislation are well known. It was potent among the causes of Bacon's Rebellion in Virginia, it kept Massachusetts in a chronic brawl with Charles II., it bred fierce discontents in New York, it raised up legions of smugglers, it added a fresh lease of life to piracy, and it had much to do with the irritation that led to our War of Independence.

The misguided commercial greed exhibited in such legislation reminds one of Æsop's dog who dropped the bone while snatching at its shadow. In the infancy of modern commerce all nations fell into such errors, and Spain was no worse than the rest. But the restrictive navigation laws of Spain were always more vexatious than those of England, because they were much more rigorously and harshly administered. Here we come upon the companion evil in Spanish colonial rule, its political despotism. If we would properly understand the revolt of Spain's colonies, we shall do well to compare and contrast it with our own revolt against the government of George III. The English colonies in America never suffered anything that could be called oppression, except for a brief moment under Berkeley in Virginia and under Andros in New England; but Berkeley's violence led to his removal, and the policy which Andros tried to enforce was quickly overthrown by a revolution in England, so that neither of these instances counts for much against the mother country. Our forefathers on this side of the Atlantic were not liable to arbitrary imprisonment or extortionate taxes, the privacy of their homes was not invaded, and they were free to speak and print their thoughts; when things went wrong they could scold and grumble to their hearts' content. They severed their political connection with England, not in order to gain new liberties, but to guard against the possible risk of losing old ones. Far different was it with the people of the Spanish colonies at the beginning of the present century. Their government, under viceroys and captains general sent out from Spain, was an absolute despotism. They were subject to arbitrary and oppressive taxation. The people of English America refused to submit to a very light stamp tax, imposed purely for American interests, to defend the frontier against Indian raids; the people of Spanish America saw vast amounts of treasure carried away year after year to be spent upon European enterprises in which they felt no interest whatever. They had no popular assemblies, no *habeas corpus* acts, no freedom of the press. Their houses were not their castles, for the minions of the civil and of the spiritual power could penetrate everywhere; a petty quarrel between neighbors might end in dragging some of them before the Inquisition, to be tortured or put to death for heresy. For that pre-eminently Spanish and Satanic institution survived in America until two decades of the nineteenth century had passed.

What was the Inquisition? It was a machine for winnowing out and destroying all such individuals as surpassed the average in quickness of wit, earnestness of purpose, and strength of character, in so far as to entertain opinions of their own and boldly declare them. The more closely people approached an elevated standard of intelligence and moral courage, the more likely was the machine to reach them. It worked with deadly efficiency, cutting off the brightest and boldest in their early prime, while the duller and weaker spirits were spared to propagate the race. Thus the ideas and methods which other nations were devising to meet the new exigencies of modern life were denied admission into Spain. In manufactures, in commerce, in the control of the various sources of wealth, she was completely left behind by nations from which the minds hospitable toward new ideas had not been so carefully weeded out. In many respects the atmosphere of thought in Spain remains mediæval even to the present day. In the government of her dependencies her methods have shown scarcely any improvement since the Middle Ages, and it was not strange that the advent of this stirring nineteenth century should bring rebellion. Some drops of the yeast so plentifully scattered by the French Revolution found their way into tropical America and set up a ferment in that oppressed society.

The countries first to feel the effects were Venezuela and New Granada, which were the most accessible to European ideas from the French and English West Indies; and the temporary overthrow of the Spanish monarchy by Napoleon seemed to furnish the occasion. The revolution which began in Venezuela in 1810 was extended to the Argentine states, and then across to Chili, until it reached and set free Peru in 1824. Meanwhile, Mexico was winning its independence, and the pentarchy of Central America soon followed. At the same time Florida was purchased by the United States, so that of all the immense transatlantic empire to which Columbus had led the way nothing remained in Spanish hands save the islands of Cuba and Porto Rico.

While Cuba has always been highly valued by Spain, its importance in the eighteenth century was small compared to what it has come to be in recent years. In the middle of the century the island passed for a moment out of Spanish control. In 1762 Spain added her arms to those of France, Austria, and Russia, in the tremendous war which those powers were unsuccessfully waging against Great Britain and Prussia. As a result, the English captured Havana and held the island practically at their mercy, but the treaty of 1763 restored it to Spain in exchange for Florida and other important concessions.[1] It would probably have been far better for the interests of civilization and good government in Cuba if the island had remained in British hands. It is significant that the sanitary condition of Havana seems never to have been so well cared for as in 1762, and the mediæval restrictions upon trade were in a considerable measure relaxed. After this brief interval the restoration of Spanish control was a reversion to the old state of things.

At the beginning of the nineteenth century the population of the island was about 400,000 souls, of whom rather less than half were negro slaves. The native Indians had long since been exterminated. The whites, mostly of Spanish descent, lived on their farms and knew next to nothing

[1] In the treaty of 1783 Great Britain restored Florida to Spain.

about the outside world. No foreign ship could touch at a Cuban port. All commerce was prohibited save with Spain, and thus the market for sugar and tobacco was narrow and the production small. Cooped up within this legislative Chinese wall, the people were densely ignorant. Nearly all the products of the soil were consumed where they grew, division of labor was scarcely known, and there was but little circulation of ideas. Under such circumstances it is not strange that the prevalent mental attitude was one of Toryism. A dread of horrors like those so near at hand in San Domingo may well have aided this conservative feeling and helped to prevent Cuba from joining in the general revolt against Spain. In 1808, when Napoleon deposed the reigning Bourbons, the Cuban provincial council resolved unanimously to preserve the allegiance of the island to that legitimate dynasty, and Ferdinand VII. was proclaimed king. European events were fast tying Napoleon's hands, or this bold action might have called down his wrath upon Cuba, even as the heroic career of Toussaint Louverture had drawn it down upon San Domingo. For such an act of loyalty Cuba came to be known as the "Ever Faithful Isle."

One effect of the French Revolution upon Spain was the slow and painful introduction of a few modern ideas. Some wholesome warnings of experience found their way through the thick panoply of dulness that protected Ferdinand VII. against wisdom and prosperity. The spirit of revolt had become so rife in Spanish America that it was thought worth while to reward and perpetuate

Cuba's loyalty by a more liberal policy. Accordingly in 1813 the ports of the Island were thrown open to commerce, and two years afterward the government monopoly of tobacco was abolished. The Cubans were also allowed to elect representatives to the Spanish Cortes, but this privilege proved to be of small practical use, and was afterwards withdrawn. The effects, however, of the new commercial policy were astonishing, especially upon the growth of tobacco and sugar. Within a few years these crops had increased fourfold. Between the beginning and the end of the nineteenth century the production of sugar has increased nearly a hundredfold. Of this huge crop scarcely two per cent goes to Spain, while England takes fifteen per cent and the United States seventy-five. These figures enable us to realize the wonderful expansion consequent upon the opening of Cuban ports. Under such conditions the population of the island has increased to more than a million and a half. The relative proportion of negroes has decreased until it is scarcely more than one-fourth, and slavery was finally abolished in 1886.

The rapid growth of the "Ever Faithful Isle" was in great measure helped by the contemporaneous revolt of the other portions of Spanish America. Thousands of native Spaniards who in former times would have enjoyed official positions or special business privileges in such countries as Peru, or Buenos Ayres, or Venezuela, now found such sources of emolument cut off. Consequently this particular stream of immigration, which had once overflowed the whole of Spanish America, became confined to Cuba and Porto ·Rico. These favored immigrants in Cuba form the class of "Peninsulars," while the native Cuban Creoles are distinguished as the "Insulars." At the present time it is supposed that about one-fifth of the white people of Cuba are Peninsulars, or natives of Spain. They have for a long time monopolized the salaried positions in church and state and managed all matters of public administration to suit themselves. The distinction between Creole and European Spaniard is maintained as strongly as ever it was in the old days of the Viceroys of Lima; and the political connection with the mother country has long been used simply to enable one-fifth of the white population to treat the other four-fifths as having no rights which are entitled to respect.

This unwholesome state of things in Cuba has been growing up ever since the general revolt of Spanish America. The liberal commercial measures of 1813 and 1815 were not accompanied by liberal measures in politics. Nothing like real self-government was allowed the "Ever Faithful Isle." On the contrary, she was governed by a series of captains general, with powers as despotic as those of the Grand Turk. Thus there grew up an antagonism between the Peninsulars, with the captain general at their head, and the Insulars, who were on all occasions made to feel their inferior position; and, as always in such cases, this antagonism was far more venomous and implacable than that which exists between political parties in free countries. The Insulars were naturally in favor of a larger measure of self-government in which their superiority of numbers might enable them to outvote and curb their haughty opponents; on the other hand, the Peninsulars clung to Spanish despotism as their chief refuge and defence. On such lines have the hostile parties been developing for the past eighty years.

During this period the Insulars or liberal party have been getting the rudiments of political education by observing what has gone on in the republics of Spanish America and in the United States. People in their situation have no opportunities for gaining political experience of the kind with which all English-speaking countries are familiar. They start with a few general political ideas and have no means of testing their value save by insurrection. The first task is to overthrow the oppressor, and every patriot of this way of thinking is sure to be "agin" the government. Between 1820 and 1830 there were several attempts at rebellion in Cuba, fomented by such secret societies as the "Soles de Bolivar," the "Black Eagle," and others; but these premature outbreaks were quickly suppressed. The chief immediate result was the tightening of the despotic control of the captains general. The government was one of martial law, even in times of peace. The unfortunate conspiracy of 1844, for complicity with which the Cuban poet Placido was executed, and the ill-starred expeditions of Narciso Lopez in 1849 and 1851, bear witness at once to the abiding spirit of discontent among the people and to the superior strength which a better organization gave to the oppressors.

From 1851 to 1868 the smouldering fires found

little chance for breaking into flame. The revolution of September, 1868, which drove Queen Isabella II. from Spain, furnished an occasion of which the Insulars were not slow to avail themselves. On October 10 the independence of Cuba was proclaimed by Carlos de Céspedes, who soon had a force of 15,000 men marching under his orders. In the following April a congress, assembled at the town of Guáymaro, framed a republican constitution for Cuba and elected Céspedes president. Mexico and several states of South America at once recognized the Cubans as belligerents, and within two months Peru recognized them as an independent power.

The war thus begun lasted nearly ten years, until it was brought to an end by the treaty or capitulation of El Zanjon in 1878. It is known as the Ten Years' War. For the first two years the revolutionary forces seemed to have the advantage, but their cause was ruined by contentions and misunderstandings arising from the interference of the civil power with the military. The broth was spoiled by too many cooks, and the single-willed despot was enabled to score a triumph over the many-headed King Demos. In 1873 the Congress deposed Céspedes and elected in his place Salvador Cisneros, the same who again was president during Mr. Flint's stay in Cuba in 1896. Some mystery hangs over the circumstances of the death of Céspedes in 1874, but he seems to have been murdered by Spaniards.

The Ten Years' War was a terrible drain upon the resources of the government at Madrid. More than 150,000 troops were sent over from Spain, and of these more than 80,000 are said to have found their graves in Cuba. The revolutionary forces were always much smaller than their antagonists, as well as inferior in arms and equipments; besides which, the Spanish navy controlled the water. The only prudent strategy for the insurgents was the Fabian kind that avoids pitched battles, a tedious policy, but apt to be highly effective in the long run. What the Cubans accomplished by such methods and by guerilla warfare was extremely encouraging. The net result of the Ten Years' War afforded good ground for the opinion that they might try the experiment of revolution once more with strong hopes of success.

That they would try it again could hardly be doubtful. The capitulation of El Zanjon was achieved only through the understanding that abuses were to be reformed. The first article of the document implicitly concedes to Cubans representation in the Cortes at Madrid. From such a concession further reforms were expected to follow. It was clear enough that nothing short of effective reform could prevent the renewal of revolution. No such reform was secured. As far as representation at Madrid was concerned, that was soon rendered a nullity by the Peninsulars contriving to get control of the polls and prevent the election of any but their own men. It is said that of the 30 deputies chosen in 1896, all but four were natives of Spain. Bearing this in mind, let us note some other features of political reform, as conceived by the Spanish mind. The power of the captain general had been absolute. In 1895 an attempt was made to limit it by providing him with a council of 30 members, of whom 15 were to be appointed by the Crown and 15 were to be elected by the people. Of course the same influence over elections which made representation at Madrid a mere farce would control the choice of councillors. It might safely be assumed that at least 10 of the 15 would be the abettors or the pliant tools of the captain general. But to guard against any possible failure on this point, the captain general can "suspend" members who oppose him, until he has suspended 14 of the 30. If even then he cannot get a majority to uphold him, he is not yet at the end of his resources. Far from it. There is another advisory body, called the "council of authorities." Its members are the Archbishop of Santiago, the Bishop of Havana, the chief justice, the attorney general, the chief of the finance bureau, the director of local administration, and the commanders of the military and naval forces.[1] Armed with the consent of these advisers, who are pretty certain to be all of them Peninsulars, our captain general goes back to his refractory council and "suspends" all that is left of it. Then, like Wordsworth's river, he "wanders at his own sweet will."

Now one of the duties of this wonderful council was to regulate taxation and expenditures. So it made its budget, and if the captain general was satisfied with it, very well; if not, he just set it aside and did as he pleased. As Caliban would say, "As it likes me each time I do: so He!" After this, it need not surprise us to be told that each province

[1] For a more detailed account see Rowan and Ramsey, "The Island of Cuba," New York, 1897.

in Cuba has its elected representative assembly, which the autocrat at Havana may suspend at his pleasure; or that the island is abundantly supplied with courts, whose decisions he is at full liberty to overrule. We learn next, as a matter of course, that if you write a book or pamphlet containing criticisms of the autocrat or his policy, you cannot get it printed; or if you are an editor and publish such pestilent stuff in your paper, he forthwith claps you into durance vile, and confiscates a part or the whole of your balance at the bank. Political meetings as such cannot be held. Clubs for charitable purposes or for social entertainment may meet after due notice given the autocrat, so that he may be present himself or send his spies; then let the teller of anecdotes, the maker of jests, and the singer of songs keep the tongue well guarded, lest the company be dispersed before supper and the neighboring jail receive new inmates.

In such a political atmosphere corruption thrives. A planter's estate is entered upon the assessor's lists as worth $50,000; the collector comes along and demands a tax based upon an assumed value of $70,000; the planter demurs, but presently thinks it prudent to compromise upon a basis of $60,000. No change is made in the published lists, but the collector slips into his own pocket the tax upon $10,000, and goes on his way rejoicing. Thus the planter is robbed while the Government is cheated. And this is a fair specimen of what goes on throughout all departments of administration. From end to end the whole system is honeycombed with fraud.

The people of Cuba would not be worthy of our

respect if they were capable of submitting tamely to such wholesale oppression and pillage. They are to be commended for the spirit of resistance which showed itself in the Ten Years' War; and it is much to their credit that, after repeated proof of the hopelessness of any peaceful reform, they have once more risen in rebellion. It was early in 1895 that the present war broke out. To attempt to forecast its results would be premature. It is already obvious, however, that Spain's grasp upon the island is considerably weaker than before. She had not recovered from the strain of the Ten Years' War when the present struggle began. Stimulated to extraordinary efforts by the dread of revolution at home in the event of ill success, the Spanish government has shown desperate energy. Never before have such large armies been sent beyond sea. Such armies, however, are not worth their cost unless they can find and crush the enemy, and thus far the Fabian generalship of Gomez has defied them successfully. A lesson has been learned from the Ten Years' War, for this shrewd and far-sighted leader accepted the chief command on condition that he should be free from all interference on the part of the civil authorities. The problem before him is, while avoiding battles against heavy odds, to keep up hostilities until Spain's ability to borrow money comes to an end. In such a policy he has much reason to hope for success.

The recent offer of autonomy to Cuba wears all the appearance of a last card played by Spain in distress. It is made in the hope of dividing the revolutionists into two parties of moderates and irreconcilables; but the few particulars thus far made public indicate that the card is not skilfully played, that the semblance of autonomy offered is too palpably deceptive. The attitude of Gomez, if it is correctly reported, seems to show that he realizes that, while there are many occasions in life in which compromises and half-measures are desirable, the present is not one of them.

For the sake of Cuba's best interests, it is to be hoped that she will win her independence without receiving from any quarter, and especially from the United States, any such favors as might hereafter put her in a position of tutelage or in any wise hamper her freedom of action. All people liberated from the blight of Spanish dominion need to learn the alphabet of free government. Cuba will have to learn it, as all the rest of Spanish America has had to learn it, and the fewer the impediments in her way the better. Undue influence on the part of powerful neighbors is sure to be such an impediment.

One often hears arguments based on the assumption that Spanish Americans are congenitally unfit for political liberty; and the numerous convulsions of the present century in Mexico and South America are cited in point. But it is easy to reason loosely in such matters; and unless our vision covers somewhat longer ranges of time, our reasoning is sure to be loose. For example, it is a maxim at the present day that Frenchmen are politically unstable and really do not know what kind of government they want; while Englishmen, on the other hand, are the very type of stability and satisfied conservatism. There has been no violent change of government in England for more than two centuries, while on the other hand since 1792 France has had at least eight such changes. The contrast seems conclusive. But if we go back a century and a half, to the days when Voltaire and Diderot were in their prime, we find just the opposite opinion current. Then it was the English who were said to be incurably fickle in politics, while the French were steady and conservative. Since the tenth century France had never deposed a king, whereas the English had unseated five, three of whom were first deposed and then secretly murdered, one was publicly beheaded, and one driven into exile. In the seventeenth century England was a monarchy, a commonwealth under the Rump Parliament, a protectorate under Cromwell, a headless body under Monk and the army, then a monarchy again, then a monarchy put into commission. Could anything ever make an Englishman satisfied with his government?

With such an example before us, we may well pause before concluding that because the liberation of Spanish America has been attended with crude experiments in self-government and occasional catastrophes, therefore it is an immutable decree of Providence that no people are fit to govern themselves except those who speak English. Our high political capacity is the fruit of slow ages of discipline under favoring circumstance, and similar acquisition, on the part of any people whatever, must likewise be the result of discipline. The first step is the removal of obstacles; and the Spanish method of governing dependencies, a belated relic of mediævalism, is an anomaly that cannot be too soon removed. All honor to the men who shall succeed in dealing its deathblow!

The visit of my son-in-law, Mr. Grover Flint, to Cuba, early in 1896, was made with the purpose of obtaining correct information as to what was going on in the island. A brief stay at Havana was enough to assure him that the information received in that city was likely to be anything but correct. He therefore made up his mind to break away and visit the insurgents, in order to satisfy himself by ocular inspection as to the various points upon which he wished to be informed. Some experience of life on the Plains as a soldier in the United States army had prepared him for the kind of adventures involved in the undertaking, and he had lived in Spain long enough to become familiar with the language, as well as with Spanish ideas and mental habits. Under these circumstances, and with exceptional opportunities for observation, he gathered the materials for the narrative which follows; in which his purpose has been to tell the "plain unvarnished tale" of what he saw and heard.

JOHN FISKE.

Christmas, 1897.

SEARCHING FOR GOMEZ

Marching with Gomez

Chapter I

A Pacifico Household

SNUG in a grove of bushy, green poplars lay a neat, one-storied Cuban homestead, Andalusian in style, with white "dobe" walls, an old-fashioned, red pot-tiled roof, and broad, shady porches. From a wing that gave an open side on the main building where it faced the west, a curl of bluish smoke rose among the trees, and a lean old negress, turbaned like a Southern mammy, bustled at her cooking. Fat geese waddled in and out of the cook-house in search of scraps, while a family of peacocks, perched over a tumble-down farm wagon, were scarcely awake after the heat of a long afternoon. There was peace and rest about the place, as if fire and machete would never sweep from the distant highway to the little home among the poplars.

On the east porch, away from the murmur of the kitchen and the stir of farmyard creatures, a gray-headed, gray-bearded, powerfully built old gentleman, with a complexion burned and dried by sun and wind, bent over a table painting, with hair pencil and a colorless fluid, leaves of written paper. A little girl hung on his shoulder, taking the leaves in turn and placing them where the sun's slanting rays and the heat given off by the earth might quickly dry them. Then a new writing loomed out on each sheet, and the old man read secret instructions from the revolutionary Junta in Havana to be transmitted to troops in the field.

Just within the open doorway the Señora and her elder daughter, Gloria, in broad white kerchiefs and black stuff dresses, busied themselves at sewing; while a boy of twelve sat swinging his feet in an American cane chair, playing at invalid with his left arm in a sling from a wound by a Spanish bullet.

Such was a pacifico household not many leagues out of Cardenas, which I surprised late on the afternoon of March 25, 1896, by squirming through the barbed wire fence of the pasture.

A ripping of tweed cloth, as I disengaged myself from the wires, brought a giggle from the little girl, and a quick glance from the old man, who rose and advanced to meet me. "Caramba, señor, you have dropped from the clouds! Whence do you come, sir, that you do not travel by the roads?" he asked, scanning me closely. My explanation that I was an American correspondent, anxious to join the rebels, and had footed it across country from the railroad track leading to Recreo, seemed to reassure him, although, saving my passport, I bore no credentials. Faith and courtesy are instinctive with Cubans of the better class.

"Your face is a guarantee," he said thoughtfully, and I was "in my house" at once.

The ladies came from within and greeted me with polite curiosity. I must be fatigued by my long walk. I must rest myself. A guest was an event, now that the country was dangerous, and I must be cared for. While I attempted to answer these friendly solicitations, the old gentleman disappeared, boldly leaving his cipher despatches unconcealed. Presently he returned with a flask of Cognac and two little glasses, — copitas, — and we drank to better times. The yellow liquor was low in the bottle, seeming to indicate the frugality of my host's circumstances.

Then I showed my new friends a "*Detente,*" that was given me, with wishes for good luck, before I left Cardenas. It was a little, scalloped strip of white flannel, embroidered in silk with a crimson heart, a green cross, and a scroll of leaves, and the motto "*Detente! El corazon de Jesus esta conmigo.*" (Be of good cheer! The heart of Jesus is with me.) It was a simple insurgent emblem, such as the busy little fingers of the faithful Cuban maidens in Cardenas stitch in numbers to be sent out secretly to brothers, sweethearts, and cousins in the Manigua — "in the woods," as the Cubans term life in the insurgent ranks. I had pinned it on my shirt; — who could fail with such a talisman? — and I think it increased the ladies' trust in a stranger. The members of the family evidently felt no further anxiety on my score; for they resumed their occupations, leaving me to my cigar.

"*A simple insurgent emblem.*"

As I rested on the hospitable porch, red beams of the setting sun tinged the green of marsh and canebrake, and lingered on the foot-hills that rose half a league away between us and the sea. Darkness fell by degrees, and, excepting sounds from the cook-house, the stillness was unbroken. Then yellow beeswax candles were lighted, and we gathered in the main room, where I took my first supper outside the Spanish lines.

The supper was a simple "mess" of beef and sweet-potatoes. It was served on a rough deal table, by an elderly man-servant, who addressed the members of the family with "thee" and "thou," and loitered benignantly in the room while we ate. It was a sombre room, darkened by heavy old furniture,—a black-walnut wardrobe, an upright desk, a case of gloomy old books, and a few high-backed chairs of unvarnished oak. The plastered walls, except where our distorted shadows blackened them, shone yellow in the taper light, with an effect like a Rembrandt picture. Only two bits of color enlivened the walls,—a tinted engraving of the Virgin in a gilt frame, and an illuminated calendar of Saints' Days and holy festivals for the year 1895, as announced by the Bishop of Havana.

After supper, as a substitute for the luxury of coffee, small cups of guarapo — sugar dissolved in heated water — were served with cigarettes; in which Gloria and her mother joined us.

My host was a doctor of medicine and a man of attainments, with the proud elegance of manner of the old school. We talked of belligerency and possible intervention by the United States. I listened to the little boy's story, how, while riding a pet donkey from a pasture near the railroad track, a train had passed and soldiers had practised their marksmanship from the armored cars, shattering his arm and killing the donkey.

So the evening passed. When the ladies withdrew, I stepped out into the night to a shed that formed part of the kitchen and watched the negro farm-hands grind cane by torchlight on a hand crusher, and boil the sap to make sugar: some for use in the family, some for the local Cuban guerilla. Then to bed in a guest chamber adjacent to the cook-house, with a door that closed only when you propped it with a heavy beam.

In the quiet of my little room, with only the moving of a night breeze through a window in which there was no glass — there never is glass in Cuba — I slept peacefully until the barking of dogs brought the remembrance of war and danger. Some one had arrived and was talking earnestly with my host, and I heard a clink, as if the flask of Cognac was doing honor to another guest. Then came a soft beating of horses' hoofs that presently died away in the distance, and all was quiet again until daybreak.

The significance of this incident became apparent when my host awoke me with a morning cup of guarapo. He disturbed me early, he said, because he had learned that a Spanish column was preparing to move through the district, and I had best pass the day in a place of safety.

Taking my grip, Pablo, the family servant, led me by a blind path among the canes to a little bayou that reached far into the swamp "for many miles," he said. A rough, flat boat lay partly in the lily pads, partly on the soft bank, and we embarked, poling down stream for, perhaps, two hundred yards, to a spot where a group of palm trees grew from an island, offering a cool shelter from the sun.

A young man in a freshly washed linen suit was there swinging comfortably in his hammock, between a palm and a clump of bamboo, and rolling cigarettes. He wore a rebel cockade on his hat, his pistol and machete hung in easy reach, and his muzzle-loading shotgun rested against the palm trunk. He was the first insurgent soldier I had met. He had ridden the country all night and was resting in security for the day. His horse, he told me, was browsing among the canes near the farmhouse I had left. Pablo had brought a basket of cold beef and potatoes, and the water was clear and sweet,

"*Swinging comfortably in his hammock.*"

"though dangerous for Spaniards — it gave them a fever," he said, so I was left with my insurgent to spend the day.

I sketched my friend and shared his cigarettes, then we napped, he in his hammock, I in the shifting shade of the palms, until noon, when we heard the train, puffing and wheezing in the distance, on the railroad track by which I had come out the day before. We heard a shot, too, but only one, and knew that some soldier had shot at a crow, a vulture, or, perhaps, a stray cow. Then, as the afternoon wore on, dark clouds with showers of rain blew down from the north, and just in time to save us a drenching, Pablo's bark glided down the bayou, to take us back for supper. The weather was to be bad, and there was no longer danger of soldiers.

News passes mysteriously and swiftly among the patriot brotherhood. After supper that evening,— and a fitfully stormy evening it was, — there came a quick slapping of unshod hoofs outside in the wet grass, and four well-armed, neatly dressed insurgents — one of them with the stars of a captain on his cross-belt — reined up and dismounted by the door. They led an extra horse for the correspondent, and after a farewell feast of cigarettes and guarapo, I bade an all-around good-by. On parting, as a practical keepsake, my host gave me a jicara,— a polished cocoanut shell such as they use for cups in the field, — through a hole in which the Señorita Gloria knotted a cord, that it might hang easily from my belt. Then I swung up with the rest and rode off in the darkness, noticing that my companions placed me in the middle; two riding single file ahead and two behind.

I was at length safe under the wing of the insurrection, far safer than the members of the family that had received me so kindly, though I did not realize this fully as the warm light from their open shutters dimmed in the distance. I was soon to learn that in western Cuba the only approach to safety lay in the insurgent field, and that all country people, who remained in their houses, were as hostages to the enemy.

I do not mention my kind old host's name for many and obvious reasons. Desolation came to his home at last, and some months ago he fell under the machete while defending a field hospital.

Whether the Señorita Gloria, with her widowed mother, her brother, and her little sister, met outrage and death, or are herded, a starving family group, among the fever-stricken concentrados in some pestilential seaport town, I have never learned.

Chapter II

Savanas Nuevas

BANKS of clouds obscured the moon, and cool showers blew in from the sea as we zigzagged by guarda-rayas[1] in the canefields, and through the tall moist grass of the pastures, up a hilly trail into the forest. Sometimes as

"*Savanas Nuevas lies among the scrubby foothills of the coast, surrounded by swamps and mountains. You approach it by a blind trail that winds from the valley for nearly a league among the forests. Twenty well-armed men could hold that trail against a Spanish regiment.*" (Letter to *Journal*, April, 1896.)

we passed a clearing and the shadowy outline of a peasant's hut, dogs awoke and bayed until we were out of hearing. Once as we splashed through a

[1] *Guarda-rayas*: aisles or passages for marking sections and carrying off cut cane.

deep pool, a great white bird arose and floated, spirit-like, into the night ahead of us. We rode silently for perhaps an hour, slipping about in the mud on up grades, and trotting when our path offered a level, until a sharp challenge, "Alto! Quien va? (Halt! Who goes?)" brought us to a stop. "Cuba," shouted the captain.

"Avanza uno! (Advance one!)" came from the mysterious sentry in the bush. Then our captain jogged forward a dozen paces with the pass-word, and called for us to follow.

We were now past the pickets in a permanent Cuban camp. From constant chopping of hoofs, the path was deep and heavy, while every wind brought to the nostrils a stench of dead cattle that mist and rain could not beat down. Boughs of trees struck my face, and I hung forward in the saddle, letting my mount flounder after the others without guidance, through criss-cross, gully-like paths and clumps of clinging foliage. So on for a bewildered interval, guarding my head with my right elbow from showers of drops and swaying branches, and clutching my horse with the "full leg," till I felt the sharp play of his forehand muscles, when a sudden turn brought us into a circle of light, and we reined up before a low rancho, where pale figures stood about a sputtering camp-fire, poking and feeding it. One, taller than the rest, turned and stepped toward us.

"Dismount," said the tall insurgent, as he singled me from my companions and advanced with extended hand. It was Juan José Andarje, major of the force, and he welcomed me to Savanas Nuevas.

It was too wet for conversation. Andarje gave up to me a couch of saplings under the eaves of his rancho, and took himself somewhere else for the night. He lighted a short taper, sticking a bit of twig cross-wise in the wax just below the flame,—a Mambi[1] trick to prevent its blowing out.

By this flickering candle-light I got my bearings, and stepped under the low roof, dodging and ducking to avoid the pistols, rifles, and despatch boxes that hung everywhere from above. My couch was of branches, with an old coat rolled up, old pieces of blanket, and empty saddle-bags for cushions. A bulky form snored on a similar cot opposite me. Between the snoring soldier and myself were three hammocks, slung from the rustic trusses overhead, near enough to each other to bump when occupied. They were for the captain and two lieutenants under Andarje, who, taking advantage of the light, came in after me.

The feeble flame threatened to go out in every gust of wind; so taking off my soggy boots, and wrapping my feet in my damp covert coat, I turned in. With sheath knife and six-shooter wrapped in my broad-brimmed felt sombrero, and tucked pillow-wise under my head, I dropped off to sleep, wondering if dawn would prove my new friends cut-throats and brigands, as Prince Iturbide, and some acquaintances, friends of the Spanish legation, had described them to me at the Metropolitan Club in Washington.

---

[1] *Mambi:* a term implying savage and uncouth origin, equivalent to "Digger-Indian," bestowed on the insurgents by the Spaniards during the last war. The word, however, pleased the rebels' sense of humor, and they now, jokingly, if not seriously, apply it to themselves as a nickname.

The sun of March 27th rose bright and clear, and Antonio, the staff cook, a merry, stumpy little rebel, was up with the birds, noisily heating a can of guarapo. The hammocks beside me were empty, so I pulled on my boots and went out to dry them in the ashes of the cook-fire.

Then Camarioca, Andarje's big negro asistente,[1] brought me a fat juicy sugar-cane, and taught me how to whittle the bark from the bottom up, and carve it into white, nutritious sections, — a fine cool substitute for bread.

"Antonio, the staff cook."

Antonio was fanning a bundle of green sticks to a flame with his hat, and I sat down on a muddy palm log by his fire, to warm my feet

An official rack for saddles.

and look about me. The clearing was scarcely a dozen yards across, and mist still hung in the trees about us. A sapling, bent horizontally from a notch

---

[1] *Asistente:* an officer's orderly, or servant.

hip-high in its trunk, formed a rack for saddles and bridles, protected by bits of oiled cloth, cracked and worn, but glistening with a fringe of drops.

About us horses stood tethered among the trees, anywhere and everywhere, feeding on cogollo (pronounced *coyo*),— rich leaves of the sugar-cane, fresh cut by the camp servants in the swamps where it grows wild;— and a sorry, sore-backed lot of nags they were, though tough and tireless, I soon found out, as our own American bronchos.

The rancho in which I had spent the night was a neat specimen of foresters' architecture, built of dead boughs, interlaced and fastened with tawny strips of the inner bark of the Majana, that furnishes the Mambis with a natural cordage strong as hemp. The thatch of broad palm leaves was faded and brown,— it was just beginning to throw off vapor under the sun's increasing rays. The ridgepole was braced between two royal palms, appropriate in dignity to a staff-headquarters; so tall that you strained your neck looking up at them.

My stout, snoring "bunkie," of the night before, who had occupied the cot opposite me, in our rancho, crawled out into the sunlight and dipped up a steaming jicara of guarapo. Then he sat down beside me. It was the cook's domain, where only distinguished guests, officers, and their orderlies were allowed to loaf or stretch and shake themselves in the early morning.

Andarje and his officers being already up and away, my neighbor introduced himself as Lieutenant Herrera, an aide-de-camp of Gomez, temporarily attached to the force. He was a tall, amiable young man with a blonde moustache, very fat and pink in spite of field life. His first remark was that I looked as though I had got wet the night before. He envied me a bath, — he hadn't had even a respectable face-wash himself for a month, — he who was accustomed to his tub and soap every morning in Havana.

Continuing his confidences, Herrera told me that he had got lost some weeks before while sent on a commission by the commander-in-chief, and had wandered in peril, dodging troops and guerilla bands. On one occasion his guide was shot at his side, and he barely escaped by hiding himself in a canefield. Gomez had marched suddenly eastward, and Herrera was awaiting his return; for Rumor, who always laid out Gomez' plans for him in advance, had it that he was about to attack Havana. Herrera thought that if I meant to join Gomez, I had better settle down and wait for him to come our way. Then Herrera asked me if I would like to see the general's handwriting, and he went back under the

"*Accustomed to his tub and soap every morning in Havana.*"

rancho, where his despatch box hung, and proudly brought me his commission, nicely inscribed on foolscap and signed MAXIMO GOMEZ.

Herrera went on to explain that life at Savanas Nuevas was beastly dull. In the Manigua one rarely spent two nights in the same place; but this was a permanent hospital camp, for the sick and wounded of forces skirmishing about the district, and the guard was strong enough to protect it in case of attack, or at least hold the passes until the patients might be removed to some point of safety deeper in the forest. Savanas Nuevas was also a sort of mail station, where couriers stopped to change horses, or get news of forces operating about northern Matanzas.

Dr. Dominguez at work.

When we had emptied our jicaras, Camarioca and two other asistentes came up, grinning, for their share, and drained the can. Then Antonio, the cook, sat down beside us and rolled himself a cigarette with the air of a man who has done a good morning's work. I therefore inferred that the Mambis took no early breakfast (in which I was correct), so I strolled off to see the camp with Herrera.

Paths cut through the jungle with machetes diverged in every direction, winding snakelike about an occasional royal palm. They were rough paths, where your toe stubbed against sharp stumps of saplings, or caught in muddy roots of tropical vines. They led past camp-fires and groups of ranchos, smaller than our own, and were sure to end in a bog, or a pool of slimy water. All this woodland was the property of Andarje's father, a well-to-do peasant proprietor of the neighborhood.

A frequent feature of the humbler ranchos was a cow skin, hairy side down, slung over the ridgepole,—a valued addition, Herrera explained to me, because it would turn the heaviest rain, and in the heat of the day collect to itself the swarming flies.

The Parilla.

The occupants of these habitations of the rank and file were mostly at home, some still sleeping under cover, some kindling fires and cutting rations of fresh meat into strips for the midday meal, some greasing their rifles and revolvers after the moisture of the day before. Most of them, scantily clad in ragged cotton clothing, exposed skin swarthy as bronze under every rent; though some appeared proudly in white linen coats, freshly washed by pacificita [1] admirers of the valley. No two hats were alike; some were brimless, and the best of them had

---

[1] Feminine, diminutive of *pacifico*, frequently used by the Cubans as is *Cubanita*, in addressing attractive young ladies.

an obviously home-made look. They were a courteous, genial lot of outlaws, and passed the time of day cheerily as we strolled along.

In a remote clearing, where the odor of camp offal and the swarm of insects attracted by it were less evident, we came upon the field hospital, and Herrera presented me with appropriate formality to Francisco Dominguez, M.D., of Havana, the surgeon in charge.

Dr. Dominguez was a busy little man, second in importance only to Andarje himself.

I saw his patients. They were each under a separate rancho, cool, among leafy paths trodden only by their attendants. There were eight of them, some uncertain of life and some convalescing,—and some very picturesque machete and gunshot wounds there were. Although proper medicines were extremely scarce, Dominguez managed to patch up the wounded with rags and diluted carbolic acid, trusting largely in merciful nature to do the rest.

At the one entrance of the camp was the picket guard; a score of powerful blacks, Orientales, like the infantry of Quintin Bandera, who had followed Maceo from the extreme east of the Island and had been lately incorporated in Andarje's force.

Four or five of these negroes had wives, very dusky females, barefooted and scantily attired, who squatted about, doing the cooking for their husbands and their particular friends. Sentry duty on the one approach from the valley was entrusted to these "buffalo-soldiers," who, like the marines on a warship, were constantly on guard, and no one was allowed to leave camp without a written pass from the officer of the day. Though illiterate, they possessed all the keen observation of the illiterate, and could recognize their officers' signatures if they could not read them.

These men were as ragged as any I had ever seen. Some had on scarcely more than a gunny-sack, held about the loins by a cartridge belt, with the merest remnant of a shirt, or pair of trousers. Some were bareheaded, but all were happy enough, continually grinning, and showing their ivory teeth and white eyeballs. Their duties were light, for they walked post for only an hour in turn, and spent the rest of the time simply existing.

Some insurgents and their weapons.

In this part of the camp, cattle brought from the valley were killed and butchered anywhere among the trees. Sanitation, by the way, had no part in Andarje's discipline. No attempt was made to burn hide or entrails, and the refuse accumulated to dry and bleach in the sun, reminding us, even at headquarters, of its presence with every shift of the wind.

Breakfast for the staff was waiting when we got

back to the rancho. Strips of freshly killed steer were roasting on the parilla, a gridiron-like structure of green sticks, built over the fire, while an iron camp kettle — a luxury of rank, and the only one to be seen in Savanas Nuevas — nestled in the embers below, bubbling and boiling with a mess of sweet-potatoes. We helped ourselves and ate with sheath-knives and fingers, on bits of clean white palm bark, that served as plates. Dr. Dominguez joined us with the contribution of an unripe orange, which we shared, each man squeezing some of its juice on his meat as seasoning; for salt is almost unknown in the Manigua.

Andarje, who had returned from the valley, brought from his saddle-bags some long brown cigarettes, saved for a special occasion, and comfort was complete.

The siesta habit is easily acquired in the tropics. Even on a march, you often grow drowsy in the saddle under the noonday heat, until white spots chase over the landscape; unless a freshening sense of danger comes to quicken the pulse and clear the head. Herrera had the habit to perfection, and examples are contagious; so I crawled under the rancho where there was rest from the buzzing flies and the rays of the sun.

Dinner was similar to breakfast, though the company was less, for the staff in active commission had gone to scout the plain below. For Dominguez, Herrera, and myself the evening wore on in idleness, talking town life, clubs, and theatres, and listening to the howling and beating of sticks, with

Departure of a courier from Savanas Nuevas.

which the Orientales of the guard accompanied their dances until dark. Herrera's nature was peaceful and pleasure-loving. He looked anxiously for the day when he might ride into Havana with the "Liberating Army" and sit down at ease once more in his own club; but this he was never to do. He died a month later in Santa Clara, from the accidental discharge of a rifle.

Night came gratefully after the long day, with clear moonlight and cool breezes. Then strange birds sang. Queer raccoon-like animals called jutias peered with sparkling eyes from the low treetops, and great land-crabs scurried into their holes at the approach of a shadow. There was silence everywhere, and the commonplace swamp forest of the day became a fairyland.

The force stationed at Savanas Nuevas consisted of twenty mounted armados, carrying Remington carbines, captured Spanish Mausers, Winchester repeaters, even three or four old-fashioned shotguns. Some wore revolvers of more or less ancient pattern and questionable efficiency. There were fifteen mounted asistentes, including hospital servants; and finally the infantry armed with Remingtons and Mausers. Thus the force, counting the commissioned officers, two sergeants, and four corporals, mustered above seventy. Every man, whatever he did not have, had a machete, and appeared tolerably able to use it.

One morning at breakfast, a scout rode in and dismounted by headquarters. "Pues, señores," he said; "soldados en Capitolio! (there are soldiers in Capitolio)." Capitolio was a hill near by, where there was a fort; so it looked as if a reinforcement had come to move against Savanas Nuevas. Then I saw our force assemble and line up by the picket guard.

Half of the enlisted men were negroes, and two were Chinamen (survivors of the Macao coolie traffic, that followed the suppression of the slave trade), shifty, sharp-eyed Mongols, with none of the placid laundry look about them. The firearms were in a bad condition, some sightless, some sawed off for convenience in handling. These men did not seem to know much about shooting, but were evidently accustomed to bang away, trusting in Providence and the fear they inspired to efface the enemy. Being a stationary force, they had little chance to practise skirmishing, and were therefore somewhat below the standard of efficiency: this I found out from observation of other insurgent bands.

Service at Savanas Nuevas was not severe. The mounted men spent their time in merely patrolling the trail, or scouting the valley below, where they cut telegraph wires and tore up bits of the railroad track. At night they rode by squads through the country in search of Plateados.[1] Whenever they caught one, he was brought in and hanged to a bough of the "Tree of Justice" on the outskirts of the camp. Thus life with its simplicity and

---

[1] The Plateados were robbers who infested the country early in the war; a terror to small planters and defenceless women. Mr. Silvester Scovel, correspondent of the *New York World*, has told of a narrow escape he had when "held up" by a company of them. As the outrages perpetrated by Plateados were invariably attributed by the Spanish authorities to the organized insurgents, the latter have been especially active in exterminating all sorts of outlaws. Every Cuban on detached service carries

its exigencies resembled that of Marion's men in our own Revolution.

So five days passed at Savanas Nuevas, with only an occasional break when a courier rode in with news from the outer world. Often these messengers brought copies of the Havana papers, which were read aloud by the camp-fire; sometimes American papers came to us and were turned over to me to translate. The insurgents were eager to know what Mr. Cleveland was up to, and whether he would grant the recognition voted by Congress. When I happened to read a passage dilating on some horrible atrocity, one of the listeners was sure to wag his head and say, "Pooh! I could have told him something worse than that myself."

The "Tree of Justice."

I saw very little of Andarje while I stayed in his

---

a cedula, or pass, signed by his commanding officer, giving the reasons for his travelling abroad. Suspicious persons who cannot account for themselves, or carry arms without the proper cedula, are tried as Plateados. So strictly has the insurgent police system been carried out that desperadoes of every class have long since ceased to exist. The "Tree of Justice," where they executed Plateados, was an institution of Savanas Nuevas.

camp, except his bluff, wholesome face at dinner; for he rode the country by night, and slept mostly by day.

Meanwhile I succeeded in raising a fair equipment. Andarje gave me a horse and saddle, and I was able to purchase a hammock and a light blanket, through pacificos, who had access to the town. I had fortunately been able to smuggle out a 44 cal. revolver which the insurgents loved to examine. It was "Americano legitimo," so clean and new that it gladdened their eyes. It completed my outfit.

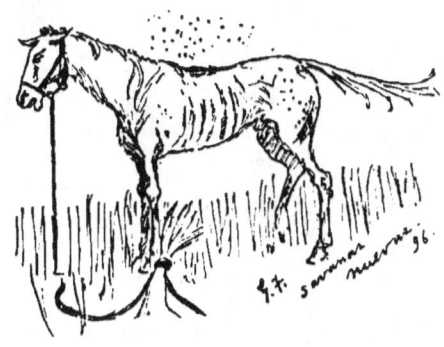

"*Andarje gave me a horse.*"

By this time I had made up my mind to go in search of the commander-in-chief, and not to "wait until he came our way," as Herrera had suggested. I went carefully through my kit and gave away everything not absolutely necessary for field service; then, borrowing an escort from Andarje, I rode to join Major Rojas, who commanded a good force of bushwhackers in the neighborhood of Cardenas, and whose assistance would be useful in forwarding me on my way to Gomez.

Chapter III

Singeing the King's Beard[1]

FOUR miles out of Cardenas, in the angle formed by the two railroads leading respectively to Cimmarones and Recreo, there is a swamp forest thickly grown with giant palms. In the rainy season it is flooded and uninhabitable; but from October to July it is a splendid place for the Cuban game of hide and seek. It is an innocent looking grove, so near the city with its garrison of four thousand troops, and from it you can watch the train with its armored[2] cars full of soldiers at a distance of scarcely three hundred yards, feeling

---

[1] Sir Francis Drake, when he burned the ships in the harbor of Cadiz, in 1587, facetiously termed it "singeing the beard of the King of Spain." — See Barrows' "Life of Drake," p. 256.

[2] Freight or "box" cars, plated laterally with boiler iron, pierced with loopholes for rifles.

its way toward Cimmarones in the morning, and moving slowly back in the afternoon.

Major Rojas, who was a wealthy sugar planter when the revolution began, made this swamp forest his headquarters with a force of sixty men. Forty of them were armados, with the usual assortment of Winchesters, Remingtons, and Spanish Mausers, but very short of ammunition. About half of them were negroes who had cut cane before the war on Rojas' estates.

The officers, non-commissioned officers, and high privates were young men of leading families in Cardenas, with a sprinkling of young peasants of the more intelligent class. One of the officers was an instructor in fencing; all his pupils had taken to the field, so he had no alternative but to go too.

Rojas' men, like Andarje's, had lived all their lives in the district and knew every inch of it. Consequently, they made excellent scouts and an effective guerilla[1] in spite of their small number. By night Rojas camped near the railroad track on a grassy savanna dotted with palms, where his men slung their hammocks or stretched their oules,[2] while the horses grazed on lariats near by.

A little before daybreak Rojas blew two shrill notes on a pewter whistle. Then the force rose, folded its hammocks and oules, saddled up, and filed, by the gray dawn, into the swamp, all but the camp servants, who rode off into the canefields to cut bundles of cogollo for the day's forage.

The horses stood saddled all day, in case of a

[1] *Guerilla*: see note at end of chapter.
[2] *Oules*: bits of glazed oil, or rubber, cloth.

sudden alarm, an invariable Mambi custom; and the force loafed, slept a little more, cooked its beef and sweet-potatoes, or was told off into foraging-parties, according to circumstances.

"*Bundles of cogollo for the day's forage.*"

At this time Weyler was attempting to enforce his orders to grind the sugar-cane, and the insurgents were actively forehanded in burning it up. It was my good luck to be a guest at one of Rojas' bonfires.

In the clear evening starlight, Rojas, two officers, four armed men, and myself left camp by a narrow cowpath, took down the bars of the snake fences bordering the railroad, and crossed the track silently. Then we filed through a farmyard on to the highroad. It was a broad road, where wagons might have easily passed each other, and it wound between stone walls and fields of waving cane. Two of the enlisted men rode ahead with carbines unslung across the pommels of their saddles, and two dropped behind.

After a mile, a turn of the road brought us out on a rising ground overlooking the bay and the city of Cardenas. Lights shone in the town, marking the main avenue of the city and public squares distinctly. It was strange to look down, an outlaw, on streets I had walked freely a week before, — yet

I was conscious of a certain feeling of pride thereat. A solitary light gleamed below us, half a mile away to our left. "That is the 'Sugar House,'" said Rojas.

We continued slowly along the high-road. Rojas blew a note on his whistle, then we halted and listened for a few moments.

"*The wall of flame rolled swiftly right and left.*"

We rode on, and he repeated the call, halting again. Presently, with a swishing of cane leaves, a mounted man trotted swiftly from the shadow of a guarda-raya to our right, and pulled up sharp, with his horse's head over the wall. "It is true, Señor Comandante," he said, "they have arrived,— eighty of the infantry,— they have camped in the ingenio, and there will be grinding to-morrow."

"Go ahead with your 'candela,'"[1] said Rojas; and we rode back to the rising ground, where we halted under a guasima tree and waited, straining our eyes over the black sweep of country below.

A soft breeze blew inland, passing through the vegetation with a rustle, as we sat there on our horses for nearly a quarter of an hour without a word.

"Look!" said Rojas, suddenly.

A faint light flickered to the left, moving in a straight line midway between us and the ingenio. Then in its wake a triangular red flame shot up, doubling and tripling and tumbling over itself, sweeping a cloud of white smoke into the sky. It was the prairie fire picture of the old school geographies, only in place of frightened, stampeded animals, tall palms rose in sharp silhouette in the foreground. Behind us every tree, every stone and blade of grass that was not hidden by our shadows stood out in orange glare, and a sweet, burning smell, with a sound like the heavy fall of rain, came to us even against the breeze.

As the wall of flame rolled swiftly right and left, the ear caught a sharp pah! pah-pah! pah-pah-pr-r-r! of Mauser rifles, like a popping of toy pistols. The soldiers had tumbled out of the ingenio and were shooting at random.

"How beautiful!" observed Rojas.

For three nights these "candela parties" continued; and the roofs of Cardenas were illuminated with our efforts. Rojas' own plantation, then in

---

[1] *Candela:* an illumination, a bonfire, — applied distinctly to the blaze of burning sugar-cane.

care of an agent, and that of his brother, came under the torch; for Weyler's proclamation decreed that all must grind whether they would or not, and soldiers were sent to protect the planters, and, incidentally, to see that they were obedient.

NOTE. — A guerilla is an irregular troop of cavalry, numbering from thirty to one hundred men. Such troops are organized by the Spanish authorities, in the larger towns and cities, from native Cubans of low caste, and Spaniards long resident in the Island. That both officers and men of these irregular forces are recruited from disorderly classes is notorious, and Mr. Stephen Bonsal, in describing their mutilations of a captive, states that the guerrilleros (members of the guerilla) of Matanzas city are "liberated convicts to a man." Although not distinguished for courage, the Spanish guerillas are formidable enough owing to their knowledge of the country and familiarity with Cuban methods.

In garb the guerillas resemble the Cubans, a resemblance that they endeavor by every means to increase. Early in the war they adopted the Cuban signal of throwing back the hat, allowing it to dangle on the hat cord when challenging, and frequently gave the Cuban challenge "Alto! quien va? (Halt! who goes?)" instead of the regulation Spanish challenge "Alto! quien vive? (Halt! who lives?)." You may detect the stripe of an advancing cavalry force, however, with a field-glass, by noticing whether the hats and carbines are of uniform pattern. Uniformity, even in half a dozen gun-barrels, peeping from a thicket, is a suspicious circumstance.

The guerillas are employed almost entirely as guides and advance guards to Spanish infantry columns, and their attempts to pass for Cubans and get the first shot, have frequently led them to shoot into each other by accident.

I have a pathetic story which was told me by José Ballete y Sierra, a recruit in Rojas' force, while waiting, as a desarmado, his turn to carry a rifle.

Two weeks before I met him, José Ballete was owner of a little plantation near Recreo. His sixteen-year-old son was seen by the Spanish guerrilleros of Recreo exchanging words with a scouting party of insurgents. After the rebels had passed, the guerrilleros came from their hiding-place, arrested the lad, and took him before the Alcalde of Recreo as a suspect. The Alcalde seems to have been a decent sort of fellow, for he dismissed the case and ordered the guerrilleros to take the boy home. As soon as they were clear of the town, the guerrilleros cut the boy to pieces with their machetes, and left his mutilated body in a field, where it was found six days later by his parents. Then the father put a star and a blue ribbon on his hat, and joined the rebels in the woods.

Although the word *guerilla* may apply to every mounted Cuban company, the Cuban prefers to speak of his troop as a *fuerza*, or force.

Chapter IV

A Skirmish with the "Gringos"[1]

I JOINED Lacret on the afternoon of April 4th, just in time to witness a skirmish, and to observe that method of fighting pursued with so much success by the rebels and so little by the Spaniards. Rojas had heard that Lacret was to camp that day with a large force at Pavo Real, an estate in the foothills, midway between Cardenas and Matanzas, and five miles from the shore. The Spanish Colonel Pavia, however, had heard so too, with the result that when we were still three miles from Pavo Real, we heard firing ahead.

We met two peasants on the road, who told us that a big Spanish column had come by rail from Matanzas and had cut across country from Limonar, and were near, very near, — Dios only knew how near. As they spoke, there came a popping like the explosion of a string of fire-crackers, then five crashing volleys rolled through the hills, followed by the sharp rattle of Mausers fired "at will," and our pacifico friends sped on with scarcely an "adios."

A puff of black smoke shot up a mile in front of us, — the black smoke of a peasant's cottage that

---

[1] *Gringo* is familiar to all who have lived in the Southwest as contemptuously applied by the Mexicans to Americans. It means something awkward and foreign. In Cuba I found it commonly applied to Spaniards.

leaps into the sky with a shower of sparks and dies away quickly. As we looked, another black cloud arose, blowing over the trees this time far to our right. Then we knew that the Spaniards were marching toward the shore, and that Lacret was probably retreating before them. So we turned our horses toward the sea

It was a pleasant, hilly district, threaded by up

"*Fleeing as from a plague.*"

and down country lanes, and cut by yellow limestone walls into pastures, canefields, and clumps of scrub forest, — a country for ambuscades and surprises.

Peasants hurried past us, fleeing as from a plague. Old men, women with babies in their arms, and little children tugging at their skirts, ran along, never looking up. Cottages were left vacant; only dogs and hens remained.

At last the crest of a hill opened up a wide view of the ocean. Below us lay rich canefields sweeping to the coastline, with only a fringe of palms and undergrowth between them and the blue sea. Skirting the palms, a long white line of mounted figures moved slowly toward Cardenas; it was Lacret's impedimenta, as the unarmed contingent of camp servants and officers' orderlies is called, and a fresh rattle of musketry told that the main force was covering its retreat.

Following a boundary wall through the sloping canefield, we ran into Lacret's rear-guard. Lacret was there himself, surrounded by his staff, peering over the country through his field-glass. A long line of armed men chewing sugar-cane and lounging in their saddles were marching off leisurely by twos, after the impedimenta, which had already passed. A trooper, shouting "Clear the way," trotted through the group of officers, leading a horse on which were two men, — one holding the other, a negro, on the pommel of his saddle before him. The latter was wounded or dead; for his head hung limp on his breast, and his ragged shirt, open on his black chest, was stained with blood. A dozen stragglers came galloping up, leaning on their horses' necks, and leaped or scrambled through gaps in the boundary wall. One of them, a lieutenant distinguished only by a star on his crossbelt, rode up to

"*His head hung limp on his breast.*"

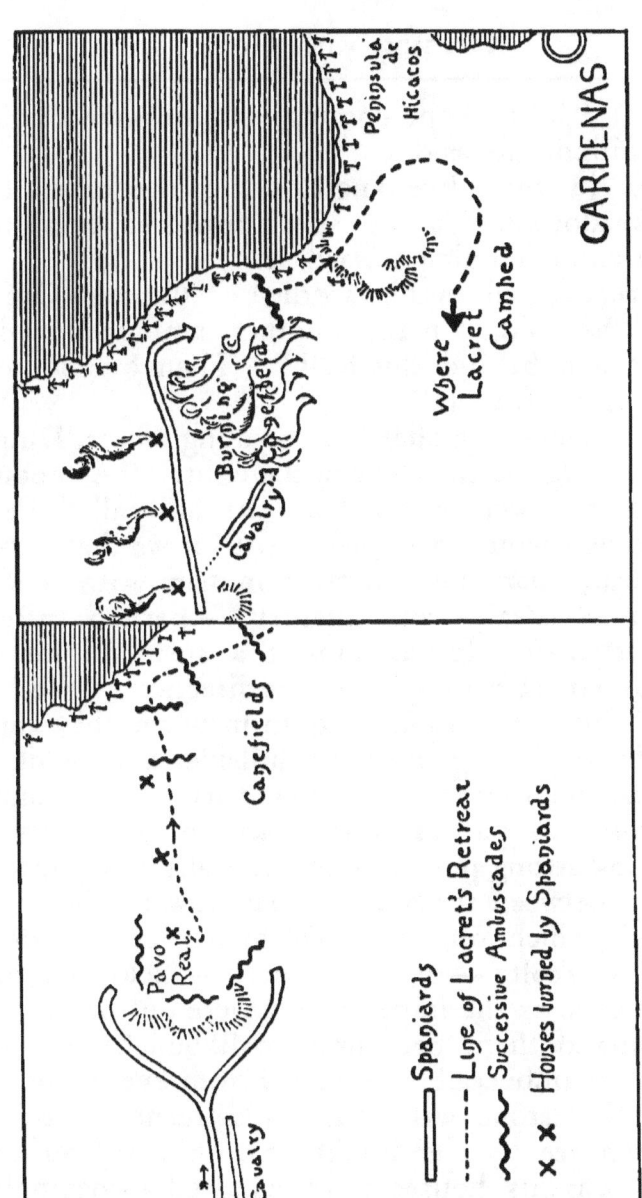

Plan of Lacret's skirmish with Pavia at Pavo Real, April 4, 1896.

Lacret. "They kept coming, and we were out of ammunition," he said.

Back in the olive angle, where the canes and palm shadows met, a gray speck appeared, enlarging swiftly and extending toward us.

Lacret turned in his saddle! "Captain Camaguey," he said, "make another ambuscade with twenty men behind this wall." Then he rode on, followed by the staff.

As we tagged on after him, a young officer, Duque Estrada, told me the story of the fight. "At noon," he said, "we were camped on the hill called Pavo Real, when scouts galloped in with news that Pavia was near, marching from Limonar, with a full column of cavalry and infantry, — perhaps fifteen hundred men. It was almost a surprise; for we did not expect troops from that direction. We had scarcely time to mount and form when they came in sight, deploying over the hillsides and fields to the west in an effort to surround us. The general sent out two parties, forty each, of armed men, who took strong positions behind walls and thickets, leaving between them a free road toward the coast, through which our unarmed men rode in safety. Lacret's escolta — or body-guard — held the hill, and as soon as the impedimenta were out of the way we followed them, dropping small bunches of men behind to ambuscade the enemy from every wooded hill or limestone wall that could furnish a cover. You can see by the smoke that they are burning all the peasants' houses we have passed, — beginning with the one at Pavo Real. They are brave to-day," — he said *bravo*, which means at once, angry, persistent, valorous, aggressive — "and have kept after us, although we have left five ambuscades and they must have lost quite a few men already."

Two scouts galloped suddenly from a guarda-raya of the canefield through which my little party had just passed. "The gringos!" they shouted; "the cavalry are coming. Many, many of them! They are coming through the cane to head us off!" Over the crest

Starting a candela.

of the hill a dark moving something appeared, approaching diagonally. Pavia's mind had expanded with a stratagem, and things looked serious.

Lacret turned back to where Camaguey was placing his handful of men for the sixth ambuscade. "Give them a candela," he said.

A negro, without dismounting, cut a bunch of palm leaves by the roadside, twisted them together into a torch, and lighted it, galloping along by the side of our retreating line of men. He leaned low from his saddle, switching the sputtering torch under the skirts of the cane shoots; another negro dismounted, climbed over the wall with a bunch of matches, and fanning vigorously with his hat, kindled a fire on the other side.

A strong breeze was blowing from the sea; the canes were ablaze with frightful heat in a moment, and the heavy smoke and flame were swept in the face of the Spanish cavalry. We had nothing more to fear from that quarter.

A popping from Camaguey's men joined the crackling of burning cane. The gray line of Spaniards was now within easy range, and the sharp pah! pah! pah! of Mausers, with a psit! of an occasional bullet, lower aimed than the others, came in return.

The Spaniards advanced a little and drew up to shoot again.

Lacret, sitting on his horse by the wall, watched the flames spreading before the wind. He was very conspicuous, wearing a tall Mexican hat, and you could hear shouts of "Tira al sombrero alto (Shoot at the tall hat)." Then we left Camaguey and rode after the main force. That was the last ambuscade of the day.

It was now four o'clock in the afternoon. The Spaniards sent half a dozen volleys in our direction, and fell back toward Pavo Real. Our column took to the forest-clad hummocks at the base of the peninsula Hicacos, and as we looked back, the whole country seemed ablaze. Four miles of sugar-cane skirting the shore was afire, and back among the hills of Pavo Real rose the blacker smoke of burning cottages.

This skirmish cost Lacret two out of two hundred armados, one of whom was buried, when the troops ceased to pursue, among the scrub trees of the peninsula. The other received a fatal wound from a stray shot at very long range, perhaps a mile, and after his troop was under cover. A nickel-covered Mauser bullet pierced the small of his back, passed through the thumb of his bridle hand, and buried itself in the pommel of his saddle.

We camped that night in the overseer's cottage on a sugar estate, three miles out of Cardenas, and as I sat at supper with Lacret, scouts reported the enemy's position in the immediate neighborhood. Pavia had made camp in a sugar-house five miles away, near Pavo Real. Three miles to the south of us, camping on another large plantation, was a Spanish column of eight hundred men which had marched that afternoon from Cardenas. To the northeast, at scarcely a greater distance, lay Cardenas with its garrison of regulars and volunteers. It was fair to suppose that with reasonable activity, Spanish scouting parties might locate us during the night and have every lane and trail about us ambuscaded by morning.

I asked Lacret if we were not in a bit of a hole, and my question surprised him.

"They will not know where we are," he said, "until they hear it from peasants to-morrow. They never dare to send out scouts: if they did, I should capture them at once. They only move about the country in heavy columns, and I can skirmish with them or evade them as I like. By to-morrow they will know that we have been here, and they will march here on principle; but by sunrise I shall be gone, and they will not know where I am, excepting by accident, until twenty-four hours later." I found that Lacret was not guilty of exaggeration.

Meanwhile the dying man was given a room to himself, and the surgeon tried to do something for him. At sundown his wound began to pain him, and his groans, "Ay, Dios mio! Ay, Dios mio!" broke the stillness of the night until death came early the next morning.

Lacret takes an evening nap.

Chapter V

"Pacified Matanzas"

BY two in the morning of April 5th, Lacret's column was on the road and daybreak found it winding from the valley of Guamacaro by a wide circuit into the hills, and back again toward Pavo Real. An advance guard of fifty armados rode a quarter of a mile ahead, then came Lacret with his towering hat, surrounded by his staff and followed by his escolta, some sixty big, black cane-cutters, naked as Andarje's infantry.

After the escolta, an impedimenta of one hundred ragamuffins, white, black, and yellow, bob-tailed along with a tinkling of pots and pans; it included the officers' orderlies and outlawed peasants, who had begged to follow the force for safety.[1] It was

---

[1] Peasants were flocking daily to be incorporated in the force; but there were no rifles, and the impedimenta was already crowded. Those in immediate danger were

mounted on all sorts of beasts, small donkeys, even mares in foal, and with feeble-limbed little colts neighing and scampering after them. One negro wore an antique Spanish dragoon sabre attached to his waist by twine, and a single gilt spur tied over his bare instep, with which he constantly goaded his horse to greater exertions by an upward jerk of the knee.

A rear-guard of fifty more armados ended the procession. The rest of the force explored the country for a league ahead as scouts, or rode the fields to right and left of the column as flankers, foraging in potato patches and leading off horses on lariats wherever they found them. The force, as usual, had marched on an empty stomach, but sugar-canes cut on the way made a frequent and refreshing "long breakfast."

As we journeyed along, dead horses by the roadside, gaps torn in the yellow limestone walls, chips and scars on trunks of trees, marked scenes of long retreats and frequent skirmishes. Vultures floated lazily over the pastures or watched us from fence and gate post with sleek indifference. The frequent banquets of the war had dulled their appetite.

One noticed that the houses of all who could

---

allowed to march with us, until they could be left in some comparatively safe camp in the swamps of the south shore. Later, west of the Hanabana river, near Cocodrillos, I met a party of three hundred refugees, the overflow of Matanzas impedimenta. They were marching on foot from the swamps, which a scarcity of wild pigs and the first floods of the rainy season had rendered uninhabitable for so great a number together, toward the forest-clad highlands of the interior, where they hoped to survive the summer. Nearly all these men were negroes, naked, destitute, — not half a dozen revolvers or fifty good machetes among them. Even their officers, two mulatto lieutenants, looked discouraged. With proper arms, this mob might have become a formidable force.

afford to live in the towns were deserted. Their owners had stripped the red tiles from the roofs, so that insurgents might not camp in them, and give the troops an excuse for using the torch. For the same reason, the thatch was removed from some of the smaller cottages, leaving only framework structures like huge bird cages. But the peasants who tilled the soil for a living had to stay at home or starve, and on them fell the fury of Spain.

"Structures like bird cages."

Their hearts were with the insurrection; they gave us what they had and told truthfully whatever they knew of the soldiers' movements. An incident of the march proved the sympathy of the average farmer.

The owner of a palm-thatched hut invited Lacret to stop for a cup of guarapo, or "Cuba Libre." As the general reined up, the countryman held out to him a cartridge box with fifty rounds of ammunition which he had found in a field, thrown away or lost by a Spanish soldier. Lacret gave the man a gold piece, yet the gold was scarcely adequate to the value of such a gift.

As the morning wore on, the heat was intense, and eight horses under heavy-weight riders had dropped by noon. The men did not seem to realize that some day the supply of horseflesh in Matanzas might come to an end. They rode with loose girths, they lolled in their saddles, sometimes with the knee over the pommel, almost the worst crime of which a cavalryman can be guilty, and they never dismounted, going up or down a hill, however steep the grade. Whenever I dismounted, as I had been taught to do for the sake of my horse, when an enlisted man in the First United States Cavalry, I was asked if the ride tired me.

By one o'clock we reached Pavo Real, and the motley force sought the shade of every hedge, wall, and clump of trees; extending like gypsy groups over the country in every direction. Pots were unpacked from the saddles, parillas were built, and an ox that had trailed with the impedimenta all that morning was led up drooling and panting to be butchered by the machete.

Under the porch of a house that, being roofless and deserted, had escaped burning, Lacret reclined in his hammock, giving out guard details for the afternoon.

After dinner I went over the trail of the Spanish troops and saw the ruins they had left. I saw an old woman and her half-naked sons poking in the square bed of ashes, which was all that remained of their home, looking for the family kettle. The sons had fled to the woods when the soldiers came, but the mother remained. "The Mambis were here last night," said an officer, riding up. "Yes, but I can't help that any more than I can help your being here," returned the old woman. "Burn the house," commanded the officer.

There were some houses that they did not attempt

to burn, but went through them like locusts. The families had come back and were crouching about, helpless and dazed at the situation. One woman showed me where they had unscrewed the top of her sewing-machine and taken it away to sell in the town; they took sheets and bedding, even baby clothes, and the pigs and poultry from the farmyard.

Twining like the trail of a great serpent across the fields and through the soft grass of the roadside, a narrow path was worn and polished by a thousand

"*Looking for the family kettle.*"

pairs of hempen sandals slipping along in Indian file. By it, at intervals, lay spoons, forks or garments that the gringos had dropped when they were tired of carrying them.

There had been a court-martial in Lacret's camp on the morning of the skirmish. A mulatto lieutenant named Sanchez — a brave man, too, they told me — had been found guilty of assault on a negro girl of the neighborhood, and condemned to death. He was hung under the porch of a deserted cottage, with a placard on his breast giving his name, the offence, and the finding of the court. I saw the body, and the Spaniards saw it too. A week later, in a bundle of Havana newspapers that came to us, we read that the cabecilla (or chieftain) Sanchez had fallen in battle, and had been left dead on the field by Lacret's retreating bands.

All that afternoon local forces kept arriving, until the entire command numbered a thousand or more. Thirty cabecillas, of northern Matanzas,— among them names that had become famous throughout the Island,— reported to Lacret, and the staff-headquarters was a busy scene of greetings and conferences.

"El Indio Bravo."

There was Major Miguelin, known as the "Indio Bravo," who slouched about, looking up acquaintances, joking with every one and repeating the story of how he had, a week before, discomfited an entire Spanish regiment. He was a bronzed, sharp-eyed little man, who boasted Indian blood, and had sworn never to cut his hair "till he should lead his forty negroes into Havana." His black locks already reached his shoulders. Miguelin was a seasoned veteran of the Ten Years' War,— a singular mixture of kindness and ferocity. He loved his men like sons, and would proudly pat them on the shoulder, calling attention to their great size and vigorous health. "What could Spanish 'yearlings' do against such fellows?"

A smooth-faced boy of twenty or so, the centre of an attentive group of older men, was pointed out to me as a person of distinction. This was Clothilde Garcia, the son of a wealthy planter, known before the war only as a spoiled child and mischievous youth. But when the revolution broke out he surprised everybody by leading a force of his father's stout farm-hands into the field; and though many Cuban gentlemen rose with small bands at the first call to arms, only to lose their followings through inexperience and the doubt that then filled men's minds, Garcia was one of the very few chieftains to successfully maintain an organized force until the liberating army of Gomez and Maceo swept the western provinces, calling every warm-blooded native to its standard.

"Inglesito"[1] (the little Englishman) was another thorn in Spain's Cuban crown. He was fair and distinctly of Anglo-Saxon type, the son of an American named Gould, yet he spoke no English, for his father died when he was a child, leaving him to the care of his Cuban mother. He was called "Inglesito" because his father was an "Ingles," as every one is in Cuba who speaks English.

Lieutenant-Colonel Rejino Alfonso was noteworthy as having been a brigand before the war. His personal history was interesting, as it threw some light on pre-revolutionary life in Cuba. As

---

[1] "Inglesito" (Alfredo Gould) has since died of a wound in Havana Province. Raoul Marti, a native of Guantanamo, of French origin, who understands English and has been in the United States, is now known as "Inglesito" and is said to be an able soldier.

a youth, Alfonso quarrelled with a civil guard and killed him, which unfortunate accident left no career open to him but that of an outlaw among the hills. Before the revolution the Guardia Civil, a select and infallible corps of Spanish constabulary, had a sort of absolute power over the timid country people. Their acts were inscrutable. If a civil guard shot or stabbed a peasant in a tavern row, it was because the culprit was "dangerous and disorderly." When the civil guards arrested a man, the chances were that he would be shot on the road "while attempting a violent escape."

Civil guards were, therefore, feared and hated, and whenever anybody had the pluck and originality to kill one of them in self-defence, it was considered a virtuous act. Consequently Alfonso became a popular hero, holding with "El Cid" a romantic place in the hearts of the peasants. Planters delighted to lend him money in return for anecdotes of his escapes from "justice." He was never a "sequestador," — a brigand who seizes people and holds them for ransom; nor did I hear of his ever being guilty of any outrage.

When the war began, Alfonso called his law-breaking friends together and asked them to abandon their disorderly life and organize a Cuban guerilla. They followed him, all but four or five, who became plateados and were finally executed by the Insurgents.

It is told of Alfonso that in the insurgent ranks he found himself face to face with an ex-police agent who for years had been most active in attempting his arrest and conviction. Bystanders, remembering the ex-brigand's fiery reputation, expected a duel at once; but they were disappointed. Alfonso advanced to meet his enemy with extended hand, saying that he was glad to count him a friend, now that they fought under the same colors.

As I saw him, Alfonso possessed attractive manners, with a frank, manly face and an honest gray eye. He was, perhaps, thirty years old, a good soldier, with an unusual knowledge of the country, — the result of professional experience.

Another popular hero, Rafael Cardenas, a major of General Aguierre's Havana division, who was soon to be appointed a brigadier-general, and who was fresh in the glory of an important exploit, — the capture of a trainload of arms and ammunition that Martinez Campos, some weeks before, had attempted to send from Havana to the garrison in Matanzas city. Cardenas' troop of Havana cavalry was noticeably better mounted, better equipped, and better "set up" than any force Lacret had with him, and the men were nearly all white. Perhaps they appeared better because of longer service; for this force was one of the first organized in Havana Province; while the Matanzas division consisted almost entirely of recruits incorporated during the invasion.

Cardenas was a young man of ancient lineage, descended from a certain de Cardenas who was secretary to Isabella the Catholic, and whose grandson was settled in Cuba before the *Mayflower* landed her colony at Plymouth.

Rafael's father, becoming blind when a young man, lived in seclusion, and wrote verses on liberty that made him famous throughout the Island, and gave inspiration to his son. Rafael was a barrister by profession; a tall young fellow with a dark moustache. He wore a blue college-man's sweater, with high tan-colored leggings, and a tall palm-leaf hat of the fine grade called jipi-japa. He sat a horse well, with a rather mediæval, knightly air. His lieutenants were George Aguierre, nephew of General Aguierre, and a young English-Cuban engineer named del Monte, of blonde, Saxon type, who has since been reported killed, a cousin of Leonardo del Monte of New York.

For a mile over the country extended the different squadrons. Everywhere fires, scarcely larger than if they had been built by Indian scouts, blazed under parillas, cooking strips of meat; but so tiny and scattered were they that no smoke was discernible on the landscape.

Half of the enlisted men as you saw them together were negroes,[1] with here and there a Chinaman. Occasionally a man was pointed out as a Spanish deserter, and in every case he appeared on an equality with the others.

The officers were of all classes, — planters or planters' sons, professional men and peasants of the more intelligent order, with a trifling percentage of negroes and mulattoes. The prevailing tone of these forces was distinctly aristocratic: in fact, they

---

[1] In 1887, of the entire population of Cuba (1,102,689 whites and 485,187 blacks — total, 1,587,876) 30½% were negroes. Statistics show a steadily decreasing percentage of negroes since 1841, when it was 58.4 (418,291 whites to 589,333 negroes). The numerical decrease of the negroes seems due to the condition under which they lived in slavery, which was continued as late as 1886. [See Mr. Maturin Ballou in "Due South," p. 279.]

were just such troops as Georgia and the Carolinas would have sent to the field early in this century. The discipline was good, and the men, though one missed many of the formalities that distinguish regular soldiers, were conspicuously willing and obedient. I was surprised to find that by a recognized but unwritten law, a professional man in good standing, or one holding the degree of bachelor of arts, was entitled to a lieutenant's commission and a servant. Occasionally officers so appointed failed to develop the slightest military capacity; some even suffered from the hardships of camp life, yet I never knew an instance of dissatisfaction at the system by the humbler rank-and-file. All of these men, officers and "buck-soldiers" alike, served absolutely without pay and on pain of a death, if captured, such as our frontier soldiers were accustomed to meet when taken prisoner by the Apache Indians.

So much for Pavo Real. On the morning of the 6th the local forces separated, returning to their own districts, and Lacret resumed his series of extraordinary, zigzag marches across the Island, that made him, to the Spaniards, a man of mystery.

Chapter VI

With Lacret and his Staff

LACRET was a picturesque, gray-headed gentleman, with a very brown sunburned face, and neatly curled white moustachios. He had a hawk nose and high cheek-bones like an old French general of the second Empire. His manners were refined and courteous. He spoke French as a second language; but barely understood English. He was of Haytian French descent.

Lacret was a wealthy man, and whenever he succeeded in burning up a big sugar-mill, the Havana papers consoled themselves by publishing items of how different bits of property or invested interests of his had been seized by the Spanish Government. These accounts were always read with delight by Insurgents and Spaniards alike, for the Cubans loved to think what a Mogul their commander had been, and it pleased the Spaniards to feel that they were getting even with an enemy.

Lacret was exceedingly neat in his costume, his belt and leggings were always well blacked, he carried a change of linen uniform in his saddle-bags, and he was very particular about being neatly shaved. The most extraordinary article of his dress was the tall Mexican hat that had attracted the attention of the Spaniards at Pavo Real. It had a silver star within a triangular crimson cockade on one side, and from it a long red cord hung about his neck and down his back like an artilleryman's aigulette. That hat was known throughout Matanzas Province. There was not another like it in all Cuba.

Lacret's valet and barber was a black man named Campoverde, a pretentious, undershot darky whom he used to discharge from his personal service perhaps twice a week. Lacret was fond of Campoverde, Calle-verde, or Casa-verde (Greenfield, Green-street, Green-house) as the staff variously and facetiously called him, and often sent him to cottages by the roadside with his long pipe to light it. The valet would trot back puffing furiously at the general's pipe, for tobacco was a luxury even for an officer, and always taking the longest way to make the most of his smoke.

Lacret had two bullets, souvenirs of the last war, both lodged in his right ankle. Often on long marches they would pain him terribly, and then it was that Campoverde might look out for squalls.

Lacret would remove one boot and ride along under the blazing sun, writhing in pain, with the bare, scarred foot thrust far away from the stirrup.

No one liked to talk to the general at those times, and the staff would whisper, "The old man is bad to-day; it is lucky there are no shots (tiros), for he is scarcely able to command." And Campoverde, who was at Lacret's left hand to carry his discarded boot, had to keep both eyes open. He knew that it was no day for trifling.

Bertrand. as sketched by Janiz.— Page 56.

Lacret and his staff made a picturesque and entertaining company. Honest old Pio Dominguez, lieutenant-colonel, and tried veteran of the last war, was senior officer. Then there was Louis Borde, of Jamaica, a relative of the general, who was second on the list, ranking as major, a refined, pleasant-spoken gentleman, an eloquent authority on the habits and diseases of canary birds; for the breeding of them in large aviaries had been his innocent pastime before the war. Physically he was the largest, perhaps the strongest, of Lacret's aides.

Two of the staff, Bertrand and Pujol, proved the Spanish saying "from Cuban mothers Cuban offspring." They were sons of Spanish officers of rank. Bertrand was a handsome young man, recently promoted from the ranks for gallantry. His father, a colonel and nobleman, a marquis I believe, had resigned his commission when his son ran off to the Manigua. Pujol, a lanky, hard-faced youth, was son of a Spanish major. Months afterwards he was bayoneted while lying wounded in a Cuban field-hospital.

There was Piedra, Lacret's secretary, whose handwriting was beautiful and rapid, Captain Elias of Tampa, a Cuban-born American, and a little Havana lawyer, something of a fire-eater and duellist, who bore scars of encounters with rapiers, — his name has escaped me.

Finally, there was Manoel Camaguey, captain of the escolta, a boastful but fearless little man who kept a careful diary of all the engagements he had ever been in, together with a list of his wounds, which he would read for hours at a time to any one who would listen. I was with him one evening when he read his journal to a peasant family until they interrupted his recital with food brought from a secret cupboard, and Camaguey won an extra supper.

Camaguey was always in a skirmish if there was one; for it was Lacret's policy, when a column pressed him, to send off the impedimenta with a guide, and gallop with the escolta to check the Spaniards and cover the impedimenta's retreat. I rarely saw him use other forces he had with him in a skirmish, if he could avoid it: perhaps because he had more confidence in his own body-guard.

General Collazo.

At this time Collazo, who had just landed his expedition at Baradero, near Cardenas, was with us, waiting to join Gomez. Collazo was to become a general, on confirmation of the commander-in-chief, and he had selected as the nucleus of his staff, Hernandez and Duque Estrada, two young officers who had been educated, and very well educated, in the United States. Charlie Hernandez was conspicuous for a fine pair of boots which he never took off. They were sportsman's boots, came to the knee and were laced up in front.

Somehow, whenever you saw Hernandez, you

saw his boots first and always considered the chances of war, and wondered who would get those boots in case an accident were to happen to their occupant. Although Hernandez shared the common danger of dying with his boots on, there was no possibility of his being buried with them on.

I had almost forgotten a little doctor named Janiz. I think he was appointed largely on account of his pleasing social qualities, for he never seemed to know what to do when a man was wounded. He would always open his little medical case and spread it out all over the table and study the instruments and then roll them up, put them back again, and turn with a sigh of relief to the good old rag and diluted carbolic acid treatment.

Janiz was a bit of an artist, and made portraits that were in great demand. One I reproduce; it was of Bertrand and did not flatter him in the least. Janiz had a knack at caricature, and a sense of humor that made him sketch men who went to sleep in chairs, or corners, in awkward poses or with their mouths open, and then tickle them with straws until they awoke. Janiz would himself remain awake, even when fatigued, for fun of this kind. Janiz and the little barrister, the alleged fire-eater, had a joke that they passed between them.

Hernandez' beautiful boots.

One would catch the other's eye and remark "Jigili-ji," chuckling; the other would reply quick as a shot, "Jigili-ji," and both would squirm in spasms of mutual merriment. I never was able to learn what the joke was.

As a disciplinarian, Lacret was a failure. He yielded to humane emotions, and was altogether too easy with his men. I remember at Pavo Real, Miguelin's scouts brought in an evil-eyed peasant, accused, on fair circumstantial evidence, of having guided the Spaniards to the attack of the day before, and who even had a Spanish pass about him; yet Lacret let him go on the ground that the evidence was not conclusive. Near Bolondron, Lacret spared two guerrilleros who had been captured by his scouts. Regular Spanish soldiers are invariably released as a matter of policy; but guerrilleros are usually regarded as traitors, and fair game for the machete.

The consequence of Lacret's kindness was to encourage stealing among the negroes, and whenever local forces camped with us, you had to be up very early, the moment the whistle was blown, to see that no one rode away with your horse. I found a contrast later, in Gomez' camp, where you could leave anything, even a purse or a pistol, lying about, and nobody would take it: for it was very well known that Gomez would shoot any man found stealing the smallest thing as quick as he could make a court-martial convict him.

With the peasants Lacret was genial and patronizing, and a welcome guest in their cottages. He played grandfather to the men, and flattered the women with an old soldier's insinuating gallantry. Where there were attractive girls of marriageable age, Lacret would join them, bringing gifts of cigarettes, or long black cigars, if he had them; for the Cubanitas love tobacco, and they would all puff and joke together very happily.

To myself, as a correspondent, Lacret was especially courteous. He detailed two negroes from his impedimenta, Alfredo and Eusebio, to be my asistentes, one of whom followed me till the day of an unfortunate skirmish; the other until I set sail from Cuba.

Noticing that Pujol was far better mounted than I,— for he rode a fiery little stallion that some scouts had found concealed among the canes on a sugar estate, while I still rode the old flea-bitten gray mare Andarje had given me,— Lacret bade us change steeds. This with a characteristic little speech, telling how foreigners should be cherished and given of the best. Pujol and I shifted saddles, though Pujol, as a friend, advised me that his was a high-spirited animal, that he, skilled equestrian as he was, could scarcely control; perhaps for an American it might be dangerous. I was mortified to deprive a companion of a good horse; but the general so commanded; and as

"*The Cubanitas love tobacco.*"

for Pujol, I was able to soothe his feelings with a small loan some days later.

Eusebio and Alfredo.

Lacret's courtesy was of the old baronial type, and before I left him he made Piedra draw up for me a commission (which I reproduce on page 66) as honorary major of his staff, "to take active effect," he said, "as soon as I chose to become a Cuban citizen." This commission was later of great assistance to me in securing guides and small escorts as I travelled in search of Gomez.

Lacret made two circuits in ten days of "pacified Matanzas," always marching long before daybreak, passing within gunshot of encamped Spanish columns, tearing up railroad tracks and cutting telegraph wires. It was the level "redearth" (tierra Colorada) country, where rich ferruginous mould tints the soil, enriching it for the production of sugarcane and coffee. Everywhere the cane was afire, and a

Map showing Lacret's two circuits of Pacified Matanzas, in ten days, and the railroads we crossed.

haze of fragrant smoke hung in the air. Sometimes

"A swearing, clattering exit of the impedimenta after the practico."

we crossed the bare hills that extend like a great backbone through the centre of the province, and moved into some new district where our presence was unlooked for. Sometimes we circled about white villages, with dots of forts and tall cathedral towers; sometimes, when halting for dinner, we would be nearly surprised, and shots from the main guard would be followed by a tumbling of pots and pans into panniers on the backs of horses and mules, and a swearing, clattering exit of the impedimenta on the trot or gallop after the practico (guide).

After one of these surprises, near Bolondron, on the 18th of May, a man called "El Japones" (the Japanese), a big, stupid fellow who had come with Collazo's expedition, was captured.

He was one of a handful of men, commanded by Elias, who "stood off" the pursuing Spaniards from behind stone-walls, and his horse was shot under him. Contrary to general orders, he separated himself from his troop and went to a farmhouse in search of a fresh mount. The Spanish advance was unexpectedly swift and "El Japones" was caught in the yard in front of the cottage. The peasants who buried him said that before he died they gouged out his eyes and smashed in his teeth with the butts of their muskets. At any rate he gave them some information, including the fact that there was an American correspondent with Lacret. When this news was reported at the officers' mess,—so I was told by Mr. Dawley, the *Harper's Weekly* correspondent who was with the Spanish regiment at the time,—a diminutive lieutenant tapped his machete, saying, "Oh! wouldn't I like to get at that Yankee; that

Uncle Sam pig, — I'd teach him to go with the Mambis."

One afternoon, within sight and gunshot of a fort, we captured a courier on a fine coffee-colored mule, with mail for the colonel of that same Spanish column. Lacret seized the official correspondence and the mule, and let the courier go his way on foot with the private letters. Duque Estrada rode the mule for some time afterwards.

On the 14th, early in the morning, we rode through a great sugar estate, called, I believe, Conchita, one of the largest in all Matanzas, about an hour before daybreak. Inglesito had burned it a day or two before under Lacret's orders. It was a little town by itself, built over the top of a broad hill. There were long buildings of stone for the employees, and storehouses for the syrup and sugar. In the centre were the mills — all modern machinery. Everything was destroyed — only blackened walls remained, in which rafters and fragments of fallen roofing still smouldered or blazed in tiny flames. The guard of Spanish soldiers had departed — and it was dismal, and silent, except for the howling of half a dozen dogs. Certainly half a million of invested capital and standing cane went up on that estate alone.

Everywhere splendid sugar-mills of obstinate planters, burned by the rebels, and peasants' huts and country houses of the rich burned by the troops, lay in ashes. Flames, and the unburied bodies of slaughtered pacificos of all ages, marked the course of Spanish columns.

The Spaniards, following our trail, usually arrived at an estate, or cottage, a few hours after we had

(One-half the actual size.)

Division Matánzas. General Lacret Morlot (No. 265). In pursuance of the authority vested in me by Article 13 of the Law of Military Organization, and considering the services lent, in the war of Cuban Independence, by the citizen Grover Flint, this Headquarters confers upon him the military rank of Honorary Major in the Liberating Army of Cuba. Savana Grande, April 20, 1896.

F. & L. (Fatherland and Liberty)
(Signed) José Lacret Morlot,
General of Division.

left it, and burned everything. The destruction of property was appalling.

There was the Socorro de Armas place,—a comfortable shooting-box, near Navajas, where we once rested for a day and a night.

De Armas was no longer living; but a steward represented the heirs and kept the house with its gardens and fruit trees, in good order.

Some of us enjoyed siestas in de Armas' salon, where we sprawled over the dignified old furniture,—sofas and tables and armchairs; some of us bathed in Señor de Armas' little tin bathtubs; some of us found old friends in his library,—works of the Badminton series, books of travel and adventure, English novels that are held classic, and Monte Cristos, and Les Misérables, and Wandering Jews, and detective stories of Gaboriau; and there was an album of popular photographs of twenty years ago,—Clara Morris, Madame Ristori, Adelaide Neilson as Rosalind, Kate Claxton in a snow scene from the "Two Orphans," Lotta in "Zip," Charles Fechter in a corduroy suit, and the elder Sothern as Lord Dundreary. We ate from the de Armas porcelain — it was handsome porcelain — and as a change from my hammock, I slept on the long, low, cushioned seat of the old family volante, which the careful steward had trundled up on the front porch.

"*The old family volante.*"

It was a clean bunk, with that fragrance of cloth and leather that you find only in private carriages, and before we left, Duque Estrada, who had no waterproof, cut a great square of leather from the volante's hood that kept him dry on many a rainy march afterwards.

An hour after we left the de Armas place, a black cloud arose behind us against the clear morning sky, and we knew that the Bungalow and the furniture and the old volante were going up in smoke.

Once in a while there was time to get our clothes washed; but like eating and sleeping, cleanliness was a matter of luck. In this connection, Lacret once remarked, "I shall bathe myself when the floods of the rainy season (*las lluvias*) begin. We all managed to shave occasionally, Campoverde acting as barber in off moments for those who had no razors. Campoverde was also staff hair-cutter by appointment. Otherwise, Lacret's camp offered no luxuries excepting now and then a chance package of tobacco, or a thimbleful of coffee — sometimes it was honest, black Cuban coffee, sometimes a liquid brewed from scorched kernels of Indian corn. It was a struggle to write, because at night tapers were hard to get, and by day, when Lacret made a house his headquarters, the staff slept all over the tables and chairs until Campoverde tipped them off and served dinner. Even Piedra, the secretary, achieved official correspondence with difficulty.

Efforts were made by those of the staff who could borrow money from the general, or had any of their own, to get clothing, tobacco, rum, anything, out from the towns. Some daring pacifico would volunteer to smuggle these supplies "for his personal use"; but meanwhile, a sudden movement of the troops would send Lacret scurrying off to another district, and that was generally the last of the pacifico and the red gold piece.

On one occasion, Charlie Hernandez and Duque Estrada sent a pacifico to Bolondron to buy them jipi-japa hats and two packages of cigars. The regular price of the hats was four dollars each, but the pacifico arranged with a Spanish sergeant to buy them in Bolondron and deliver them to him at eight dollars apiece, with a corresponding advance for the cigars. The sly sergeant, to save appearances (he knew the supplies were for insurgents), smuggled them out through the lines in the coffin of a dead man who was to be buried in a cemetery on the outskirts of the town.

By the 20th of April the entire force was beginning to show signs of wear. The horses were all in bad condition from constant marching, so Lacret moved to the southward of Bolondron.

There at Savana Grande, in the pasture country, where the tall palm forests and swamps of the south shore begin, Lacret held another mobilization of local forces. It was a sparsely settled district, with little danger of surprise from troops.

The headquarters had been a pot-house, and a number of alcoholic luxuries still remained, for the Spaniards had not yet been there. The proprietor was crafty; every flask of brandy or liquor you bargained for was the last, and the price advanced as swiftly as that of the Sibylline books. (Transactions of course were in confidence "between gentlemen.")

The vicissitudes of del Monte.

It was at Savana Grande that I met an old acquaintance. Years ago, when I was a small boy in New York and used to attend dancing classes, I knew a very swell youth named Leonardo del Monte. His family had a large estate in Cuba where they did a great deal of entertaining. Every afternoon del Monte promenaded Fifth Avenue in a silk hat and a long frock coat, with the gait that they call in England, the "cavalry stoop." He was several years older than I, but I often thought of him and wished I might grow up to look as distinguished as del Monte.

I was sitting on my host's porch, when a young man, a very seedy object, came limping up. His left shoe was tied on with a string, because the upper part had given way, and his right foot was bandaged in a sort of splint cunningly contrived from bits of cedar cigar boxes, and he wore a straggly beard. He asked me in English if I thought there was any possibility of getting a drink round there. I talked with him and found it was Leonardo.

Some months before del Monte had received a Remington bullet in his foot that smashed the bones and gave him no end of trouble. He had been in a swamp hospital for two months, but getting sick of its flies and stench, he left as soon as his foot was a little better.

Del Monte was a civil engineer, a graduate of Stevens Institute. He was then on his way to practise his academic knowledge of high explosives in dynamiting a railroad bridge near Cañas. Whether he succeeded or not I never learned.

Chapter VII

The Prefectura Pedrosa

THE Prefectura Pedrosa is in the district of Pedrosa, where canefields and pastures end, and the everglades and palm forests of the south shore begin. It is a short day's march from Navajas, a large garrison town, and consequently not an entirely safe neighborhood. To reach it you must follow winding paths, through stretches of porous gray limestone, every crevice of which is so luxuriantly grown with pineapple, bananas, and malanga vines, that it is a splendid place for ambuscades. The paths are of brick-red dust that penetrates like the alkaline dust of our western plains: it rises in the air from under your horse's hoofs and works into your clothing, and is hard to wash out.

The prefect lived with his family in one of three

comfortable palm-thatched cottages, on the edge of a forest. This first representative of the Civil Government I had seen, was an intelligent peasant, who carried a rifle and dressed neatly, like an officer of a local force, with the usual tricolored cockade on his hat. He exercised his duties as magistrate and only authorized killer of cattle and dispenser of beef to the country people of Pedrosa. His prefectura was one of the post stations within a day's march of each other that extend along the south shore from Cienfuegos, in Santa Clara, to the big trocha in Pinar del Rio.

Here for the first time in the Manigua, I could write under a roof and on a table, with plenty of light, and without expectation of sudden alarm. I could also arrange to forward correspondence through the lines to my agent in Cardenas.

Did the reader ever guess at the history of the tardy correspondence from the insurgent field he occasionally found in his morning newspaper during that period of the war? Of the many letters I wrote from the Manigua, some of which I reproduce from memory in these chapters, the greater part were lost, or destroyed by the couriers to whom they were entrusted. Many a letter that reached its destination had to be smuggled past the guards of a town, perhaps in a basket of fruit, a cheese, or a cocoanut shell by some pacifico, who delivered it to my agent at the risk of his life and passed that risk along with it.

I had arranged lines of communication through Cardenas and Matanzas; but in both cities my agents were arrested, though it was long before I learned of the fact. The time was already past when a letter dropped in the postoffice of any town would be sent on its way with an unbroken seal.

And these letters were queer-looking documents. They were written on almost anything; sometimes on the blue or orange wrappers of a cake of chocolate, sometimes on the fly-leaves of old books from deserted houses.

Early in the campaign I had lost my saddle-bags, with ink, pens, paper, and other supplies of the kind, and so I bought or borrowed pencils from peasants as I travelled along. One letter to the *Journal* arrived in New York with every other leaf missing. The agent, in the uncertainty of smuggling it out, evidently did not believe in trusting all his eggs to one basket.

All was quiet at Pedrosa that morning. Nothing moved over the country but the shadows, until that afternoon a courier, who knew Matanzas Province as a New York policeman knows Broadway, rode off to the northward, with a bulky letter addressed to an imaginary person in Cardenas.

There was a hospital in the forest at Pedrosa, just such a swamp hospital as Leo del Monte had complained of. It was there I met Madame Hernandez, the pretty young wife of Dr. Francisco Hernandez, formerly Maceo's staff surgeon and a graduate of the University of Madrid. She was assisting her husband as a trained nurse, and when the prefect presented me to her, she was under a rancho of palm leaves, fighting mosquitoes and tearing lint for the wounded.

Madame Hernandez had sacrificed every comfort in life, except that of being with her husband, for the Cuban cause. She had just returned from the field, where for three months she had accompanied her husband, riding on a side-saddle, with Maceo's staff, in some of the hardest battles the fighting Cuban general ever had.

In action, they told me Madame Hernandez always sat calmly on her horse in the hottest fire, ready to gallop to the side of a wounded officer or enlisted man. On one occasion, Maceo, seeing her tending a wounded negro soldier within range of the Spanish guns, rose in his stirrups, waved his hat and shouted " Viva la Reina de Cuba! (Long live the Queen of Cuba!) "

Madame Hernandez was diffident, and little inclined to talk about herself.

" Do you ever feel nervous under fire? " I asked.

" Ah, no, Señor," she replied; " I feel no fear, because I know one only falls when the time comes — so, you see, I couldn't feel frightened, and it does not matter whether the firing is near or far away. Then I have my duties to attend to, which makes a difference. The first time I was under fire I did feel a strange fascination and interest, and then somebody was wounded near me, and I went to attend him."

" Have you personally witnessed any of the atrocities that the troops inflict on the country people?"

" Not exactly! You see we were always on the

march, but the troops followed us, killing many poor people and burning houses. I knew of one very sad case, however.

"General Maceo and our staff camped with a very good and kind family at Lomo del Gato. There was an old man and his young married daughter, who had lately become a mother. She was a very sweet woman, and her husband, I think, was with the insurgents. After we left, the Spaniards came and our scouts brought in stories from the country people of what they did there.

"They entered the house of our kind friends, sacked it, and cut the old man down with machetes. They killed an old negro servant and two mulatto farm-hands, and left their bodies by the road unburied. The daughter was in the room when they killed her father, and she tried to rush between them and the old man. They cut her about the right arm, which she raised before her face, and wounded her with thrusts of bayonets. The wet nurse ran to the door and held up the little baby before her, begging for mercy. A soldier, standing outside, put his rifle to the infant's head and shot the poor little thing dead. The daughter refused to be cared for by a Spanish surgeon, but they put her in a shed near by, for they had fired the house, and the regimental surgeon ordered quicklime put on her wounds. She died from shock and pain.

"This is the story the peasants tell in Lomo del Gato. You hear such stories all over the Island — I believe they are all true — though it seems incredible that people could act so nowadays."

I asked Madame Hernandez if there was no

less exposed place for her than at Maceo's side in action.

"There was no other place, even if I wished,— and after all one is as safe at a general's side as anywhere," she answered. "Our headquarters was the saddle, and at night we stopped wherever we happened to be. Then, you know, I am not here for my own comfort."

At night, on that campaign, Madame Hernandez slept, as I learned from Lacret, like any Cuban soldier, in a hammock between two palm trees, or under the porch of some cottage. She never felt fatigue, she said, because she had too much to do.

She was in Maceo's hardest battles. She was at Pavo Real, where the Spanish General Luque was wounded and his column driven back before a charge of Maceo's cavalry. At Rio Hondo she was with the first line of skirmishers, who accounted for fifty-four Spaniards in three hours and laid their bodies side by side on the high-road. At Moralitos and Jesus Nazareno she rode tirelessly in an all-day skirmish, when the insurgent army engaged three Spanish columns. She was at Jaruco when the town was taken and sacked. It was there that the Spanish troops entered after the insurgent forces had retired, shot down seventeen non-combatants, whom they dragged from their houses, and sent thirteen more to the dungeons of Morro.

NOTE. — I remember Dr. Hernandez as a tall, gaunt man, extremely pallid and emaciated. I clip the following from the *Boston Globe* of August 3, 1897, without comment.

"Havana. Aug. 2. — A correspondent who has returned from the Isla de Pinos secured an interview with Mrs. Hernandez, widow of Dr. Hernandez, who was Maceo's physician.

"Mrs. Hernandez was captured by Spaniards after her husband was killed near Sancti Spiritus, and deported to the penal settlement of the Isla de Pinos. Mrs. Hernandez says that her husband, who was in the last stages of consumption, was hidden in Managua hospital, accompanied by herself and two faithful negro attendants, all unarmed.

"Her husband was at the point of death and too weak to move when the Spanish forces, under Col. Orozzo, approached. . . . She hoisted a white flag with a red cross, but the troops fired upon the house, killing one attendant and wounding the other. She advanced to meet the Spaniards, beseeching the commandant to cease firing, and announced her husband's name and rank. . . . The soldiers surrounded the house. . . . Col. Orozzo dismounted and entered the building, and Dr. Hernandez made an effort to rise and greet him, when Orozzo deliberately drew his revolver and sent a bullet through the sick man's brain. The soldiers tore Mrs. Hernandez from her husband's body, hacked the corpse with machetes and set fire to the building. . . . They forced her to march before them with arms shackled all of that day. . . . Arriving at Sancti Spiritus, after further ill treatment, she was thrown into a common prison with male criminals. Weyler condemned her to indefinite confinement in a penal settlement.''

A cup of guarapo by the roadside.

Chapter VIII

Marto's Men

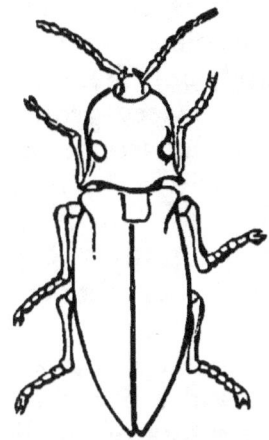

A Cocuyo (actual size).

FROM Pedrosa eastward to the Hanabana river are rolling pastures lighted at night by reflections of distant candelas and the gleam of the great fire beetles, called cocuyos,[1] — insects as big as June bugs, with a spark brilliant enough to read by if you catch one in a handkerchief. In times of peace, young men catch cocuyos and present them to their sweethearts, who tangle them in their mantillas, or pin them on their bosoms confined in little bits of lace. In war time, the cocuyos, as they sail along a few feet above the ground, might pass for the glowing cigars of horsemen, moving at a trot toward and away from one another, and for this reason one may still smoke and ride through the long grass within a few yards of a Spanish sentry without attracting attention.

---

[1] The cocuyo (sometimes cocujo) is by far the most brilliant insect of its kind known to naturalists. Half a dozen of them confined in a wicker cage will supply a light equal to that of a small candle, and in the old slave days they served to illuminate the cabins of plantation negroes.

By night, this silent open country is safe travelling. Only stray cattle and roving insurgent bands cross it, and there are patches of woods that offer hiding places by day. It is a desolate district. Wherever country houses have stood, only beds of ashes and blackened "dobe" walls, with weed-grown gardens, remain, and the railroad line to Camaronas (on the Bay of Cochinos) was abandoned early in the war.

The Hanabana river is easy to ford, for, until the rainy season, it is only a rush-grown gully. On the eastern side, rich pastures, forests, and canebrakes begin and extend to Cienfuegos.

The district about Cienfuegos is what a Cuban would call "muy malo" (very bad), and a Spaniard loyal and faithful. That is, there are lots of small towns almost within gunshot hearing of each other, all of which have guerilla forces, composed of as villanous a mob of jail sweepings as could be gathered anywhere in the world. These guerillas are the more confident and ferocious because in that part of the country the Cuban forces have been demoralized, and led oftener than otherwise by men who would rather run than fight. Atrocities committed by the Spanish guerillas about Cienfuegos have been of such mediæval ghastliness that no one ever believed them, and reports of them are handled gingerly by news editors.

There are some good insurgent forces, however, one of them commanded by Desiderio Marto, a tall one-eyed man, who made the forests near Yaguaramas his headquarters, with something less than one hundred men, half infantry. Even Marto's men could not do very active fighting. Their tactics consisted in burning cane, shooting at Spanish forts by night to keep the soldiers awake, circling around the towns, and having small hand-to-hand skirmishes, when possible, with the local guerillas;—the semi-offensive warfare that lack of ammunition makes necessary for the insurgents in Cuba. Marto's men rarely camped two nights in the same place, and so they were secure against preconcerted attack. The camp was ready to move at a moment's notice. All they had to do was to throw the camp kettles in a big straw pack-saddle on the back of the star mule, blow two notes on the whistle, meaning "To horse!" and march off through forest paths or among canefields to some covered spot a mile or so away and camp for the night.

Marto's troopers were noticeably proficient in a natural form of the skirmish drill that is so much studied by our United States cavalry. They rode the country in single or double file, according to circumstances. Whenever palm groves and clumps of underbrush made a cover to the right or left, flankers in twos or threes galloped forward, without command, sometimes for two hundred yards, poking into every thicket that might conceal an enemy.

In the United States cavalry service we have a drill in which odd numbers, of specified sets of fours, trot or gallop to one side of the column, and even numbers to the other, or ahead, as the case may be, as scouts and flankers. It would have worried an American cavalry officer to see files leave the column at will; but the ease and security with which Marto's little force travelled, proved the value of practical training that comes from actual experience and necessity.

There was a dense patch of forest, scarcely half a mile across, in the fork of two high-roads, where four of Marto's officers had cut a clearing and constructed large and comfortable ranchos for their families. This was the safest spot to be found in an otherwise dangerous region. Blind paths led to the clearing, where you had to climb over trees felled diagonally across your way until you became sweaty and irritable. The horses were left nearer the road, but the inner clearing was sacred — designed for a place of absolute safety as long as the war might last. Consequently even the entrances of its two approaches were skilfully concealed, and you lifted certain fallen trees and replaced them on passing in or out.

These families were shut off from the world. They got their water from natural wells in cavities of the limestone, — the sort of limestone you found at Pedrosa. Only the officers and their asistentes entered occasionally, carrying rations of beef and sweet-potatoes, in gunny sacks. On a very small scale it was a type of the communities on the southern coast in the Cienaga Zapata, the great swamp lands of the Shoe, inaccessible from the mainland except by a narrow trail through everglades and jungles, where cattle and wild pigs abound and the insurgents have established hospitals, tanneries, and workshops.

Two of the four families were colored, with a swarm of naked pickaninnies tugging at their mammy's skirts, or burrowing in the red soil. The girls wore glass beads around their necks like little savages.

When a sudden cloudburst came, for the rainy season was setting in, the negro children gathered in two black, wriggling broods, peering with white eyeballs from the shelter of their ranchos. The white children also were naked, as all peasant children under five or six years old are in Cuba, and brown as little Indians, with abdomens distended

"*When a sudden cloudburst came.*"

from vegetable diet. They were less neat than the blacks, or perhaps the soil on their bodies showed more — they were only decently clean for half an hour every other day, when their mothers washed them all over. The families were friendly enough, but instinctively whites and blacks kept apart.

When the rain fell in torrents, only a vigorous shovelling kept the floors of the ranchos from flooding, but nobody minded that, and there was a sense of security very unusual in that part of the Island.

Captain Benigno Ortiz, a thickset colored man, with a positively refined softness of manner and speech, was my host. He was a devoted father, and confessed to me, as he sat in the midst of his family, — "I am naturally valiant, especially if I forget myself, but when I think of these children I feel fear of bullets." Thinking of his pickaninnies, Ortiz was always studying and devising fresh obstacles for the paths leading to the world of war and danger outside. "I could alone with fifty cartridges," he said, "hold one of these entrances against an entire guerilla."

Ortiz was by birth a native of Santo Domingo, and spoke a purer Spanish than the average Cuban. The ambition of his life was to send his two little boys to the United States, — "even as far as Jacksonville" to be educated. "For learning," he said, "is the comfort of life, and in the United States there is great learning, even more perhaps than in Havana or Spain."

There were two roosters, two parrots and five hens in the settlement, and the roosters caused all the trouble. They crowed continually, and their crowing, when the moon was high and the forest still from the song of wild birds, could be heard to a great distance. "This," said Ortiz, "is dangerous, and these roosters should be killed. They imperil the lives of our children, even of our wives." But the wife of the man who owned the roosters, a white woman, was obstinate. "When have the Spaniards ever thought of coming here, I'd like to know," she said, "and besides, one is a very fine game-cock that was loaned to us to keep." There were daily discussions on this point, and the proprietress of the roosters, whose husband was away in service, finally cut out the tongue of one of them as a compromise, but it was found that the cock crowed almost as loudly as before, only it was a labored, unmusical performance. "When an alarm comes," whispered Ortiz, impressively, "I will cut their throats," and the matter was temporarily dropped.

The children's games were all warlike. They played Spain and Cuba with sticks for guns, and carried on skirmishes in the underbrush. Sometimes it was a game of prefectura, where one child hid a broom horse in the thicket and another played Spaniard and scouted about with a wooden machete to find and kill it. The first sound the babies mastered was "Alto, quien va? Cuba," and "Pah, Pah," "Poom, poom, poom,"—for often sounds of shots came from the high-road, and the infants learned to distinguish between the bark of the Mauser and the slow detonation of the Remington.

There was at this time, as guest of the woman who owned the roosters, Madame Paulina Ruiz Gonzales, wife of Captain Rafael Gonzales, an officer of Pancho Perez, brigadier-general of the Santa Clara division. Some months before she had left her home in Corral Falso by night, and met a party of insurgents on the outskirts of the town.

She rode off, astride an extra horse, to the force of Manolo Menendez, where her husband was at the time. She was too plucky and too proud to be one of the impedimenta, so she begged Pancho

Perez to let her carry the flag. Two days after she carried the standard[1] very gallantly under a hot shower of Mauser bullets, and was appointed lieutenant for bravery. On the fifth of February, at Mango Largo, she led in two machete charges against the guerilla of Corral Falso. With the standard slung from her left arm, she rode with a machete in the front rank, beside Pancho Perez himself. Here she gave the machete to two guerrilleros. One she struck three times, shouting "Viva Cuba Libre," and cut him down from his saddle. Both lay dead on the field when the guerilla retired. She had two horses shot under her. One in the engagement of Villa de Habaco, on the last day of March, and the other when Manolo Menendez' troop rode into an ambuscade near Bolondron. She had already taken part in ten battles and skirmishes, always under gun-fire, and where the machetes fell oftenest, but she had never been wounded.

The "flag captain" and her autograph.

[1] With both Lacret and Gomez, flags were packed away in some staff officer's saddle-bags, and displayed only on grand occasions, when a flag-pole was cut and trooper detailed to carry it.

Madame Gonzales wore a linen coat and a short skirt that showed a pair of striped trousers beneath. She was twenty-one years old and very pretty, with regular features, soft dark eyes, glossy black hair that curled over her forehead, and a gentle, persuasive voice. She was slim as a poplar and very graceful.

They told me she held an honorary commission from Pancho Perez as capitana banderada or flag captain. General Perez was then lying wounded in a field-hospital in the peninsula Zapata, and she was awaiting his return, to once more carry the standard of the Santa Clara division.

When I met Madame Gonzales, she had lost her hat, and I made her accept my own, an American cow-puncher's sombrero, and showed her how to give it the proper "Denver poke." This readiness on my part to incur sunstroke paved the way to an interview.

"Were you ever afraid?" I asked.

"Gracious! no, Señor," she answered, with a little laugh. The thought that one could experience fear seemed to amuse her mightily.

"Did you not feel a little strange when you heard the first volley and saw men falling about you?"

"No, no, Señor, I never felt afraid in my life, but in my first action I was impatient. My horse could not go to the enemy quick enough. I rode my first charge without giving the machete to any one. We were all hurried together and crowded from this side and from that. I saw the machetes flash near me, and heard the rattle and clash, but I found no one in front of me. Then it was all dust and the enemy had gone. Our men were all crowding about the flag, and cheering, but figure to yourself, Señor, I had met nobody and I felt I had come out for nothing, though they told me the centre where I rode cut the line of soldiers right in two. As for me, I heard shots and the dust choked me, and I was crowded to this side and that but I could strike no one, and I had to put my machete back, feeling that I had not struck for Cuba."

"Would you like to kill a Spaniard?" I asked.

"But no, Señor, I would not for the world kill any one, but figure to yourself, when you ride against an enemy, that is a different thing. You strike for Cuba and you think only of Cuba. I have struck with the machete, but it was not as if I had hurt any one. They fell, but you know it was for Cuba and I would not hurt any one."[1]

---

[1] Interesting stories have been published about Amazons in the Cuban field, but Madame Gonzales was the only one it was my fortune to meet.

There are women, mostly negresses, with some of the smaller local forces who have followed their husbands, sharing the hardship of the always moving camp and the chances of a stray bullet. They carry machetes, as tools rather than weapons, wear bloomers, even trousers, and sleep in hammocks or on bits of rubber cloth on the hard ground; but they do not fight in the skirmish line with rifle or shotgun, like the men, for they form part of the impedimenta. With the impedimenta, they remain in the rear when the attacks are made, or are hurried off in advance of the main force when it is time to retire.

Gomez disapproves of women in the field, and calls it an "escandalo." The "old man" does not permit even heroines in his own camp.

Chapter IX

The Zone of Cienfuegos

"*He wore an anxious look.*"

HOW the prefect of Soledad escaped nervous prostration I never could understand. He lived with his attractive wife and two pretty little blonde daughters in a comfortable thatched cottage, not three hundred yards from the high-road in the demoralized zone of Cienfuegos. Soledad was only two leagues from Cartagena, an equal distance from Santiago, and a short half-day's march from both Las Lajas and Santo Domingo,—all towns with jailbird guerillas that rivalled each other in outrage and villany.

The prefect had four men under him, two of whom scouted the roads by day and two by night. Luckily the country about Soledad was wooded and there was a fair chance of escape, even in case of surprise. The prefect always wore an anxious look, and his reply to a salutation was invariably, "No hay novedad (There is nothing new)."

The prefect of Soledad was by turns butcher for the pacificos of the neighborhood and green grocer for the civil and military commissions that frequently crossed the Cienfuegos district, going eastward or westward, and his duties of killing beef, gathering vegetables from the peasants, or attending to his private farming, kept him very busy.

Map of the zone of Cienfuegos, showing its numerous garrisoned towns and principal railroads.

In spite of the constant danger that was part of his home life, the prefect sometimes went out of his way, as I thought, to look for trouble.

On one occasion, with a cabecilla named Pepe Aguilar and only three men, we took supper at a house on the highway scarcely a quarter of a mile out of Cartagena, leaving our horses hitched in the yard while one man mounted guard at the gate.

The visit was an interesting one, especially as the hostess was a woman noted for her patriotism, who had recently equipped a field-hospital with drugs purchased at her own expense and smuggled out from town beneath her skirts; but had the guerilla of Cartagena known we were there, they might have given us a rub to escape.

The insurgents have a proneness to this sort of recklessness. I remember dining with Lacret and several of his officers outside of his camp one night, on invitation from a peasant. It was an adventure of the sort that cost the Cubans one of their most distinguished generals, Bruno Zayas, who, with two officers of his staff, accepted the hospitality of a pacifico, were betrayed, and surrounded by a force sent to capture them. Zayas shot himself, and his officers were cut down, game to the last. It was from exposing themselves to treachery in a similar manner that a Colonel Sanchez and five of his men were caught and shot near Sagua a few months later, and more recently Brigadier Aranguren swells the list of victims of misplaced confidence.

This Pepe Aguilar, by the way, was a thickset, bullet-headed young man, of genial bearing, but not a very soldierly character, for he always seemed to be foraging on his own account, or making love to peasant girls near the town by night, and sleeping by day when his force courted ease in the woods. As a sample of his discipline, the prefect and I once rode into his camp at midnight without being challenged.

Another instance of demoralization was the condition of the force of a negro named Aniceta.[1]

---
[1] Major Aniceta Hernandez.

The prefect had found in the woods remains of cattle killed without his knowledge, and I was with him when he tracked and discovered the perpetrators and found them to be members of Aniceta's force, who maintained a little prefecture of their own in the forests, where they lived in lawless ease and did no fighting.

Some weeks afterwards, with Gomez, I saw this force again. Rumors of their inactivity had reached the commander, and he sent one of his fighting regiments to the Cienfuegos district to gather them all in, and had them drawn up before him in his camp at Pozo Azul, near the Camaguey border. There the old general gave them a lecture that made them wince more than the steel of the Spaniards. Every man of them felt that the eye of the great war chief was on him personally. He had heard, he said, that they had been macheted, cut up, and made to run like sheep by a small Spanish guerilla. He had travelled the entire length of the Island and had never heard of such a disgraceful thing before. He would put them, he said, in the future where they would have to fight; and he thereupon divided them up among his forces, giving instructions that every one of them should be put as often as possible in a place of danger. As for Aniceta himself, he must have overslept, for he was captured by Captain Piniera of the Lajas Guerilla and shot in the town of Las Lajas.

Type of an elderly Maja.

These forces were what they called "Majaces." That is, composed of men who carry arms and look valiant, but live on the country and do not fight. They get their name from a huge snake, called "Maja," that kills chickens and destroys hens' eggs. It is a big, dangerous-looking reptile, but perfectly harmless.

Another Maja officer of the district was Captain Pinos, who commanded thirty men, and was the most candid specimen, for a timid man, I had ever seen. Pinos always ran at the first shot, and never denied it, for he judged that life in the long grass was too pleasant to be sacrificed lightly. He was an ox-eyed, middle-sized man, with flowing dark moustachios and a sad agree-with-you-sir-perfectly-I-am-a-blackguard manner. Without a blush, he told how the Santo Domingo guerilla had nearly captured him the day before. It was a story of a long chase, where the followers of Pinos owed their lives to the endurance of their horses alone. It was a gallop through the forest, every man for himself, with the relentless guerilla in full cry behind. 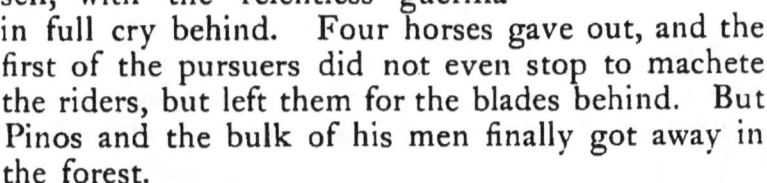 Four horses gave out, and the first of the pursuers did not even stop to machete the riders, but left them for the blades behind. But Pinos and the bulk of his men finally got away in the forest.

A lieutenant of Pinos', who stood by, told how he also escaped by a miracle. With his young mulatto asistente, Chicho, he was left in the extreme rear. Three of his comrades had already fallen, and his own horse was panting and weak-kneed and could not last much longer. In the middle of a deep arroyo, Chicho's horse planted his feet in the mud and refused to move. The lieutenant's horse just behind halted in his tracks too. Then Chicho turned in his saddle. "Hide in the swamp grass, Lieutenant," he said, and the officer slid from his horse and ran for a few paces to a fallen palm tree, behind which, in the deep mud and undergrowth, he threw himself at full length and lay without moving. He scarcely dared to breathe, and his heart, he said, "worked like the big driving wheel of an engine in a sugar-mill." In a moment, the guerrilleros were upon Chicho, and he fell from his saddle under blows without a word.

Half a dozen of the guerrilleros urged their horses in pursuit past the arroyo. Others stopped to "calentar la sangre (warm their blood)" with a hack at Chicho's body, causing a blockade in the narrow trail behind. "There must be another nañigo[1] about here," shouted an officer, pushing past the files and galloping by. "No, my captain," said one of the guerrilleros, "it is the horse of one whom I shot myself from the saddle some distance back."

Then one of them took Chicho's belt and machete as souvenirs, and the guerilla moved on. Pinos' lieutenant lay motionless, half covered with slimy water, not daring to lift his head until dark.

Then with his story, he found his way back to

[1] *Nañigo:* a term of reproach. According to Bonsal it was originally applied to negroes addicted to mysterious voodoo practices.

Soledad. Whether he waited to bury Chicho or not, he never said.

The flight of Pinos was similar to one described to me by Captain Mario Carillo, an assistant of the Administrator of Finance of Las Villas,[1] who travelled through this district a short time before I did, under escort of a force very similar in character to Pinos'. They encountered a guerilla and fled precipitately, though Carillo told me the numbers of the two forces were nearly equal. The rebels ran as fast as their grass-fed horses could go, with the guerilla trotting along a hundred yards behind. When a horse gave out, the rider was left to shift for himself, his comrades scarcely looking over their shoulders. The guerilla kept up the pursuit, led by a tall mulatto who lifted his right knee indolently to the pommel of his saddle and macheted stragglers with that up and down chopping stroke from the shoulder that native Cubans know how to give. It is the stroke of the forester when he clears brush from a wood-path, not the long, swinging cut of the trained cavalryman, who leans out of his saddle and strikes with the full weight of his body, but it is nearly as effective.

One of the insurgent party on a slow horse found himself last in the retreating line, but he did not despair. The way was narrow and riders could only pass each other with difficulty. He dug his spurs frantically into his horse's flanks, and crowded on the rider in front of him. Drawing his revolver, he covered his comrade from behind, shouting, "Halt, you coward! turn about and fight!" The

---

[1] Colonel Ernesto Fonts y Sterling.

trooper reined up in surprise, and the man with the slow horse, taking advantage of his momentary hesitation, brushed hurriedly past. Holding up each trooper in turn, the man on the slow horse worked his way along the line until he led the retreat, and, needless to say, escaped unharmed.

Another queer character was Colonel Aoulet, lieutenant-governor of the district of Cienfuegos. He had a very small force under him, acting as a sort of body-guard. He was very reckless, and would pass the night anywhere at all without bothering to post sentries, seeming to rely entirely on his ability to jump and run in any given emergency. It was very difficult to tell just how many men Aoulet did have, because his escapes were so sudden that he usually left most of them behind. He was always devising complicated schemes for destroying the Spaniards, and at this time he was at work on a history of the war in Cuba, which he wrote of evenings, in a heavy notebook that he carried with him.

I spent one night with Aoulet, in a peasant's cottage on the "King's High-road," just out of Cartagena, and most of that night I sat up listening to the distant baying of dogs, and awaiting the arrival of a guide the local sub-prefect had promised to send me. I was the only man in the party awake. These unmilitary methods did not appeal to me, and I was glad to leave Aoulet to make and record history without my assistance.

There were exceptions to the general demoralization, for all the Cienfuegos cabecillas were not majaces. Marto was certainly a most conscientious and active officer, and I was once with Manolo Menendez near Santa Rosa, when with forty armed men he went out of his way to attack two Spanish guerillas combined, nearly two hundred strong.

On that occasion Menendez led a helter skelter attack, shouting, "All who have long machetes to the front!" but the gringos were too numerous, and after an exchange of shots, we retired. Menendez got a pistol bullet in his upper arm, and we squirted carbolic acid into it, and then tied it up with an old white shirt. One of "ours" was killed.[1]

For nearly a week I remained about Soledad, trying to get a guide or a small escort to cross the railroad line into the Santa Clara district; for Gomez was now reported to be circling between Sancti Espiritu and Santa Clara city. From Sagua to Cienfuegos the railroad was very carefully guarded. There were forts the entire length of the route, at short distances from each other, and large garrisons in adjacent towns.

This important railroad was called the Central Trocha. It was patrolled by night, and the roads crossing it were often well ambuscaded. In fact, every effort was made by the Spaniards to prevent communication between the rebel forces on either side of the line. It was therefore safest to slip quietly through the trocha with a very small party and a good guide, or cross it in a weak spot with a force numerous enough to take care of itself.

[1] It is interesting to note that put under different influences these Cienfuegos forces act differently, although recruited from the same material. If the leader likes fighting, the men will fight pluckily; if he likes to run, they will run with equal cheerfulness.

Chapter X

Typical Atrocities — The Olayita Massacre[1]

ON the second of May I rode with the force of Major Manolo Menendez near the town of Soledad. At evening we passed by a little hamlet of half a dozen houses. The peasants recognized us as insurgents and came out to meet us in great excitement. This was their story: —

"His hat . . . remained."

The Spanish guerrilleros of Las Rodas had passed there that morning, and, finding no insurgents to fight, they halted before the house of Desiderio Vida, a man of thirty, who supported his mother, his wife and children, by his labor as a small farmer. The captain of the guerilla entered the house with

[1] See also the story of the murder of the American correspondent, Charles Govin. Appendix B.

three of his men and addressed Vida, in the presence of his family, with abuse and profanity.

"Thou art a Mambi. Come, scoundrel, tell us what thou knowest of the Mambis."

Vida protested that he knew nothing. Calling him a traitor, a shameless one and a nañigo, they dragged him from his house and took up their march, leading him, with his arms tied above the elbows, off among the canefields until he was lost to sight of his home. The neighbors dared not follow, and there were no witnesses of the murder.

Desiderio Vida was led from the roadside into a little arroyo or gully. Here he was cut down, and his body was left, to be found by his neighbors, after the departure of the guerilla. "We will bury him," said Menendez; "you shall see how they mutilate our people."

Vida had been buried already when we got there, but I saw the place where he fell, the hollow in the tall grass, and the blood that stained the plants as thickly as when you have slaughtered a bullock; his straw hat — a very faded old hat, that no one cared to carry away — remained. There was a cut in the brim an inch from the band, where a stroke of the machete had fallen. It must have sunk in his shoulder. With the next blow, the crown was cleft, and the clotted blood inside was scarcely dry when I saw it.

The excitable nature of the Latin, if it feels fear, must suffer terribly. There were distinct indications that the victim had been ill at the stomach from fright.

The peasants told me that Desiderio Vida had no less than a dozen wounds on his body when they found him, and that his left arm was nearly severed from his body. This was but a sample of the murders that became so frequent in all parts of the Island soon after the accession of Weyler.

One of the peasants who told me the circumstances in the Vida case, had an American wife, a red-headed New England woman, who threw up her hands and cried, in English, "For Heaven's sake, don't tell our names! — they'll kill us all — they'll kill us all."

The terror inspired in the peasantry of Central Las Villas by the guerilla bands was pitiable to witness; for no fireside was free from the danger of their visits. Men and women existed in dull unceasing dread, praying that Mr. Cleveland, "who could do anything," would interfere to help them; and the old Spanish proverb, "To-morrow will be another day"[1] had a terrible significance. At the sight of an approaching column of horsemen children scurried from their parents' doorways to hide in the brush, and in the barbed-wire fences enclosing farmyards one found openings through which the families might escape more easily to the shelter of canefield, or forest. Riding near Villa Clara with an escort of twenty Matanzas troopers (armados), who were all negroes and scantily clad, a marked contrast to the neatly dressed, ribbon-decked men of Las Villas, we were frequently mistaken for a Spanish guerilla. Passing a cottage, the peasants greeted us with

[1] "*Mañana sera otra dia.*"

cheerful smiles, though they still trembled from the agitation that our first appearance had caused.

And those who fell into the hands of the guerrilleros did not always meet as speedy a death as did Desiderio Vida, if one is to trust to the stories one hears in the district. The country rang with tales of the unspeakable methods employed by the guerilla officers in torturing men who were marked for vengeance, and every prefect could furnish memoranda of horrors. Many of the atrocities told me by scatter-brained pacificos were subsequently repeated to me by men of good standing, who had them on evidence they believed truthful. I myself saw, when with Lacret at Manjuaries, a negro who bore unmistakable physical evidences of having survived tortures of an unnatural character, which he testified had been inflicted upon him by a detachment of Spanish soldiers and civil guards, and I obtained from Lacret's staff surgeon a certificate as to the nature of the permanent injuries the man received. This document, written on odd scraps of paper, I have managed to preserve, though it is of interest only to medical men.

I had the fortune to see with my own eyes, and sketch with my own pencil, the remains of some victims of the Olayita massacre, perhaps the most striking atrocity that has taken place during the present war. These ghastly evidences of the manner in which it is possible for Spanish soldiers to conduct themselves, are still to be seen among the ruins of the Olayita plantation, fifteen miles to the southwest of Sagua la Grande.

Charred remains of at least seven victims of the Orayita massacre as I saw them under the driving wheel of the sugar mill, on May 6th, 1896.
Grover Flint

Typical Atrocities

At Olayita, in the latter part of February, 1896, the Cuban forces of Quintin Bandera skirmished with two Spanish columns under the command of Colonel Arce. The insurgents took up a position about the ingenio of the Olayita plantation, and retired southward, after having inflicted a heavy loss on the Spanish troops. As soon as the insurgent column had marched away, the Spanish infantry made a general charge on the sugar-house and its

The ingenio, Olayita.

surrounding buildings. There were no less than twenty-three pacificos, innocent non-combatants, plantation hands and their families, employed on the estate. The administrator was M. Braulio Duarte, a French citizen, and the proprietor was a certain Domingo Bertharte.

Here is the story of the massacre, as told without variation by peasants of the neighborhood.

On the approach of the Spaniards, M. Duarte locked himself in his house, a small, two-storied frame building, lay down on his bed, and wrapped himself in the French flag. The troops burst in the door, dragged M. Duarte outside, and cut him to pieces with their machetes on his own doorstep. The flag of France was soaked in blood.

An indiscriminate slaughter of the plantation hands and their families was now begun. Men, women, and small children were dragged from their homes and cut down in the usual brutal manner. The ingenio and all the surrounding buildings, the storehouses and the cottages of the plantation negroes, were set on fire, and the bodies of the victims, dead or dying, were thrown among the flames. Only one escaped, a Chinese coolie, who succeeded in making the woods near by with six Mauser bullet holes in him.

None of the pacificos, as I have it from insurgent officers who were there, had taken any part in the skirmish, but lay, quaking with fear, in their houses as long as the firing continued.

On the sixth day of May, I rode with the cavalry squadron of Colonel Robau and Major Saienz over the fields of the massacre. It was a hurried visit, for a column was then after us, and I could devote but thirty minutes to a study of the remains of the butchery that still existed. The sites of the cottages and outhouses were gray heaps of ashes. Of the sugar-house itself, a tin roof still remained, covering a mass of rusty machinery and charred timber.

In the trunk, under the great driving wheel, I counted the charred bodies of seven victims; uppermost of all, wedged between the wheel and the masonry, lay a negro woman, with a baby in her arms. Her clothing had been burned away, but the charred flesh remained, and a portion of one of her leather slippers. Of those parts of the body that had been most exposed to the flames, the bones were visible. The negress lay in an almost natural position, clasping the infant tight to her breast with a hugging, clutching embrace that death had only intensified. The body of the child was but little disintegrated by the flames. The other bodies in the pit were reduced to charred skeletons. The negress and her child had evidently been the last thrown in, and their remains had dried without decaying.

There were other bodies, they told me, in the débris of the central part of the building, which had fallen in, but I had not time to look for them. I was also told that the bodies of two other women and two little girls had been thrown into the burning cottages and entirely consumed.

Beneath the ingenio there was a cellar, in which were furnaces for heating the great sugar-boilers above. There was a little bakeshop in this cellar. I went down a short flight of steps to the chamber where the furnaces were, and there I found the remains of a Chinaman, one of the coolies employed about the place, perfectly preserved in a mummified state.

I examined the body very carefully. There were wounds of the machete about the back and legs, as though the coolie had been driven into the cellar with blows, but none of them fatal. The body was writhed in intense agony, and the face fixed in an expression of extreme horror. Parts of the clothing, a loose linen coat and trousers, were singed, and there was every indication that the man had been locked in, and forced to die from the heat of the burning ingenio above. The flesh had become

The body by the furnace underneath the ingenio.

parchment, and each muscle and line of facial expression, drawn by suffering, was intensified by the shrinkage of the flesh.

In the little passage that led to the bakeshop lay the body of another Chinaman with a gash of the machete in the back of his head. His expression and the contortion of his body were similar to those of the first, and distinctly indicated that he must have died under the same conditions. On the floor by his side lay a paper score of the loaves of bread baked for the settlement that morning. Though the wound in the back of his head was deep and some stains of blood remained on the floor, it was evident that he died by the torture of heat.

Three months had passed, and these bodies had dried without the slightest trace of decomposition.

"*On the floor by his side lay a paper score of the loaves of bread baked that morning.*"

They probably remain to this day in as perfect a state as when I saw them; and whoever visits Olayita will probably find in that cellar a good briarwood pipe that I laid down while I stopped to sketch the bodies.

In the cane, fifty yards from the ingenio, I found the corpse of a laborer who had attempted to escape. His head was completely severed from his body, and the clothing, such as remained, bore traces of machete wounds, and was thickened and stiffened with dried blood. The shoes and hat had been removed, if not by the Spanish soldiers, by the poor people living in the neighborhood, who never allow such relics to go to waste. Another pacifico, I was told, lay in the canes near by, but I did not have time to look for him.

I saw the grave of M. Duarte and that of his secretary, for after the massacre took place a Spanish officer had given orders to bury them near the ruins of their cottages. The remains of eleven of the twenty-two victims were as I have described them, and will so continue until the Spanish Government sees fit to remove them, or so long as the insurgent government chooses to preserve them as a relic of the war; for protected from the moisture of the rainy season by the cover above, they will be preserved in the pure warm air for an indefinite period of time.

I have been told that a brother of M. Duarte has presented the case to the French Consul, and that disavowal of the assassination, with a comfortable solace to the nearest of kin, is likely to follow.

I made it a point, in riding over the Island, to inquire, in every district, about the latest Spanish atrocities. The answer always was like this:—
"There were five pacificos macheted outside of the town last week! Two weeks ago ten were shot!"

Often bodies of pacificos, of all ages, obviously laborers and farmers, lying in the canes on estates where insurgents were supposed to have camped, or thrown in the brush by the roadside, proved these statements. Even at this time, when there was some attempt to deny and conceal acts of the kind, it would have been a conservative estimate to allow twenty pacificos, murdered in an irregular off-hand manner, to every town big enough to have its name on the map. And this was before Weyler began his policy of concentration[1] and reconcentration, that has already accomplished a greater destruction of peasant life than one can recall in the annals of mediæval warfare.

[1] What concentration means, Appendix C.

Lying among the canes.

Chapter XI

Crossing the Line

I MET Colonel Robau's squadron, with which I visited the scene of the Olayita massacre, by a mere accident. In fact I was lost, travelling with my two servants, an armed man, and a guide — who did not know the way. It was a splendid force of one hundred men all fully armed, and veterans who had swept down the Island with Gomez and Maceo six months before in the invasion of the western provinces to Pinar del Rio. They had just returned from Maceo's command, having cut their way through Weyler's big trocha. Robau, who is now a brigadier, was not with the force at this time, and Major Saienz was in command.

A little north of Olayita there is a line of forest, and here we caught a cow and killed her for breakfast. Two Spanish columns had been skirmishing through the country the day before, and everything, canefields, cottages, even foliage on the borders of forests, was aflame. The Spaniards had passed by the Olayita estate, and the ruins were smouldering again, for they had started a fire under the already charred timbers of the old sugar-house. Everywhere there were carcasses of horses and cattle drying in the sun, for the Spaniards were killing all the live-stock they could find. One big white stallion galloped limping after our party, attracted by the other horses, and I tried to catch it, but it was frightened and would not let me get near. I could see, however, that its hindquarters were hacked with machetes, its tail was nearly cut off, and one of its hindlegs was partly hamstrung. The temptation to shoot it was strong, as it is in the western plains to shoot the maimed cattle one finds dying slowly by the railroad tracks, or worried by packs of pitiless coyotes; but ammunition was precious.

We camped that night in the woods north of Olayita. Early on the following morning there was an alarm of "Boots and Saddles!" for a party was seen approaching in our trail, that might be a guerilla,—perhaps the advance guard of the column that had been burning the cane the day before. This turned out to be a mistake. They were old friends,—a detachment of Lacret's escolta with Camaguey in command. Lacret's wound had been bothering him excessively and he was laid up for rest, in a little prefectura near by, with half of his escort. He had sent the other half with Camaguey to carry me to Gomez, who was now reported to be very near, on the other side of the Sagua line. There were twenty men, all good big negroes, and I now had escort enough to cross the line under any circumstances.

That evening we marched to within half a mile of the railroad, but we did not cross because there was some delay in getting a guide, and besides it was raining heavily; so we camped on a deserted farm, and the officers made a cow-shed, consisting of a thatched roof and upright supports (there are no barns in Cuba), their headquarters. All these structures, like the peasants' huts, are alive with fleas that live in the clay soil of the floors; therefore we went through the performance of tearing palm thatch from the roof, lighting it in torches, and giving the floor a flame-bath and a coat of ashes to kill them. We did this until the fleas were supposed to be dead. Then those of us who had hammocks swung them under the uprights, and the rest turned in on the ground.

Next day the rain fell in constant showers. We killed two steers for the entire party in the evening, and got ready to cross the railroad line a little before sundown. A train passed, and we could see the smoke and hear the armored cars feeling their way along. When darkness came, the column got under way. We forded the Sagua river and rode across pastures and between hedges, and through the farmyards of a little settlement. It was dark and stormy. We stole along slowly, halting at times, waiting for the scouts to examine the country ahead, and then advancing again. Saienz was not anxious to skirmish with the patrols, because his men had scarcely five rounds of ammunition apiece and had no idea when they could get any more. The peasants came out and whispered with us as we rode along. They gave us cigarettes and cigars that they had made themselves.[1] From time to time the word was passed from one to another up and

---

[1] In these central districts of Las Villas, tobacco grows freely, though inferior to tobacco of Vuelto Abajo, which supplies the foreign market. One found many slat-sided sheds where the rich leaves hung to dry, and the country people were expert in the art of rolling cigars.

down the line,—"There must be no loud talking." "We are going to cross: we are going to cross," was repeated from man to man.

Finally there was one long pause. Somebody, with a pair of nippers, was cutting the barbed-wire fences on either side of the track. Then the order came down the line to advance at a trot. The whole party clattered over the embankment and across the steel rails with a noise that seemed very loud after the precautions we had been taking to keep silent, and then we took to an open pasture on the other side. "Now we are in Free Cuba," said Camaguey. A little to the east side of the line we halted and bade "Good-by" to Robau's men, who rode back at once. We had not ridden far when there came shots behind us;—our friends had run into a patrol, but Camaguey said it amounted to nothing and he guessed they could take care of themselves, so we kept on into "Free Cuba," for east of the Sagua and Cienfuegos Railway there are fewer towns, and up to that time the country had been comparatively little harassed by Spanish columns.

Before making camp that night, we stopped at a good-sized farmhouse, and the proprietor offered us coffee and home-made cigars. There was a tall young girl, a sallow blonde, who was noted throughout the country as an extemporaneous poetess. The neighborhood regarded her as a marvel, and we listened attentively while she stood gazing up at the bunches of roots and herbs that hung from the rafters above, and solemnly recited sonorous rolling verse with an inspired look. There was no apparent beginning or end to these verses, but I took note of some fragments, of a patriotic character, which I reproduce without a direct attempt at translation: —

> Salgan traidores, tiranos, que los esperan el Mambis
> Con la dulzura de aqui del bello tipo Cubano
> Salgan á explorar villanos, las fuertes contribuciones
> Salgan á operaciones para que cobran vilmente
> Trozo de plomo caliente, de los cincuenta millones.
>
> Publica Aurora Brillante, al Cubano con razon,
> Siguiera la Insurreccion, sin detener un instante,
> Machete y bala constante hasta con ella acabar,
> Salgan, tiranos á implorar de nuestro mano el perdon,
> Que sera la salvación, que España podrá alcanzar.
>
> Ahora se va nuestro general valiente que marcha
> Pinar del Rio; su mandato y poderio,
> Procede severamente, dirije su contingente
> La grandeza de Ultramar ya no podran disfrutar.
> De racimo de la uva porque,
> Su querida Cuba, Maceo se la va quitar
> Colon, Cienfuegos, Matanzas, y en Remedios
> Guerreros de confianza, cobardes cojen sus lanzas
> Preparan sus batallones, salgan en operaciones,
> Detengan el contingente, y veran pelear decente
> Estos valientes campeones.

The music and rhythm of these lines would be lost in English. They sing of the tyrant legions that sally forth at dawn and of the vigilant rebel who watches their movements from afar, of the insurrection spreading everywhere, of the machetes that will remain drawn until the final triumph of the insurgent arms, and of the tyrants begging peace and pardon in the end. They exult in Maceo's march to Pinar del Rio, his tried warriors (guerreros de confianza) checking the timid battalions and finally grasping from Spain her beloved Cuba.

These lines, which a scholarly Cuban gentleman tells me outrage every known rule of metrical composition, were nevertheless very impressive as delivered by the sallow poetess. After her tribute to Maceo and his followers she diverted her inspiration to our party in a most complimentary way, dwelling on the patriots risking a bad pass (the central trocha) travelling tirelessly to meet the great general (Gomez), and of the bold correspondent (myself),

"We were challenged by an advance guard of Gomez' escort."

from the frozen north, who would spread tales of Cuban heroism abroad. The gift of extemporaneous verse-making is not an uncommon one among the Cubans.

That night we camped on a hill from which the lights of the town of Esperanza could be seen distinctly; and took up the march toward Santa Clara at dawn the following morning. Our guides from stage to stage were men from the local prefecturas — and Camaguey signed receipts for their services with great show of formality. From one of them we learned that Gomez was now scarcely six leagues away, and for the very first time in my field experience, news of Gomez' whereabouts proved true. At noon, two days later, near the town of Camaguani, our party was hailed from a neighboring hilltop and challenged by an advance guard of Gomez' own escort. Half an hour afterwards we climbed a hill that commanded a broad view of the fertile valley of the little river called Sagua la Chica, where the smoke of burning farmhouses and volleys like the rolling of distant thunder indicated the presence of a Spanish column. On the summit of the hill we found the commander-in-chief in camp, with his staff, under a cow-shed; while the horses of his escolta, grazing on the slopes below, and wisps of smoke from a score of scattered parillas, told that the command was resting from the morning's march.

As we filed past headquarters, a straight little white-bearded man, in a gray cloth suit and riding boots, with two golden stars on either lapel of his coat, came out to meet us, peering with a sharp eye from beneath his broad hat brim, that was cocked a little to one side, while a group of neatly dressed officers remained at a distance behind.

This was Gomez, the man who has made his name famous in three continents.

MARCHING WITH GOMEZ

Dr. Hernandez.   Gomez.   Colonel Bosa.

[Drawn from a photograph taken in the field for the New York Journal, by Mr. Karl Decker.]

Chapter I

The Man under the Hub

HE is a gray little man. His clothes do not fit well, and, perhaps, if you saw it in a photograph, his figure might seem old and ordinary. But the moment he turns his keen eyes on you, they strike like a blow from the shoulder. You feel the will, the fearlessness, and the experience of men that is in those eyes, and their owner becomes a giant before you.

He is a farmer by birth, the son of a farmer, with an Anglo-Saxon tenacity of purpose, and a sense of honor as clean and true as the blade of his little Santo Domingo machete.

When the revolution broke out in Santo Domingo, he served as a lieutenant in the Spanish army against the land of his birth, in her struggle for independence.[1] He was fighting for rank, I have heard him say; but the example of the Domin-

"Gomez' little Santo Domingo machete."

---

[1] "Not so much to serve Spain as in reality to combat one of the many political bands that in that time divided San Domingo, did General Gomez become one of those that proclaimed the re-establishment of Spanish rule on that Island." So wrote an eminent Cuban whom I questioned on this point.

ican patriots, and the methods of his brother soldiers, made him think. In later years he came to believe with the Cubans that Cuba should be free, and when others dared only whisper, he proclaimed his sympathies, and was relieved of a captain's commission in consequence.

When the Ten Years' War broke out, in 1868, Gomez, and Modesto Diaz, another Dominican and ex-Spanish officer, were among the first to offer their swords to the insurgents. Both were experienced soldiers, energetic and of the character of iron.[1]

"In great part the successful resistance of the Cubans, during the first years of the war, was due to the unwavering resolution of Diaz and Gomez."— So wrote a correspondent of the *New York Herald*, James J. O'Kelly, who visited the insurgents in Oriente in 1873 and made an extensive study of Spanish prison interiors in consequence.

Of Diaz, a story is told that illustrates the extraordinary value, at that time, of a man accustomed to irregular warfare.

When the insurgents besieged Bayamo, early in the war, a Spanish column of seven hundred men hurried from Manzanillo, under the command of a Colonel Campillo, to raise the siege. Had they arrived, defeat would have met the rebels in their first important undertaking, and the insurrection might have died in its infancy. Diaz, with a dozen armed peasants who had never heard a shot fired,

---

[1] After resigning his commission in the Spanish army, Gomez cultivated with his own hands a small farm near Bayamo. While at his toil, the Revolution of 1868 broke out and he left the plough to enlist in the rebel army as a private soldier. Gomez thus became the Cincinnatus of the patriots of the Antilles. After the close of the Ten Years' War, Gomez accepted a commission in the army of Honduras.

and two hundred slaves carrying machetes, awaited the regulars at the ford of the river Babatuaba.

As the advance guard attempted to cross, Diaz, who was a good shot, opened fire on them from behind a stout ceiba tree. The twelve peasants lay in the brush out of danger, loading the pieces and passing them to Diaz, who sustained such a rapid and telling fire that the troops imagined their advance disputed by a strong party. The advance guard fell back. When the two hundred cane-cutters came crashing through the brush, seemingly a wing of the entire Cuban army, hesitation was succeeded by retreat. Next day Bayamo surrendered.

Starting in as a drill master, Gomez worked gradually to the front and was given command of the Central Department on the death of General Agramonte. The Cubans were then hampered by a complicated civil government, and a cabinet council that insisted on attempting to conduct the war. Gomez proposed the plan of invasion, with the idea of carrying the rebellion boldly from the forests and mountains of Oriente and Camaguey to the gates of Havana, thus bringing to open rebellion a populous country wherein disaffection had hitherto smouldered beneath the surface like Nihilism in Russia.

But the council would not consent; they disagreed, hesitated, and disapproved. An invasion was deemed a wild undertaking, so Gomez gave the Spaniards the battle of Las Guasimas, where over six hundred soldiers were cut down by machetes. It was a brilliant victory; but ammunition was far scarcer in those days even than now, and men were less plentiful, because the war was conducted in a dilatory manner. Gomez' force was too crippled in resources even to hope to march into the enemy's country.

So the Ten Years' War degenerated into a sectional struggle, and never, at its heat, had as many as eight thousand properly armed men.[1] Even then it was a class question, enrolling almost entirely the aristocratic Cuban-born planters, and the slaves to whom they had given freedom. It did not appeal practically to the peasants, who dared not offer more than their sympathies; for them there was too much to lose and too little to gain.

As the revolution remained sectional, so the wealth of Cuba, the canefields of the central provinces and the tobacco of Vuelta Abajo, remained unimpaired. Spain could support the war from the actual products of the Island, and their pawnable value.

All this Gomez saw; but it was a case of too many cooks, and the cause did not advance. The treaty of Zanzon, with its luminous Castilian promises of reform, was accepted by the insurgent chiefs, — Gomez among them.

So the war ended. Diaz died after it was over; but Gomez lived to be the man under the hub, to whose genius alone is due the credit of having lifted the Cuban cause from a rut and pushed it successfully from Cape Maisi to the Point of San Antonio.

At the beginning of the present war, Gomez was offered the command of the forces such as they might be or might become; and he accepted, with

[1] Armados, in the Cuban sense. See note on organization of the Cuban Army, Appendix A.

the distinct stipulation that the commander-in-chief of the army should have supreme and exclusive control of all military matters. On assuming command, therefore, Gomez was free to begin his old plan of invasion of the entire Island. He had only his thin skirmish line of soldiers, with scarcely four rounds of ammunition apiece; but he had as his second in command, Antonio Maceo, — a cavalry leader who combined cool judgment and strategic capacity with the reckless dash of Custer, — the veteran Lacret, and Quintin Bandera with his negro infantry from Oriente.

In Matanzas and Las Villas small forces had already taken the field; but they had no organization, and were hidden in the forests and mountains like bands of robbers; and by the Spanish authorities they were regarded as such.

But the march of Gomez and Maceo into Havana Provinces brought the revolution to the door of every plantation owner and peasant in the Island. The thin skirmish line marched into Havana Provinces through a country then occupied by upwards of one hundred thousand royal troops, taking small towns as it went, seizing small forts, and always gaining in numbers and equipment; for everywhere recruits flocked to the tricolor as insects swarm about a light.

By January, 1896, the rebellion had extended through the entire Island, and Gomez was able to put in force his second plan — that of destruction. Proprietors of plantations were forbidden to grind cane on pain of having their crops destroyed; many confided in the protection of Martinez Campos and saw their plantations go up in flames. Others did not grind, and their canefields remained standing. In February Weyler came in and ordered the planters to resume grinding throughout the Island. Then their canefields were universally destroyed.

The burning of cane means only the loss of the crop for one year; for fire simply destroys the leaves and chars the stalks, leaving the root unharmed. Sugar can be made from burnt cane, but it is of poor quality. The planters still attempted to grind,—many of them grinding with burnt cane, according to Weyler's orders. Then the insurgents burned not only the cane but the sugar-mills also, and millions of invested capital went up daily. This was carrying out Gomez' idea of destroying everything of value in the Island, and depriving Spain of any possible revenue. Gomez is fond of repeating the story of the semi-civilized Indians who once inhabited Cuba, and who threw their gold into the rivers at the approach of the Spaniards, knowing it to be the cause of their persecution. So the invasion accomplished not only the spread of the rebellion throughout the Island, but it succeeded in cutting off Spain from every possible revenue in that direction, and in injuring her credit abroad.

Gomez has told his own story of the invasion in a little book published in one of the secret presses in the forests of Oriente, entitled, "My Escort."

It is a story of the hardships of his landing with José Marti, the skirmish at Dos Rios in which Marti fell, and the meeting with Maceo. He tells

M. GOMEZ.

Mi Escolta.
(Boceto Histórico)

ORIENTE.
IMPRENTA "EL CUBANO LIBRE."
1897.

Title-page of Gomez' pamphlet — two-thirds actual size.

of the dodging of Spanish troops sent against him by Martinez Campos, and especially of the heavy line of troops massed by Campos on the boundary of Camaguey. When he learned of the last movement, he said to General Borero, his chief of staff, "We are saved. The fact that they try to intercept us shows that Camaguey is all ready to take arms, and that our friends are waiting to receive us."

"With my general staff as a nucleus," he writes, "I began to organize the army and prepare a plan of campaign.

"By this time General Roloff and Serafin Sanchez had successfully landed their expedition near Tunas, Sancti Spiritus. The only force I had with me, for I did not wish to weaken Maceo's force in Camaguey, was my own escort of a hundred men. I cautioned the captain of it to find out the sentiment of his men, because I had given my oath not to turn back until I had reached the most western provinces; and I wished to be accompanied only by resolute men.

"'General,' answered my captain, with the pride of a Camagueyano, 'these men will follow you anywhere. They are prepared to march at the hour you say wherever you will lead them.'

"On the last day of October I crossed without difficulty the Jucaro Moron trocha into the district of Sancti Spiritus. While waiting for Maceo I made a campaign of continuous marches and countermarches, with the object of tiring out the enemy without consuming our ammunition. We had the fortune to capture Fort Pelayo with fifty rifles and twenty-three thousand rounds of ammunition. After that I skirmished round about the city of Sancti Spiritus

A corporal of Gomez' escort.— Page 12".

[Encarnacion Herrera, wounded at Desmayo and Mi Rosa, perhaps the tallest soldier in the Cuban army.]

and besieged the fort of Rio Grande. I wished to be especially active, so as to attract the attention of the Spaniards and leave an easy passage of the trocha open to Maceo, whom I knew to be advancing at the head of his division of the invading army. We were now well under way and ready to move into Las Villas. The activity and heroism of General Maceo did the rest. Without firing a shot, Maceo crossed the trocha on the 29th of December and we met at San Juan and matured our plans for the invasion.

"The first step was taken, and thus the most difficult part of the work was accomplished. Any hesitation, a step backward, a defeat at this time, would have been extremely dangerous for the revolution. We had to march forward, boldly and continuously, trusting in fortune and our knowledge of the country.

"On the 2d day of December we met the enemy at La Reforma, on the 3d day we were victorious at Iguara, on the 9th at Casa de Tejas, on the 11th and 12th at Boca del Toro. Afterward came Mal Tiempo, Calimete, Coliseo, and Guira de Melena.

"I do not propose to relate the details of the rough, almost daily combats that marked the invasion of 1895–96, in all of which my aides-de-camp and the men of my escort were to be seen in the front ranks. It is only necessary for me to give a list of my personal staff and of my escort, including the names of those who have fallen, and a list of the wounds received by those who are still with me. Many have fallen, but they have been worthily replaced by volunteers. Very few I have chosen myself. In this manner the ranks of the brilliant train of patriotic young men who have been at my side in the hour of danger and who follow me to-day have been continually renewed. Let me mention for a moment some of the most striking characters among my followers:" Here follows a list of the principal members of Gomez' staff; from which I select Bosa and Miguelito.

"Miguel Varona (Miguelito) is a boy fourteen years old, who has been with me from the first. He has the health and the disposition of a grown man, and there is no action of all the hard ones that we have seen where he was not in the front ranks, although sometimes I have desired him to go to the rear.

"Bernabé Bosa, captain of my escort, who ranks as colonel, has been promoted from a lieutenant for gallantry in the field. He is thirty-eight years of age, married, energetic in character, and of amiable disposition, beloved by the soldiers. He is a splendid rider and swordsman, a sure shot, and a man who appears well in both civil and military life. He is of great use to me as an interpreter of English. He saw service first in the war of '68, under such generals as Reeve, Benitez, and Morejones. He can never forget the tragic end of his father, and the sufferings of his mother, who was obliged to witness the murder of her two brothers. It is a sad family history, but almost every Cuban has a similar one. There are very few women in Cuba whom Spain has not caused to shed tears — very few who do not mourn a son, a husband, or a lover, for this is a country that Spain has never loved, but has always wished to hold in bondage for lust and brutality, as a Sultan holds a slave."

Chapter II

Gomez' Staff

AT first I thought Gomez' staff officers a less courteous lot than the aides of Lacret. They were less inclined to lionize the foreigner, and were perhaps rather more attentive to their own affairs. But I noticed that these aides were alert and prompt in obedience to a degree I had not before witnessed in the Manigua. Their very appearance was businesslike, for they carried carbines, in addition to their pistols and machetes of their grade. The soldierly discipline inspired by Gomez showed in his staff as it did in the men of his escolta, and of the local forces who had once been under his eye.

Gomez never camped in houses. He preferred not to inconvenience householders, he said; and besides, he knew that a house is always the first point of a sudden attack. There was not, therefore, the general staff mess that I had seen with Lacret.

Every officer above the grade of alferez[1] — a sort of extra second lieutenant — was entitled to one asistente. Two staff officers usually messed together. One asistente of the combination cooked

---
[1] Derived from the ancient Castilian title of honor, "standard-bearer."

and did most of the "rustling" for the mess, leaving to his colleague the care of the horses for all four. Colonels, lieutenant-colonels, and majors each had two asistentes, and could therefore mess comfortably by themselves or in combination.

In any case, every asistente was supposed to do his share of foraging and keep an eye open for patches of sweet-potatoes, for trees where the banana-like plantain might be cut in luxuriant green bunches, for the twining malanga vine with its tuberous root, that serves the peasant for bread, — and for every sort of fruit that could be found.

On making camp, when the impedimenta dispersed, the asistentes slung their masters' hammocks in spots designated by them, and hurried to put up the shelter tents of canvas, or oule, or to construct ranchos, as a cover from sun and rain.

Occasionally an asistente had a knack of climbing to the top of the royal palms, — sometimes to a height of fifty feet, — by aid of a rope hitched about the trunk and about his waist. Then he would cut great leaves for thatching, each broad enough to shelter a man; and strips of the green pliant bark that grows under the crest of the palm: useful as a covering for the ridgepole, or even as an impromptu mackintosh.

These palm trees could also be cut down, but it was a long, hard job; for though the trunks were endogenous, mere bundles of soft fibre within, the outer bark of a tall tree is an inch thick and hard as seasoned oak.

Some asistentes had great skill in building ranchos, and could put up one in an hour that would turn the heaviest storm. The asistentes were always negroes,—servants from choice, receiving no pay from their masters, but occasionally presents of cast-off clothing, tobacco, and spoils of war, if there were any. Of course, unless he had a good master, the ambition of an officer's servant was to get a rifle, by some turn of fortune, and become an armado, though many were happy enough to keep out of the firing line.

The number of Gomez' impedimenta varied continually. It included the servants of officers of the forces travelling with him, and sometimes scarcely counted fifty. The men of the impedimenta camped with their own commands, and formed again for the march when camp was broken.

"*An impromptu mackintosh.*"

It was Gomez' policy to make widely scattered camps; a policy that led the Spaniards to invariably overestimate the strength of his force, and was of itself a safeguard in case of surprise; therefore it took more or less time for the impedimenta to form; but never long enough to delay the column; for, except in retreat, the impedimenta marched last, just ahead of the rear-guard. The men that composed it were as freakish in costume and equipment as those I had seen with Lacret; but better mounted, because horse-flesh was more plentiful in Las Villas than in Matanzas.

In spite of the non-aggressive disposition of the impedimenta, it is on record as having captured a garrisoned town. It was during the invasion of Havana Province by Gomez and Maceo, when the horsemen of the great cavalry leader, and the awful infantry of Quintin Bandera were sweeping the Island, and La Reforma, Calimete, and Mal Tiempo were fresh in the minds of Spanish soldiery. The advance guard of Gomez was to take a certain town: accounts differ as to the name of the town, and I repeat the facts as I heard them. By a mistake of the guide, so the story goes, the armed force took the wrong road and marched past the town before they knew it. They did not go back; for their orders were "Forward, always forward, to Pinar del Rio."

"A fat stingy Spaniard for host."

But the unconscious impedimenta, scrambling along half a mile behind, took the right road. Before them lay the town they believed already theirs. They saw the chapel spire, the red roofs, and "dobe" walls, and visions of little shops, with shoes and clothing, and rope for bridles and lariats, and sugar and coffee, and perhaps a little fonda, with a fat stingy Spaniard for host and a storeroom with casks of wine and jugs of rum, rose like a mirage before them. Full of enthusiasm, the impedimenta took the trot, then the gallop, and tore into the hamlet with howls of "Viva Cuba, Muera España — Viva Cuba Libre!"

In the main street the garrison, two hundred strong, were drawn up, ready to surrender to the "Liberating Army." Too late the desarmados saw the flash of Spanish rifles, and the bluish, red-trimmed uniforms; but the surprise was mutual. The Cuban, Hannibal, who commanded the impedimenta, rose to the occasion. He accepted the surrender, collected the rifles, and spared the lives of the Spanish regulars. The equilibrium of all parties was restored, and another armed regiment was added to the muster roll of the Republic.

Gomez' own cook, a Spaniard born, named Moron, was an exception to the rule concerning asistentes, for he rode on a fine buckskin mule with the general staff, the pots and pans clinking in his saddle-bags. That Moron, occupying a position of trust, should be a Spaniard, was not so surprising when one considers that in the Cuban ranks are many Spaniards who, from sympathy or as deserters, have cast their lot with the rebellion. Miro, an able leader, is one of these.

Moron was always in Gomez' sight; in fact at Mal Tiempo he rode beside Gomez in a machete charge, and even from his mule macheted a Spanish soldier. It was the same machete, by the way, that he used for chopping the general's meat.

At Moron's elbow rode his scullion, Grillo (significant name for one of his profession!), on a good

Moron, ranking cook of the Cuban army.

but a smaller mule, with more of the cooking utensils in his saddle-bags, — and the two were forever quarrelling; that is, Moron was laying down the law and Grillo was talking back; for Grillo was an impudent little negro of eleven or thereabouts, and very mischievous, with a spirit of his own. Grillo was always getting into trouble. Once, I remember, Gomez' field-glass was missing, and they traced it to Grillo, who was seen looking through it, back end to, at the last camping place, and had left it in the grass. Gomez drew his machete and gave Grillo some good "planazos" with the flat of it, and the scullion was sent back with two soldiers to get it.

Gomez had also another asistente, a light mulatto, a Dominican, I believe; but he was less privileged, and travelled with the impedimenta.

At this time Gomez had, as chief of staff, Brigadier-general Zavier Vega, a tried soldier of the last war, a Camagueyano, slow of speech, but big hearted and brave. Gomez was very fond of him and trusted him.

The general's secretary was Antonio Colete, ranking as a lieutenant-colonel — a well-educated man of thirty, who wrote official letters in a clear, flowing hand and possessed a smattering of French and of general literature. Colete was, by profession, an architect of Havana.

There were half a dozen others whose names and records Gomez has given in his little book, "Mi Escolta." Some of them bore old and famous names and looked it; others were of the bluff peasant type, sturdy and honest.

These aides were supposed to be very exemplary as well as valiant. They were presumably not addicted to luxuries any more than their commander himself. Gomez, if invited by a planter to take a copita of brandy or rum, would sometimes accept, saying that he occasionally took a little as he was now a very old man; but as for his aides they never touched liquor at all.

There was certainly no open conviviality; but often when we remained over a day in one district, or from our circular marches there was likelihood of our return, arrangements were made with obliging peasants by those who had money, and supplies bought through pacificos who had access to the towns were brought into camp, as I had seen them when with Lacret.

There were two officers who attracted my attention from the first, Pedro Guitierrez and Miguel Varona (Miguelito), whom Gomez particularly mentions in his book.

"Miguelito" was a pet of the old general's. He was a son of a brave officer and companion-in-arms of Gomez during the last war. Miguelito's hammock was always swung near that of the commander-in-chief, and he sat at his mess. In the first days of the invasion, Miguelito came on foot to Gómez in Camaguey, begging permission to go with him, to carry a rifle as a soldier. Gomez took the boy under his wing, and there he has remained ever since, throughout a long campaign and in many hot places. He was stout for his age, and they say that at both Calimete and Coliseo, Miguelito rode in the first ranks, and struck down men with his machete. He held the rank of lieutenant, and made a very good aide-de-camp. He was, of course, the youngest officer in the Cuban army.

Guitierrez was a youth from Puerto Rico, full of the glory of war, and really quite plucky. He was a haphazard little man, always running into gun-fire

Grillo. — Page 136.

just for the sake of being there, and often when there was no earthly need for it. I have heard Gomez reprimand him on that score, yet the "old man" did so with rather assumed severity, for not every member of the staff was so enthusiastic, even on "straight duty."

Guitierrez wore, when it rained, a beautiful plum-colored mackintosh, with a cape and a double row of silver-plated buttons, each embossed with the initials G. C. It was the mackintosh that Spain issues to that select corps of constabulary, the Guardia Civil, and Guitierrez had captured it somewhere. "When I was a boy, in Puerto Rico," he said, "I thought those Civil Guards terrible fellows. I did not know how one could manage them; but now," here he tapped his Winchester, — with which I do not believe he ever actually hit anything in his life, for he shot quick and carelessly, — "now I think no more of killing a Civil Guard than I do of spitting." And he spat on the ground to show how little such an act concerned him.

Guitierrez was a good fellow and good company. He had an emotional side that showed itself occasionally on very wet days, when the weather was what the French call *triste*.

"I have been with the general since the first of the war," he would say, "and I am now one of the few left of the original staff. I shall fall some day; I sometimes feel that I shall never live to see it over and Cuba free."

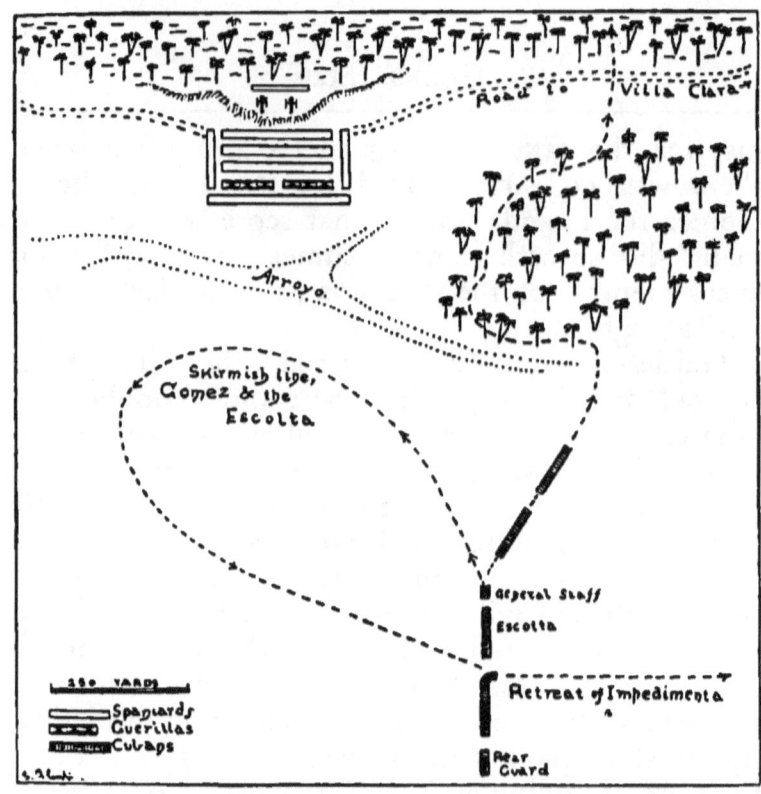

Plan of Gomez' skirmish with a Spanish column on the plains between Manajanabo and Savanas Nuevas, Santa Clara Province, May 12, 1896.

Chapter III

Manajanabo

ON May 12th, I saw an attack made on a Spanish column, fairly in the open, on the plains near the ruined fort of Manajanabo. Gomez crossed to the western side of the Sagua that morning, and breakfasted at noon at a small sugar estate, on a hill overlooking a flat, fertile valley, where tall poplars, and here and there a reach of glistening water, marked the course of the river. The railroad from Santa Clara to Sancti Espiritu ran at a closing angle with the Sagua; for we saw the smoke and heard the whistle of a south-bound train.

It was a comfortable plantation, where the proprietor was his own manager and employed half a dozen hands, — the sort of plantation that will be starved out of existence, when Cuba is free, if the sugar trust once thrusts its grasping arm into the country.

There was a mill worked by a horse, driven blindfolded in a circle about the crusher and receiving vat, all under a roof, no wider than that of a band stand in Central Park, and a trough that carried the sap to the boilers, where, under a shed a few yards away, sugar was made and stored. It was an ingenio too small to build a moral effect on, that paid its little contributions to the insurgents, and was allowed to grind enough "for private purposes." There were two iron boilers full of steaming guarapo when we got there, and many bags of rich, brown sugar.

"They filled even their hats."

With the sugar, our negroes, especially of the impedimenta, made havoc, filling saddle-bags, tin cans, pockets when they had them, even their hats transformed into baskets, which they bore off upside down on their heads. After breakfast and rest, we took the march down across the savanna by the river, with the afternoon sun on our backs.

Gomez had with him his escolta, eighty well-armed and well set-up men with an established reputation for gallantry, and two troops of fifty men each, one commanded by Major Ramon Guerra, the oldest soldier in the Cuban army, the other by an officer whose name I think was Legon; behind came the impedimenta, of asistentes and camp-followers, with twenty troopers detailed from the escolta for a rear-guard.

It was three o'clock when one of Guerra's men of the advance guard rode back and touched his hat to Gomez: "A column marching on the high-road toward Santa Clara," he said, "with a

"*Their heads and their horses' heads visible above the tall grass.*"

guerilla one hundred strong as advance guard, my general!" Gomez reined up, pulled his beard for a moment, then he cocked his eye on the country ahead, and gave quick orders over his shoulder to two aids, who galloped off, one to the head of the line, the other to the impedimenta. Then we rode on.

Looking back to where the impedimenta wound along, only heads and shoulders and horses' heads visible above the tall grass, I saw it strike from the trail, followed by the rear-guard, to the rising, hilly ground on our right.

Ahead was a wall of palm forest, where sunlight

brought out the white trunks against the shade within. To our right front, between us and the forest, was a palm grove. Toward this grove Guerra's troop turned, still at a walk. As we approached the forest the Spanish guerrilleros showed in full view, drawn up in two white lines, facing us. Behind them lay the Santa Clara high-road, skirting the forest within short carbine range of the grove toward which Guerra was making. They waited, uncertain whether we were friends or foes, while a bluish-gray bunchy mass formed behind them, thickening as a dust-hidden thread of infantry wound from the high-road into it.

Gomez led his sixty men of the escolta diagonally from the trail toward the enemy, opening as they advanced into a wide, irregular skirmish line, shouting to one another, repeating the order, "Deploy! open wide! deploy!"

The Spaniards saw our column split, and their movements became hurried and ant-like; they might still have extended to occupy the palm grove before Guerra's men got there, — but they did not. The infantry squirmed itself into a square, the last stragglers of the marching line closing up at a jog trot. There was a tremor in the two guerilla troops, as if "gathering" for the order, "Draw sabre! Forward!" but they did not charge. It was only a swiftly executed "twos left, column left," at a trot, that brought them within and behind the halted infantry ranks.

There was a white flutter of a hundred legs as the guerrilleros swung from their saddles, and stood to horse in the very centre of a solid square, — the

Major Ramon Guerra.—Page 142.

[He is upwards of ninety years, and learned to fight, he says, in the Ten Years' War, under General Ryan, whom he regards, next to Gomez, as the greatest man in history.]

most magnificent target conceivable — one that would make an American marksman's trigger finger quiver up to his elbow. As usual, the Spaniards made in every respect the least possible advantage of their natural surroundings.

The men of the escolta were now at a distance from the enemy, varying between two hundred and two hundred and fifty yards. Our other two troops were already scattering into the palm grove, and the impedimenta was safe away among the hills. Gomez' two trumpeters struck up a merry quickstep, and the shooting began on our side.

The Cubans say that if you are not wounded in the first volley, you will not be at all unless Providence so expressly desires; therefore, I waited to see the rifles go up with interest. A sparkle of moving steel ran along the bluish-gray line, then the line wavered in a thin mist of exploding, smokeless powder, and a crash came like the swift tearing of a giant strip of carpet. Another crash! and another! Five distinct crashes; and the five cartridges that each Spanish rifle carried in its magazine were expended. The popping of our men, who shot from their saddles, seemed slight and puny.

The Spanish volleys now came irregularly, swelling to a rah! rah! rah! sound, like a confused succession of college cheers. The sun caught on the waving blades of the officers, who were threatening and slapping the soldiers to preserve the alignment.

Our shots must have told, for the Spanish line wavered like cane swayed by the wind; they were shoulder to shoulder, the front rank apparently kneeling with the butts of their pieces on the ground.

Bullets sped by — every near one with a slight hissing sound as when an insect darts past you. Sometimes they would turn blades of grass, or strike in the ground with a sharp snap, like the report of an air-gun. This was all that told that we were under fire of several hundred European regulars.

A puff of white smoke blew up from some slightly higher ground to the rear of the square, and a heavy report followed. Then another puff and another report. Two field-pieces were firing alternately; but we never heard a sing or a sound of the shells, which must have travelled back to the little ingenio where we had breakfasted.

Gomez, not expecting an action, rode a cream-colored mule, and a mule is a nuisance under gun-fire. The commander-in-chief scarcely enjoyed himself; for the mule was rearing in an absurd manner, swinging on his hind feet up and down like a hobby-horse.

This rain of bullets, so high, but so thick, began to tell after a while. Several horses were shot, several limped from wounds. Guitierrez was near me, when his horse stumbled, and lay down with its head in the air. A shot had gone through the fleshy part of Guitierrez' leg, through the saddle, and through the horse.

Guitierrez said, "Caramba" or a word that begins with the same letter and means something more irrelevant, whipped off his bridle, and unstrapped the saddle. Two crimson spots were painted on his gray striped trousers. He continued shooting on foot.

Meanwhile, the men of our other two troops

opened a cross fire on the enemy from the palm grove, at a range of under two hundred yards.

For fifteen minutes the fire of the escolta continued, while the two buglers spelled each other in prolonging the quickstep. Then our line of skirmishers was thinned by the retiring of three men wounded, and the carrying off of one man killed outright. Others, like Guitierrez, whose horses had dropped, were walking to the rear, carrying their saddles and packs on their heads. Why the Spaniards, whose cavalry far outnumbered Gomez' escolta, and who were near enough to sweep through us before we could possibly have rallied for a solid front, left all the fighting to their infantry, I could not see.

The signal to retire blew, and we turned back to follow the impedimenta. "There was a deep arroyo, and we could not charge," observed Gomez,[1] between the jumps of his restive mule.

Our friends in the palm grove kept on firing, and the Spaniards remained where they were. As we came into long range, bullets fell faster and nearer, snapping into the ground, lively as hail.

When you have once turned your back on an enemy, there is an instinct to hasten, and you begin to realize that he is shooting at you. We kept a dignified walk, but we moved right along, and spoke and jested less frequently. Comparing our pace to that of the men on foot, and those holding

[1] Gomez knew well that the grass-fed mounts of the rebels, even in the excitement of a charge, have not actual strength enough to keep the run over a deep ditch or up an incline. It is also noteworthy that since the first few months of the war the Spanish infantry have become exceedingly cautious not to expose itself in open order, or even in company squares, if their tactics include that formation, to a charge of insurgent cavalry. I base this criticism on their behavior at Manajanabo and Saratoga.

L

the wounded on their saddles, and the dead man who was slung over a led horse, we, the unharmed, seemed in a hurry. There is something sad and anticlimax about a retreat, even if it is a part of the original programme.

A strip of meat lay in the path, dropped by the impedimenta, whose trail we followed. A staff officer dismounted, picked it up, and hid it carefully in the long grass. "If the Spaniards were to see it," he said, "they would say that we threw away all our provisions in our retreat."

We were out of gun-fire at last, and rejoined the impedimenta, which we found waiting on a hillside. Then we marched a mile to a tributary of the Sagua, where there was good grass for the horses, and as soon as the wounded men were sent off to the nearest prefectura, we had a supper of beef strips, and turned in.

"*A mule is a nuisance under gun-fire.*"

Chapter IV

Our Last Skirmish in Las Villas

BY dawn, Gomez was on the road back toward Manajanabo, with sixty men of the escolta ahead, twenty as rear-guard, and the impedimenta tinkling along between. The Spanish column, when darkness had put an end to the firing, kept on toward Santa Clara, and camped on the San Antonio estate, just off the high-road, and quite near where we spent the night.

It was daylight when we passed the gringos, and, as a precaution to guard against their attacking us, ten men from our advance guard, led by an aid named Tejedor, who on this occasion caught a Mauser bullet in the groin, deployed into the brush and began shooting into their camp. The troops were quick to form, and returned fire in volleys; but the nickel-capped bullets pierced only leaves of the trees, or flattened on the stone-walls that bordered the high-road. Meanwhile our main force passed out of range.

There is a great deal of safety in skirmishing with an enemy so fond of the defensive as the Spaniards. In fact, the glories of recent Spanish military history seem to be heroic defences, like Valladolid and Saragoza, where retreat was impossible, rather than gallant charges and attacks. To-day, with something of the same spirit, the Mexicans celebrate Jalapa, Churubusco, Chapultepec, and Resaca de la Palma, as the Greeks might celebrate Thermopylæ.

Further along, where the road curved over a hill, we had a bird's-eye view of the Spanish camp. The soldiers were drawn up in a clearing a hundred yards square, about the farmhouse which served as staff-headquarters. It was an oblong "dobe" house, with white walls and a red-tiled roof. On its porch a field-glass showed a group of officers, with their horses tied to the railing. Orderlies ran to and from the outlying buildings, perhaps in use as hospitals, and the infantry were still firing steadily into the wood, in the direction of the high-road. Somewhat back of the house was a well, with a covered circular top and a great arm, or sweep, that four men continually struggled to push around, pumping water into a long trough of cemented brick, or "dobe." Around the trough were gathered the guerrilleros, watering their horses by squads, and forming again back under shelter of the trees. Framing this scene of activity, a dense foliage draped the country, sweeping to the base of the rocky hill we were climbing.

As the Spaniards saw us, there was a flurry among them. The infantry ceased firing. Two field-pieces were dragged from somewhere amongst the trees, unlimbered, and turned on us. Six shells came our way,— one near enough for us to hear its metallic scream. Then we passed over the hillside and saw no more of that column. They marched into Villa Clara that same day, with a large number of wounded,— we had no means of knowing just how many, — and as for the dead, of those who fell on the field, or had died of wounds during the night, it was said that they threw them into the farmhouse and the adjoining sheds before they broke camp, and made a bonfire of it all — a method they have of concealing their losses.

We went into camp at noon on a savanna bordering the Sagua river, where a cow-shed served as Gomez' headquarters. Here we were joined by the two troops who had carried on the skirmishes from the palm grove on the day before. Scattered among the palms, they had kept up firing until sunset without losing a single man, and then they had crossed the Villa Clara road and camped in the thick of the forest beyond.

Here for the first time since leaving Marto's camp, I was able to take a bath. I had been suffering from a constant itching, beyond that caused by any parasites I had ever known, and I settled down to the belief that I was attacked by some horrible skin disease. On taking off my flannel shirt, for the first time in two weeks, I found it full of a kind of insect that I had never seen before. They were much larger than bedbugs, though similar in appearance. I showed them to a trooper who was washing his horse in the river, and he said they were the terrible caranjanos that Cubans say were brought from Spain by the Spanish soldiers.

The only way to get rid of them is to boil every article of clothing. So, without specifying for what purpose, I borrowed a leaky tin pail used for cooking potatoes, and rode from camp with Alfredo. I boiled my wardrobe secretly, and from that day I discarded my flannel shirt; for in the Manigua wool attracts and encourages vermin. Perhaps for that reason, as well as from economy, cotton is supplied the troops by the Spanish commissariat, and is exclusively worn by the Cubans.

Somehow the rumor of my affliction spread, and Moron heard it. Moron was a good friend of mine, for every morning before we broke camp he was careful to send me, by Alfredo, half a jicara full of hot coffee. To be sure, he did so by Gomez' orders; but the cook of the commander-in-chief is enough of an autocrat to forget such things once in a while, or to occasionally not have enough to go around, if he feels like it. The blight of my caranjanos fell on Alfredo, and Moron forbade him to sit by his cook-fire. My other orderly, Eusebio, was naturally a neat boy, and besides, he looked after our horses, so he escaped the ban for that evening, at least. With Alfredo and caranjanos I was soon to have another experience.

The general's mess was ampler that day than usual, for Moron had time to spend on his cooking. There was a rice stew with bits of chopped beef in it, plantains, and a dessert of creamy white cheese, which we ate in slices dipped in honey poured from a bottle into our jicaras; and there were water-cresses that Grillo had found somewhere in the river. Then there was more coffee than usual,— a jicara full for every member of the general's mess, which, besides Gomez himself, consisted of General Vega, his chief of staff, Colete, Miguelito, and myself.

For almost the first time in the field, I had succeeded in getting a bottle of brandy and a bundle of cigars through a prefect of the neighborhood. There is one luxury in sleeping in a hammock,—that is, you can smoke before going to sleep without setting fire to anything. So a day ended which I look back upon as one of the most luxurious since I had been in the Manigua.

On the following day, Gomez had his last skirmish for that season in Las Villas. A large force of Spaniards had arrived in the neighborhood, and were in camp two miles away. From midnight on there was shooting; for Gomez promptly sent a party of local infantry to keep the gringos awake. By daybreak on the thirteenth, the firing was nearer. The infantry were retreating in our direction, and the troops had turned out and were following. By six o'clock, our camp guards were engaged, and the impedimenta were already retreating into the mountains of the Grupo Cubanacan. The retreat led through an up and down, hilly country, thickly wooded, with here and there pastures within stone-walls.

The Spaniards advanced more swiftly than I had ever seen them. Instead of keeping to the roads, as usual, they swarmed into the woods, blazing away through the underbrush, pushing our men back by weight of numbers alone, over rugged hills and stone-walls, until they were on the very heels of the impedimenta and still within hand-shaking distance of the enemy. Gomez was angry and blamed the guide, who had led us by a bad way. Three hours of pursuit had not lessened the ardor of the regulars. Few of Gomez' officers had seen anything like it since the war began. At last a rocky hill rose before us, and an open path wound over it corkscrew fashion, in plain view from below. Here there was trouble with the impedimenta. They were exposed to a fire that drove over our heads and pattered among them like hail.

One of the impedimenta was shot, and fell with his horse directly in the narrowest part of the way, and it took several minutes to get him out. To hurry matters, the impedimenta, as it reached the summit, split in three parties, making off, for the sake of speed, in different directions over the brow of the hill.

Then the road was clear, and it was the turn of the staff, and the rear-guard, Guerra's men, to go up.

Gomez led, and there was scrambling and swearing and lashing of horses as the staff and rear-guard followed, jostling one another. If a horse fell, a man jerked off saddle and bridle as quickly as he could and beat the crouching animal, with drawn machete, out of the pathway. When a man lay down and called for help, volunteers dismounted, took him on their shoulders, or on their horses, and hurried him along.

I observed no unnecessary delay, even on the part of the reckless Guitierrez, who rode just in front of me, digging his heels into his horse's flanks and looking straight ahead, and the cavalry drill-master's "four feet from head to croup" was forgotten.

At the top, Gomez paused and gave old Ramon Guerra orders not to let the Spaniards up, even if he had to hold them back with the machetes. When the last of the rear-guard had joined us, the trail was open,—a sunny, glistening path, encumbered by four dead horses. One horse that had fallen, scrambled to his feet, goaded by flying pebbles and ricochet bullets, and came limping, with drooping head, up the trail after us.

The Spaniards did not try that pass, and our retreat became more dignified. Seven troopers were reported severely wounded, and three dead men were being carried, slung on led horses.

The insurgents never desert their wounded. It is part of their religion to stay with them: I have never

Carrying the wounded.

seen or heard, on good evidence, of an exception to this rule. As Gomez says, "The wounded are sacred."

The impedimenta were signalled to halt, and from it stout negroes were detailed to carry the helpless. Hammocks were borrowed from those who had them to lend, and the wounded were borne in them, slung on poles on the shoulders of their comrades. Two men carried a pole for a hundred yards or so, and rested it on crotched sticks that they drove upright in the ground at each halt, while they caught their wind and mopped their sweaty brows.

A third man shouldered those crotched sticks and changed places with the first pole-bearer who gave out.

Nine more were wounded, but able to take care of themselves; among them, General Vega, Gomez' chief of staff, received a ricochet ball in the ankle that took in a bit of his leather legging with it, and bothered him for many a week afterwards.

Burying the dead.

We moved slowly, supposing the Spaniards far behind. The impedimenta had disappeared among the hills, and the staff carelessly jogged along with the last files of the rear-guard. On a bluff overlooking the country was a cottage, and from its door a middle-aged woman with three small children gazed at us, trembling, for they had heard the approaching roar of musketry. We dismounted to reconnoitre with field-glasses. Fully one thousand yards back, through an open spot on an opposite hillside, we could see Spanish infantry straggling in another direction, and an officer on a white horse was looking back at us through his field-glass.

It was already eleven o'clock, and we stood in a bunch, passing the glass from one to another. Gomez was prominent in the foreground. Suddenly from the leafy vale below came the barking of Mausers. A detachment of Spaniards had come upon us by another trail, and were shooting at short range, — not two hundred yards. Colete was wounded in the groin, as Tejedor had been on the day before. The soldiers had begun firing as they came up. Had they waited until enough were together to send a good round volley, they might have got more of us, even our commander-in-chief; but we did not wait for volleys. We lost no time in mounting and hurrying after the rear-guard, leaving the mother and children screaming, "Ay, Dios mio!" in each other's arms; for the gringos were coming, and they knew not which way to run. Colete's wound did not prevent his riding with us without assistance. Those were the last shots that day.

A mile further on we halted. Deep in the woods, some distance from the road, a temporary camp was made for the wounded, and the dead were buried. Graves were dug with poles made from saplings sharpened to a point with machetes. Some thrust the poles into the ground to turn it up and soften it, and others scooped out the loosened earth with their hands. The equipments of the dead were removed before burial, and portioned among those who needed them most. A man tried on the hat, leggings, and shoes of his late comrade as he lay on the ground, and kept them if a fit, or if not, passed them to his neighbor; for in the field it is so difficult to get clothing of any kind, that the Mambis cannot afford to lose through sentiment.

From our point of view, the day was a victory;

Dressing General Vega's wound.

because two columns, acting in combination, had chased us as a brace of hounds chases a hare, and failed to bag us all. Yet our loss — twenty wounded and three killed outright, nearly all on the open hillside where the impedimenta came under fire — was far greater than usual in such skirmishes.

My man, Eusebio, was among the missing, and I never saw him afterwards. He carried my only bottle of ink, too, which was no small loss. Alfredo from that day did double work.

As for Alfredo, he answered muster cheerfully with the impedimenta; but when I asked him for the remainder of the brandy I had entrusted to his care, he told me that on that terrible path a bullet had shattered the bottle in his very hand, and in default of evidence to the contrary, I believed him.

Early that afternoon, we were resting in a peaceful camp, on a branch of the Sagua, near the pastures of Palo Prieto, and the toil of the morning, with its loss of life and blood, was already forgotten.

News that Gomez was near spread through the immediate country. Several peasants who had never seen the commander-in-chief visited the camp. One elderly pacifico had the temerity to visit headquarters with his whole family, all faithful Cubans. This, in spite of the fact that it was a time of alarm and surprises, and they would all have suffered if they had been caught going to or away from the camp. There was a mother and her daughter in gowns of brilliant calico only brought out on feast days. Their hair was dressed with great formality, and they were powdered to the ears, as Cuban women are on state occasions. The mother wore a Spanish mantilla and carried a huge sky-blue sun umbrella.

They brought gifts of eggs and cheese, and a fine live pullet, that Moron might carry in his pannier, and roast at the general's pleasure. There was a little boy in a freshly washed linen suit, and a little girl with close-cropped hair, and as a great honor they were presented to the general, who shook hands with them genially.

The pacifico was a well-fed, gray-whiskered old

man, who bared his head to Gomez with great respect. He had an elder son, he said, who had followed the invasion, and was perhaps with Maceo. He had not heard of him these many months.

Such visits were common as we marched through Las Villas, when there were no soldiers about. They were formal and did not last long. Gomez was always gracious when visits were made with proper show of formality, and would ask these peasants questions about their families, and what they had sacrificed for the fatherland, which was sometimes embarrassing, so that often they were abashed, and bowed themselves off even more respectfully than they had come.

"*They brought gifts of eggs and cheese, and a fine live pullet.*"

Chapter V

Into Camaguey

WITH the skirmishes about Manajanabo ended Gomez' series of illusive marches between Villa Clara and Sancti Espiritu, — marches that kept the Spaniards in pursuit, staggering under a pitiless sun or chilled by the first rains of the wet season, through a country where hunger drove the men to devour unripe fruit, and thirst drove the officers to excess in gin and brandy, each day swelling the list of sick and wounded. For the insurgents' losses were slight; men simply grew more gaunt and ragged, while horses became sore-backed and raw-boned. Then General Bruno Zayas, who for two weeks past, with perhaps five hundred men, had been campaigning in conjunction with Gomez, pushed through the middle trocha toward Matanzas, and Gomez struck eastward through the hills of the Matahambre range toward the wooded lands of Camaguey.

There were good, broad roads and comfortable farms and pastures with roaming cattle and wild horses. The pacificos were sleek and well-to-do, and often had rich gardens by the very high-road,— a contrast to the ashes, desolation, and terror of western Las Villas and Matanzas.

Once Gomez paused as he saw a farmer ploughing by the roadside. "Why do you work?" he cried; "don't you know that you are working for Spain, who will seize your crops? Don't you know that you make the land richer for Spain, and that for your work she will be less ready to abandon it? To support your family? It would be better if you fed them on roots in the forest or left them to starve,

The farmer by the roadside.

as my men have left their wives and children and parents to starve for the sake of the fatherland. You work when you should destroy. When the war is over there will be need and time for ploughing. Until then only the machete should be lifted."

Passing a cottage, a pretty young woman with a babe in her arms, and a fair-looking man carrying a rifle, showed themselves at the door. "Bring that man to me," commanded Gomez, a little theatrically. "Here, one of you staff officers, examine his cedula. So you are of the prefectura?" The man hung his head. "Ah, afraid to answer, — so neat, too, so clean, so well dressed; what! this woman has no husband and is not your wife? Is this the way you enjoy yourself while we are wearing out our skins. Colonel Bosa! where is Colonel Bosa? Here, disarm this fellow and put him among the asistentes."

Then, turning to the woman, Gomez continued less roughly, "It is the fault of you, such women as you, willing to amuse yourselves when the country is in danger; making majaces of weak men when the fatherland lacks defenders."

Eastward of the Las Villas line the country became more sparsely settled. We were entering the timber land of tall mahogany trees, draped with creeping vines and parasite plants, and giant ceiba[1] trees, that in the last war were often hollowed into canoes and bore messengers with despatches to the neutral shores of Jamaica and Santo Domingo. On peasant farms there were chopping-blocks of mahogany in the kitchens; and horse-troughs, some half a century old, were made of it. Everywhere fruits were beginning to ripen, — guavas and mangoes, mamees and rose apples.[2] Sometimes as we crossed

---

[1] The ceiba lifts a massive trunk for fifty feet into the air, and then branches into a dense canopy of foliage. It towers above the surrounding vegetation, almost equalling in height the royal palm. Native negroes believe that the ceiba is a magic tree, haunted nightly by spirits — a superstition that is shared by the negroes of Santo Domingo, Jamaica, and Nassau.

[2] Lemons grew plentifully in every garden and by the roadside. Besides being useful for the "mess" as seasoning, they were useful in operations of veterinary surgery I had now every day to perform. My horse, owing to the awkward construction of my *criollo* saddle, suffered from a severe saddle-boil, and I could allow him no rest. Every afternoon, on making camp, Alfredo held his head, while with half a lemon, I cleansed away the proud flesh from the wound — for we were now in a country

a savanna there were traces of insurgent camps; — charred parillas, bones of cattle, and low, grass-built wickyups by the roadside, wherein sentries of travelling forces had spent a night. Wild pigs abounded in the forest, and sometimes ran out from the underbrush in squealing broods, dodging our horses' hoofs. Sometimes we made right or left low cuts at them with the machete; but to capture one it was best to dismount and give chase on foot. It was a country where the prefects could cultivate crops undisturbed, plantains in abundance and sweet-potatoes, — which, once planted, grew in such profusion that on the farms one had to continually plough about the patch to prevent the tuberous roots invading the entire soil.

ALFREDO, IN HEROIC POSE.

where it was safe enough to unsaddle, though the rank-and-file, as in Matanzas, were not permitted to do so. Then I squeezed the juice of a fresh lemon into the wound and scattered wood ashes over it as a protection from flies. This was heroic treatment, but the best I could offer under the circumstances.

Into Camaguey

Our camps were often built by rivers, which gave me a chance to bathe. One morning I had the horror of again finding two caranjanos in my shirt. Back in Matanzas I had bought a ragged waterproof coat from a pacifico, that proved useless to turn rain, but served as a wrap at night. Alfredo carried this coat strapped to his saddle by day, so I remembered Moron's suspicion, and guessed that the caranjanos came from my asistente.

When we halted at noon I borrowed a tin pail, and rode, followed by my unsuspecting servant, to the river. Alfredo built a fire, and I boiled my clothing as before and bathed. When I was dressed, I ordered Alfredo to strip and boil his garments, too. This was an indignity, and he demurred. He pleaded that his clothing scarcely hung together as it was, and that a washing, let alone a boiling, would destroy it. And was he to go naked? Because he was black was no reason for his having caranjanos. There were others, white men, who, if the truth were known, had caranjanos, too. I told him to go to the impedimenta, and I would ask General Gomez for another asistente. Then he weakened, and I made him swim and duck his head three times, while his only shirt and pantaloons boiled and bubbled on the bank.

We crossed the Jucaro-Moron trocha without a shot, north of Moron. Four skirmish lines were thrown across the railroad track,—two covering the approach from the north, two from the south. It was a clay flat, thickly grown with scrub trees. Along the line in either direction a white speck of a fort was visible. No patrols came out, and the scouts boasted that it was because they dared not venture against so large a force. There was something in this, for two Americans, who crossed with a guide a short time afterward, brought tales of a hair-breadth escape from a patrol of cavalry who followed them some distance from the line.

The security of the country encouraged majaces, and Gomez despatched parties in all directions to "round them up." Every evening a silent, abashed line was drawn up before headquarters, while officers, soldiers, and asistentes crowded in anticipation of the lecture to come. Finally Gomez would come out from under his piece of canvas with a towel in one hand that served for a handkerchief, and look them through from under his bushy gray eyebrows, with his hawk's eye.

"Ah-h-h, ma-ja-ces, neat, well-fed ma-ja-ces, living in hous-es, on fresh pork and chicken and milk, the food of the women and children, swindling the republic, what do you do for the fatherland?

"Do you wear the weapons of

"Ah-h-h, ma-ja-ces, neat, well-fed ma-ja-ces!"

"Do you wear the weapons of the republic for ornaments?"

the republic for ornaments, and ride her horses for pleasure?

"You, you say your father was dying, and you left your force to be with him in December, and it is now May and he is still dying? And you over there, you with the face of a guerrillero, you say you were wounded. Look at my men. Every one of them is wounded. I am wounded. I will have the surgeon examine us and see which is the sicker man, you or I.

"You deceive the republic, but you do not deceive me. I will make you serve your country, if only as examples for others. I will keep my eye on every single one of you.

"Officer of the day, take these men to the impedimenta, make them walk with the infantry."

So, each day the active forces were swelled with men who had long waited for arms, and the impedimenta filled with those on whom the hardships of war had hitherto fallen lightly.

"*I will have the surgeon examine us and see which is the sicker man, you or I!*"

"*I will keep my eye on every single one of you!*"

In camp no breach of discipline was too slight to escape correction from the commander-in-chief; and when at rare intervals a grave offence was committed a formal court-martial was called and its findings were read aloud to the forces assembled. One court found a stripling of barely eighteen years old, guilty

A bit of camp discipline.

of sleeping on his post at sentry duty, a crime punishable with death. But Gomez, who rarely condones a fault, pardoned the culprit on account of extreme youth, after giving him a fright and a public lecture on the seriousness of his offence, and sent him to the impedimenta "until he should grow up."

Couriers soon began to arrive from the Civil Government, which still lingered about Najaza. With them came officers newly landed by the expeditions of Calixto Garcia, and Ruz. The last came with commissions issued by the ambitious government: they were captains without companies, first lieutenants without commands; and bearing the stars of those grades, they reported to Gomez. These commissions were directly in violation of the printed Articles of War, and Gomez tore them up, detailing their bearers, as untried and unpractised in war as militia recruits, to the nearest forces as second lieutenants and alferez.

With the Garcia expeditionaries, came Dr. Eusebio Hernandez, a man of position, and well known to the leaders of the revolution as an active partisan. Dr. Hernandez represented the best class of Cuban. Energetic, of high intelligence, and good family, he had studied his profession in Paris and Madrid, and removed, in 1894, to Havana, where in one year he achieved a brilliant reputation as a specialist in women's diseases. Dr. Hernandez had already been offered the position of Cuban commissioner to the South American republics; but there were Cubans enough working abroad, he said. He believed in the utmost independence in civil and military jurisdiction. He saw in Gomez the Washington of the revolution, and in the government of Cisneros a counterpart of our Continental Congress of 1776. He therefore preferred to report directly to Gomez for orders and counsel.

I mention Dr. Hernandez especially, because I came to look on him as the perhaps ablest civilian enrolled in the Cuban cause.

From the day of his arrival, Dr. Hernandez came to Gomez' mess with Colete, Miguelito, and myself.

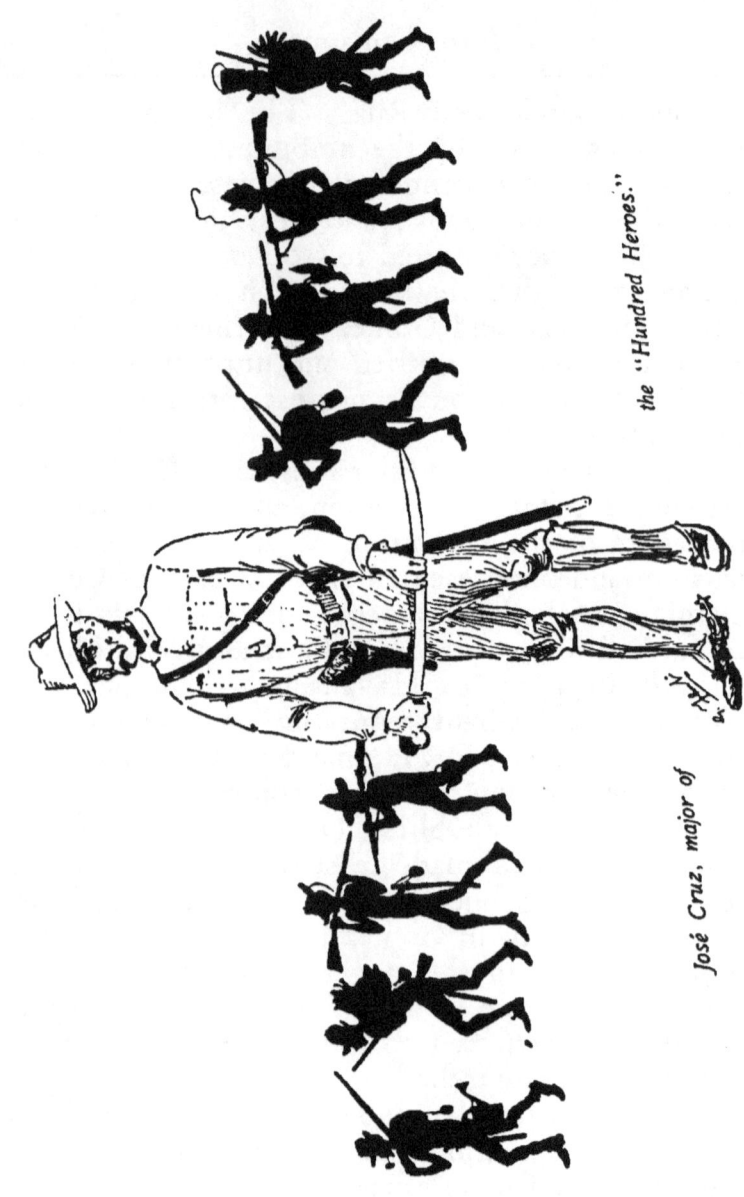

He replaced General Vega, who was temporarily absent. I had an extra spoon in my pack: Hernandez had none, so I was able to add to his equipment, and one day I saw that Gomez no longer wore his chased silver spurs, but a common pair of iron ones. At supper I saw the silver spurs on Dr. Hernandez' heels, and I knew from this token of the general's esteem, that he was now, as Gomez would say, "one of the family."

The mess had become luxurious. We were in a country famed for honey. On every farm, deserted or otherwise, there were hives by scores, in hollow palm logs; and when there was time on the march, the men would try to smoke them and scrape out the rich comb with their machetes. The asistentes vied with each other in capturing bits of comb for their masters, and the air was often filled with angry bees. Sometimes bottles of perfectly white and very fragrant honey, made from certain white flowers that grew only on certain hillsides, — honey such as I had never before seen, — were sent to Gomez as gifts of state. It was the land of the celebrated white Camaguey cheese, that is eaten as dessert, dipped in a jicara of honey, or with sugar — if there is sugar. Although our column was swelled to nearly six hundred men by the addition of one hundred infantry (commanded by the veteran, Major José Cruz, of Puerto Rico),[1] provisions were still plentiful; for these forest districts had not been exhausted by travelling armies.

The appearance of the company of infantry that now marched as our rear-guard was unique and pathetic. Somebody called them the "hundred heroes,"

---

[1] He fell at Saratoga, June 13, 1896.

and they certainly bore out the Frenchman's saying that the infantry proves its valor less in fighting than in walking so much. Ragged to the skin, travel-worn to the bone, of all colors and sizes, with their Remington or Mauser "Long Toms" across their shoulders, — any way at all, — they filed along like bits of moving earth on the landscape. In the forest trails that our horses' hoofs had cut into mud gullies, they slipped along, leaping from one side to the other in search of firmer footing, or struggling knee-deep through pools and rivulets. They carried cooking-utensils queer and various; even old watering-pots taken from deserted gardens. They were hard up for everything,— shoes, hats, equipments of every sort. Fortunately for them, they were soon to be refitted; for near Najaza, some of the first cartloads of supplies from the government workshops were portioned among them.

An incident of the march indicated another variance between our general and the Civil Government, with a possible stretch of prerogative by the latter.

It was at noon one day, that a lanky old fellow with the face of a vulture was arrested and brought before Gomez. He had a servant and three stout mules grunting under a weight of merchandise, rich as the pack of a peddler in the Arabian Nights.

He had a formal permit from the Civil Government to sell these goods,— bought in the towns, and carried out by bribery of Spanish officials, — to peasants of the neighborhood. This was in direct violation of Gomez' proclamation, forbidding trade of any kind between the town and the peasants. The old speculator's goods were scattered on the ground in heaps. He had several hundred cigars, a thousand packages of cigarettes, bundles of shoes for women and children, rolls of calico and linen stuffs, a number of trinkets and knick-knacks, four demijohns of rum and brandy, some dozen pounds of hard bread, and two bags of coffee. This, when he found himself in trouble, he swore was all for his personal use.

Gomez tore up the Government permit and parcelled the bread, and coffee, and tobacco among the soldiers, excepting the staff and escolta. The shoes, calico, and knick-knacks were given to some peasant women of the neighborhood to keep, — or divide among their friends, — and the rum and brandy was poured out on the ground, where it settled into the dry soil, leaving a rich aroma. Then the old fellow was sent on his way with a warning, and we took the march; our happy, ragged soldiery puffing clouds of pale smoke into the air from their newly acquired cigarettes and cigars.

By this time my equipment was in a sad condition. I had no rubber coat that would turn a rain, — I had no shelter tent, — I was nearly barefoot, with not a sound garment about me; for though my belt was heavy with gold, I could buy nothing. Gomez had already remarked, with what I thought at the time unnecessary frankness, that it was hard to tell which was the more ragged — my asistente or I; so I determined to delay in some district until I could refit and join the commander-in-chief later. Gomez,

Gomez' letter of introduction to Carrillo.

TRANSLATION. — Headquarters of the Liberating Army, "Pozo Azul," 21 May, 1896. To Major General Francisco Carrillo. Remedios. General: The bearer of this is Mr. Grover Flint, correspondent of the American newspaper, "The Journal," and in that capacity is at present a member of my staff. During my absence in the Villareñas districts, Mr. Flint will remain with you. I trust it is unnecessary for me to recommend him to your highest consideration. You will afford him every assistance in equipping himself completely and fittingly, that he may join me on my return, and place at his disposition every means of sending his despatches abroad. Wishing you health and glory, your General, M. Gomez.

therefore, gave me a letter of introduction to General Carrillo, who was permanently stationed near Remedios; but at the last moment I decided to remain with the "old man" and rough it.

I give a reproduction of the letter to Carrillo. It was written by the secretary, but signed by Gomez. It is a fair sample of correspondence from headquarters.

Gomez' staff barber at work.

Chapter VI

Gomez' Moral Campaign in Camaguey

RAIN fell intermittently day and night during the last week in May, and the forest trails became sloughs, wherein horses splashed to their knees, covering the backs of riders ahead with black mud. The rivers were swollen, and in the shallowest fords, water rippled above the saddle-girths, and your mount fought for a footing. Marches were therefore short, and made in the mornings. Of afternoons, Gomez had offenders from all parts brought before him, and the journey was like riding the circuit with a British magistrate of the last century. Evil-doers were run to ground and majaces were punished. In Camaguey many officers had become demoralized. They were not hard pressed enough to fight in self-

"Horses splashed to their knees."

defence, and they grew fond of ease in camp and cottage. Samples of discipline like the following were common.

Scene. — A bit of worn canvas stretched on poles between two palms. Beneath it Gomez in a hammock, with Colete sitting in the grass, writing, at his side. Bosa, Miguelito, and half a dozen alert ayudantes in background. Soldiers and asistentes in groups to right and left.

Enter, in a cloudburst of geniality and clean linen, fat, elderly man, with white moustache and red face. He gives his horse to an asistente. He wears a shiny pistol-belt and crossbelt with the stars of a major, top boots, and silver-mounted machete.

The major. — "Ah, citizens, gentlemen, my respects to you all. My respects to the commander-in-chief. I report at my general's order. I trust my general is well." (Removes his hat and bows before headquarters.)

"*I trust my general is well.*"

Gomez (testily). — "Lift up the tent. Let me see the man. I can't see the fellow." (Arranges his spectacles and peers from beneath canvas.)

"Ah! indeed! A com-an-dan-te. How many men have you?"

The major. — "About fifty, my general."

Gomez (raising his voice).—"Answer my question directly; how many men have you?"

The major (embarrassed).—"Just fifty-five, my general, and forty rifles."

Gomez.—"Are your men well, in good health? Have they ammunition?"

The major.—"Excellent, my general, with some forty rounds per man."

Gomez.—"How near does your family live?"

The major (in mild astonishment).—"Two leagues, my general."

Gomez.—"Go to them to-day. Prepare your equipment, turn over your men and your arms to Colonel Bosa at once. To-morrow I will send you to Pinar del Rio, to Maceo, where there is fighting, where you will have to fight."

The major.—"My general."

Gomez.—"Monday you allowed the Spanish convoy to pass through your district without attacking them. You have men, you have arms and ammunition, you are strong; how is this?"

The major.—"But, my general, I did not know they were coming."

Gomez.—"But you should know; it is your business to know. I knew. Every one knew. The asistentes knew. It is easy enough to go one way and let the Spaniards go another." (Rising and addressing his officers.) "Here, who wants an asistente? Here is a good strong man for an asistente,—but no, you must fight; you shall be a private soldier. Tear off those stars which you disgrace; you are a common soldier."

The major.—"But, my general, remember my

services in the last war. I fought in the Ten Years' War."

Gomez. — "The more shame you. This is as if I said I had money but I spent it; I had health but lost it. Do you think the war is already over? It is not when a man comes here saying, 'I am of ancient family, or I am a college professor, or I am a millionaire,' that he is respected; but only when he can say, 'I fight.' White or black or yellow, 'I fight' is a man's glory here. We respect men for service alone, and your service does not entitle you to respect. Oh, I have heard of you many times before. It is my duty as commander-in-chief to make you fight as a common soldier. Here, Colonel Bosa, take this private soldier away."[1]

And before the column was half way through Camaguey a major and three captains were privates of the escolta.

At Pozo Azul, a prefect, a tall, sharp-looking fellow, was tried on five indictments, for misappropriating government property and levying small sums of money, illegally, on farmers of the neighborhood. He was sentenced to death; and as evening fell, the troops were drawn up, dismounted, on three sides of a quadrangle. Then an aide of Gomez trotted to the centre of the square and read the indictments and the finding of the court-martial. Amidst silence, the prefect, his arms tied behind him, was marched across the quadrangle to the open side, followed by four ragged sharpshooters of the infantry and a corporal. His eyes were bandaged, and he was placed standing with his back to us all,

---

[1] After Gomez' scolding, the major was reduced by court-martial in due form.

six paces in front of the firing squad. There was a pause. No one moved but the corporal, who turned toward the aide as the four marksmen levelled their rifles. Then the last rays of the sun flashed on the lifted machete of the aide, and the corporal gave the order "Fuego" in a whisper heard only by the four and those nearest them.

The prefect's knees swayed under him, and he fell writhing to one side, on his back and left shoulder, with his face buried in the grass. The four bullets had passed through his head. Then the trumpeters blew "Attention!" and "Forward, March!" and the troops swung off within a pace of where the corpse lay; many straining over their shoulders to catch a glimpse of the features, others passing nonchalantly as if it were an everyday occurrence.

Two days later a burly negro corporal, of vast breadth of shoulder and a gorilla-like cast of features, was found guilty of gross insubordination. He had twice threatened an officer with his carbine. He was shot at evening also.

He died as coolly as any man I have ever seen. With an air of disgust he waved off those who wished to bandage his eyes, and leaning easily on a snake fence, in a sleeveless cotton shirt, with his powerful black arms outstretched along the upper bar, he looked into the barrels of the firing squad.

"Fire at my breast," he said; and when we marched by, as was customary, he had fallen easily, his head resting against the lowest bar of the snake fence, and his eyes open and staring up to the sky, with no other expression than annoyance fixed on his hard features.

Gomez' Moral Campaign in Camaguey 179

These rigid enforcements of discipline were reported through the Island eastward and westward by travelling commissions. They made Cubans think; and laws drawn up by the itinerant government and printed somewhere about Najaza became something more than pretty compositions under pretty coats-of-arms. Cubans felt more than ever that the republic existed in earnest, and their respect for themselves and their leaders increased.

It was on the afternoon of June 2d that scouts brought in Captain Manoel Gonzales, a dandified little man, with neatly trimmed black whiskers, a gay silk kerchief, and a fine jipi-japa hat. His high leather leggings, machete scabbard, and belt, his saddle and bridle, and saddle clothes, were all beautiful examples of Creole luxury. In his saddle-bags were certain papers, a pack of playing-cards, a complete change of clothing, and underclothing, a pocket mirror and

Gonzales' beautiful machete.

comb, a bottle of scents, and several white handkerchiefs, fifteen good cigars, and twenty packages of cigarettes. He carried a nickel-plated Winchester rifle and a Colt's revolver. All these were piled on the clay floor of a cattle shed that served as headquarters, and Gonzales, at Gomez' orders, was

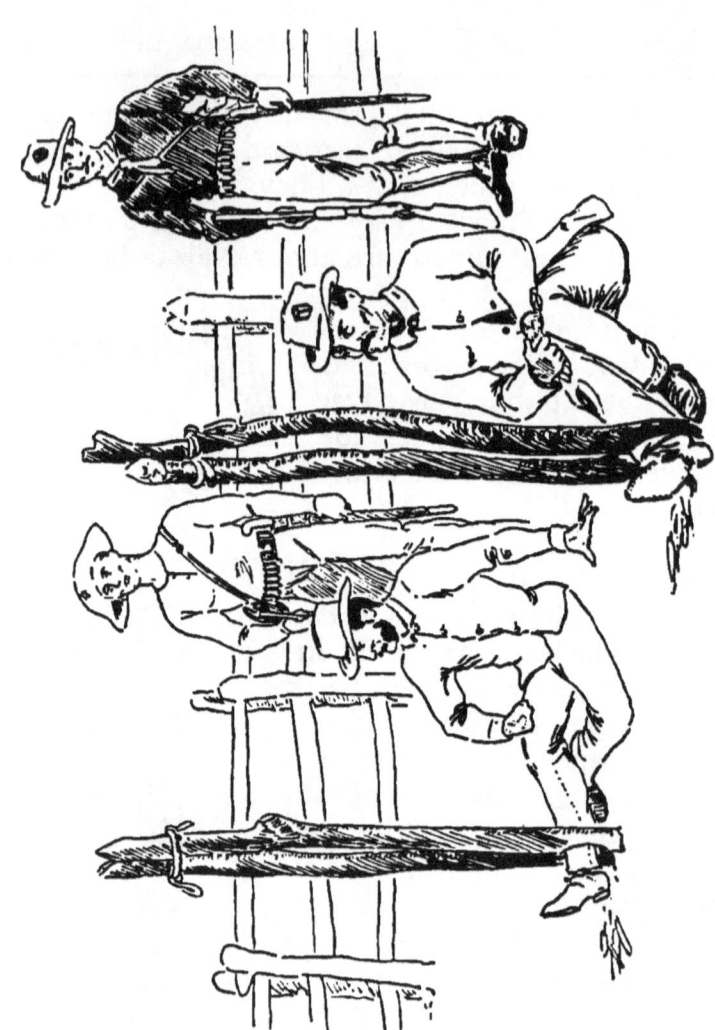

Gonzales in the stocks.

(Sketched on June 2d. The man on the left is Gonzales, the other an ordinary maja.)

put in the stocks beside an offender of less importance.

When a suspicious character is under arrest in the Manigua, one of his ankles is thrust between two stakes driven into the ground. Notches are hacked to fetter his limb more firmly, and the stakes are tied together above. There, with a sentry standing over him, he is left, safely secured, to ruminate on his misdeeds.

Everybody knew that Gonzales had been a brigand before the war. Then he had a pack of cards, and soldiers of the republic are forbidden to play at cards or have them in their possession. His cedula showed that he had been absent from any organized force since February, and in his belt were found one hundred gold centenes[1] and nearly one hundred dollars in silver. A court-martial was called, and things looked black for Gonzales. It meant either reduction to the ranks, or death.

The money was sealed in a bag, to be sent to the Minister of Finance, and in the distribution of his outfit, which in any case was too good for a " buck " soldier, I came out with his belt, its lining still marked with the fat coins, his machete (a stout Collins cut-and-thrust blade, Paraguay model, made in Connecticut), and four of the good cigars.

Besides the pack of cards, and the cedula, which proved him a sort of deserter, there was only circumstantial evidence that Gonzales had resumed his profession of brigandage. He was not an intelligent man. He talked too much for his own good. And the court-martial was determined. They sat

[1] A centen is equivalent to something over four dollars, American money.

on him from seven until midnight. His counsel, a young Havana lawyer, defended him manfully.

I had slung my hammock near the oule, under which the court was held. Lying in it, I listened to the defence, and dozed at intervals. Gonzales had been absent, he said, from the presidency on an important commission; it was to buy paper and ink. This had taken him from February until June; but they were difficult things to purchase. He carried the playing-cards merely to amuse women and children at the houses where he was entertained; he was unaware of the strict significance of the order concerning cards, etc. As for the money, it had been lent him from time to time in small sums, say two and three dollars, by admiring friends. His counsel's attitude was, "For Heaven's sake, don't bully my man, but prove something if you can."

I was already asleep when a change from noisy discussion to stillness, as the trial reached a climax, awoke me. I heard the faint but distinct voice of Gonzales, " In fact, gentlemen, *I have* led the life of a bandit." Then there was a pause, and the light flickered, as a damp wind rustled through the palm tops, and I fell asleep.

The merry notes of the " Diana " sounded to the lifting of a curtain of mist at daybreak on the 3d. The troopers, with saddles packed, were mounting when the sun was high, and aides trotted off with orders to the encampments of the different forces. The assembly followed "boots and saddles," and the escolta moved to a sloping savanna, turned

"Reveille" on a rainy morning.—Page 182.

"twos left," and halted. Then came Guerra's and Calungas' and Sanchez Agramontes' expeditionaries, and finally the neutral tinted company of infantry, half seen in the tall grass, filled a side of the quadrangle. The soldiers halted, dressed and waited. There was a gap left on the southern side, where a gnarled guasima tree, with a trunk as big as a barrel, stood alone by itself.

Gomez rode up followed by Dr. Hernandez, and halted in front of the escolta. The rest of the staff fell in line behind him. On the lower end of the square stood Gonzales, his arms tied above the elbow, behind him a corporal and four rifles from the infantry.

All were waiting, when Gomez trotted to the centre and pulled up short. He turned his big white stallion slowly about on his hind quarters by the weight of the bridle rein and an easy touch of the spur, and drew his little curved Santo Domingo machete. Then with his white beard in the air, his clear voice came in quick, sharp sentences.

"Soldiers, before you a man, Manoel Gonzales, is brought, tried and condemned by court-martial, for breaking the laws of our commonwealth. He was guilty, and having held a grade in our army, he was a dishonor to all of you who offer your lives and labors for the fatherland. I have sentenced him to be shot. By the execution of such as he, we uphold our honor, and by the death of every rascal, we secure peace to our nation when she is free. Long live free Cuba!"

Three vivas rose, and Gomez, trotting back, pulled up in front of his aides.

Gonzales walked across the square. He was pale and he puffed hard at a cigarette held between his teeth. As he passed Gomez, who sat motionless with machete still drawn, he dropped the cigarette from his mouth and turned. "A word, only a word, with the commander-in-chief." The corporal looked at Gomez, but saw only a shake of the head. "Forward, forward, hombre, man alive," he said, putting the flat of his hand on Gonzales' back, with a slight push. Then Gonzales hung his head and walked on.

Gonzales was not brave. His life had been easy and was something to lose. He was placed against the guasima tree and tied to it by one of the asistentes with a stout lariat, while another lighted a cigarette and placed it between his lips. Gonzales was limp, and the jaunty little air of yesterday was gone. There was no pride to replace it. One of his own neat white handkerchiefs was quickly tied over his face. Then, with arms behind him and the rope about his waist, his chin sunk on his breast, but the cigarette remained between his lips. The asistentes jumped to one side.

There was a flash of Gomez' machete and four shots. Gonzales was not dead. He hung forward, choking and swaying on the rope. The corporal drew his revolver and held its muzzle against Gonzales' ear. Then there was a smothered report, followed by two shrill notes of the bugle—"Forward!" The escolta took up the march, and the other troops fell in behind, while Gomez trotted off to the head of the column.

The little group of asistentes remained to bury

Gonzales. They were ragged fellows, and their perquisites were the neat white suit, that one washing would make good, a pair of serviceable boots that were good stock in trade, even if they did not fit, and the jipi-japa hat, that had fallen to one side.[1]

---

[1] "A Revolution," wrote Dr. Hernandez, "gathers to its breast all classes of men; but with the distinct understanding that the bad become good and the good practise every effort to become better, otherwise its standard becomes a refuge for those who desire to follow more conveniently, and with less danger, criminal and disorderly lives. In such a case a Revolution, even for Liberty, would not justify the vast and unavoidable destruction of life and property wherever its flag is unfurled."

Chapter VII

Gomez and Hernandez

The tax-collector in "cepo de campaña."

IT was at the trial of a tax-collector of the Civil Government, whose name I have forgotten, that I first saw Dr. Hernandez distinguish himself. This tax-collector appeared on the day that Manoel Gonzales was detained, recognized him, shook hands with him knowingly, and after that unfortunate gentleman was tried and shot, he left camp, giving a plausible pretext to the guards who demanded his pass, and faded away like the mist.

It was clear that the tax-collector had lied to the sentries, and that he had broken the regulations in leaving without permission. He was known to have money about him, and Gomez, on the theory that an honest man knows no fear, sent a detachment to run him down. He was captured in a prefectura on the fifth, and promptly brought into camp. The circumstantial evidence that he was dishonest seemed sufficient to put him in the stocks, call a court-martial, and divide his equipments among the staff.

There was difficulty in finding a man to defend the prisoner, because every one believed him guilty, and the defence of a criminal is an unpopular task; but Dr. Hernandez, seeing that he was without friends, undertook it. The trial was longer than that of Gonzales. It was begun early in the afternoon and ended at midnight.

Hernandez made a psychological study of the prisoner, sifted the evidence, and became convinced of his innocence. He demonstrated that the man's accounts, as receiver of taxes for the government, were straight, and that he could not have appropriated public funds. The man was merely a physical coward. He had witnessed Gonzales' execution, and had heard of the shooting of the prefect and the negro corporal. He formed an exaggerated dread of Gomez' discipline, and so ran away out of ordinary timidity. He lied to the guards as a timid man would be likely to do. When Hernandez closed his defence, the court acquitted the tax-collector, with a trifling sentence for the irregularity of his exit from camp, and his equipments were returned to him.

The result of this trial caused a temporary estrangement between Gomez and Dr. Hernandez. Gomez would not confirm the finding of the court. He simply called the affair off, and peremptorily ordered the tax-collector out of sight and out of camp. Gomez did not believe the man innocent, and Hernandez did. Gomez thought that Hernandez had been influenced by an emotional kindness of heart, to save the life of a criminal who had ingeniously covered his tracks. Whatever Gomez thinks, he says, with Spartan directness, and without regard for the feelings of anybody.[1] Hernandez felt hurt, and from that day until just before the Saratoga fight, Hernandez did not mess with Gomez, but with General Castillo, who had succeeded Vega as chief of staff.

It was four days later that additional evidence came out in the tax-collector's case, which justified Hernandez. Gomez, old soldier though he was, had erred for once. As Gomez never spared any one whatever comment he considered just, he was quick to admit it when in the wrong. He said something to Dr. Hernandez, and that evening the doctor turned up at supper and was again one of "the family."

In those first weeks of June it was my privilege to linger of evenings, by headquarters, and hear the war discussed in every phase by Gomez and Hernandez. Of the ultimate success of their cause, neither had the shadow of a doubt; but when the trouble would end, neither could prophesy.

Both were painfully aware of the suffering and death that every additional day meant for untold hundreds of helpless old men, women, and children. Yet the dragging on of the war was not without advantage, because it trained Cubans in self-denial; it disciplined the disorderly element, and gave the

---

[1] Once as I was making a pencil sketch of his horse, Gomez caught me at it and looked over my shoulder. "A very bad drawing," said he kindly, but in a tone of deep conviction, "I would advise you to follow some other career."

little Civil Government a chance to spread its wings and gain experience before attempting to fly alone.

As Hernandez said, "the life of one entire generation is not too great a sacrifice to the prosperity of countless generations to come."

For Hernandez, there was the glory of conflict, and the opportunity to develop his rather unusual abilities. For Gomez, continuance of the struggle meant daily hardships and lack of rest or comfort in illness, a life delightful to a young man, but trying for one of advanced years. For Gomez there was the chance of a stray bullet that might prevent his seeing the aim of his life — the work of his brain and hands — completed.

Gomez had long since ceased to count on assistance of any kind from the United States. Concerning recognition I heard him say, "I have a mind to forbid any man's speaking that word in camp. Recognition is like the rain; it is a good thing if it comes, and a good thing if it doesn't come."

Gomez distrusted Americans. He thought them mere sharpers. "They continually fill their newspapers with sympathy for our cause," he would say, "but what do they do? They sell us arms at good round prices, — as readily as they sell supplies to the Spaniards, who oppress us; but they never gave us a thing — not even a rifle."

Gomez held the old-fashioned theory of the moral responsibility of journalism. He did not realize that successful newspapers are struck off nowadays like so much calico, with no other moral purpose in view than an extensive sale. Gomez held the editor of the *New York Herald* in extreme contempt. "The

Fragment of a letter from Gomez.

TRANSLATION. — General Gomez believes, as do his followers, that if the war does not soon end, Cuba will offer to the world a sad picture of utmost misery and strife. Since they realize that Cuba's wealth is the cause of her bondage they are determined that everything must be destroyed. In the Field, 25 May, 1896.
Maximo Gomez.

fellow [*el tio ese*] publishes news in one column that is favorable to us, in another he calls us brigands; can he not take one side or the other, or none at all, like an honest man?"

These talks, which were not for publication, were held of evenings, when the weather was fine, under Gomez' bit of canvas. They were never long; for Gomez retired early, after the bugle sounded "Silencio." Often before reveille the "old man" was awake, writing private despatches or personal letters, in his hammock, by the flickering light of a yellow Mambi taper fastened on a stick driven into the ground, while an aide stood guard and the camp slept. Of afternoons, when not on the road, he dictated to his secretary, read letters, or dozed the siesta. But at supper-time, when fresh green leaves were spread at Gomez' feet, and the saucepan, with its mess of soup or chopped meat and plantains, was put before him, and we gathered with our tin plates, knives, and spoons, and squatted in a semicircle, our asistentes standing attentively behind, topics of the day were discussed over again.

Hernandez sometimes dreamed of the future of free Cuba. He favored a generous extension of suffrage to include respectable foreigners settled in the Island practically on application for citizenship. With the rebuilding of ruined ingenios, and a development, that corrupt exactions of Spanish officials had hitherto rendered unprofitable, of the great mining, timber, and cattle interests of the eastern provinces, followed by an extension of the railroad system, and in every branch of electrics, an enormous demand would arise for every sort of skilled labor. An ideal class of immigrants would be drawn to the country, and the resultant blending of Latin and Saxon races would produce a sturdy nation, active and progressive in commerce, — in fact, Hernandez saw in the Cuba of the future, an England of the Western Hemisphere. Hernandez admired Americans for their strength and vigor, and was a close student of our constitution, which he held to embody the proper theories for successful self-government.

Gomez, as a practical soldier, did not venture to speculate on Cuba's future in detail. It was looking forward enough for him to see Cuba under her own flag and government. Neither of these men approved of any scheme of annexation to the United States, or saw any conclusion of the war short of absolute independence. As Gomez said, "Autonomy might have been accepted, if offered in good faith, very early in the war; but since the time of Martinez Campos, it has been out of the question." These unyielding views on annexation and autonomy were universally held by fighting Cubans in the Manigua.

Gomez' hobby was the punishing of evil-doers. On meeting General Serafin Sanchez some weeks later, he said as he embraced him, — a rare mark of esteem from Gomez, — "When I see an honest man, I feel a year younger; but these rascals, these scoundrels" (referring to General Suarez, whom he had just cashiered), "they put me back six months. But we'll send them all to the guasima; we'll hang them all before we get through!"

After a skirmish, Gomez was invariably genial and inclined to jest with those nearest him, often pacing up and down in front of his shelter-tent. His humor was homely and honest, sometimes slightly coarse.

On one occasion, lecturing an officer who was to be tried for cowardice, Gomez turned to the breathless audience clustered behind him. "A brave man," he said, "may be forgiven many things. He may err, he may sin; but there is good in him. I would go down to the infernal regions with a brave man. But a coward cannot be trusted. A coward will lie, a coward will thieve, he will abuse women. He—" here Gomez caught the glance of a buxom matron who had come, with her two dark-eyed daughters, sight-seeing, to camp. "He would be an old goat [cabron], he would let another man make love to his wife."

It is not usual, in armies, for a commander to publicly reprimand officers, even non-commissioned officers. It is supposed to destroy the authority of their rank; but Gomez, I think, did so for a purpose. He was surrounded by men unused to weighing points of honor with nicety. Though well meaning, they were ignorant of many things, and these lectures, generalizing on what a man owed to himself and to the fatherland, gave them new ideas. Gomez' sayings were widely repeated, and the moral tone of the army was raised. He reprimanded a soldier once for selling his horse to another. "Have you no self-respect?" he said. "You sell for personal gain a horse that, like the arms you carry, is the property of the Republic, and is entrusted to you. You sell what is not your own! It is as if a child sold to another the eggs or milk from the farmyard of their common mother."

There were cases where Gomez' jests skimmed over the heads of those at whom they were aimed. I clip from *Harper's Weekly* the naïve account by T. R. Dawley of his first meeting with Gomez. Mr. Dawley evidently did not win the commander's good graces.

"To talk with the great man," says Dawley,[1] "it was necessary for me to crawl under his canvas, for he made no attempt to crawl out, and the canvas was not high enough for a man to stand up under. After having answered his few questions concerning myself, he said to one of his aides, in a pretentious way, —

"'Take him to the deposit for correspondents.'

"I had heard of deposits for horses and cattle, deposits for sweet-potatoes and coffee, but a deposit for correspondents struck me as something new; and I was not long in discovering that it was a feature of the camp as novel to the aide whom Gomez had directed to conduct me, as it was to myself."

A "deposit" (deposito), as Mr. Dawley explains, is a place where you put either animals or things. It was exactly as if Gomez had said, "Take him to the pound."

"Gomez," wrote Sylvester Scovel, "has all his life dominated undisciplined men by severity and power of will: his temper is vile."

Mr. Scovel, who made the invasion with Gomez and saw more of him than any other correspondent, played a part in a scene that opens another side of Gomez' character.

[1] See *Harper's Weekly*, May 19, 1897.

It was in the days of doubt, and Gomez, probably under great pressure, gave loose rein to his always fiery temper. For one cause or another, he several times gave "planazos" to certain of his officers, arousing a vindictive spirit among them, — almost the inception of mutiny. Scovel had won the confidence of both general and staff. He heard the whisperings about the camp-fires and saw the sullen looks; and he knew that the hot-blooded man of Latin race will often sacrifice obvious duty and the interests of his country, to regard for "his honor."

One day Scovel wrote a letter to his paper. It recounted in glowing colors the successes of the march, and the hopes of the insurrection. He closed somewhat as follows:—

"The success of Cuban arms depends on the unity and co-operation of the rebel forces. The temper of the commander-in-chief has lately become so uncontrolled as to endanger good feeling among his officers, and act as a disorganizing element. But surely the old commander who has given the best years of his life to the Cuban cause will restrain himself in time."

Scovel handed this letter to the interpreter to translate aloud to the commander-in-chief, and he sat down near by, nerving himself for a hurricane. At the closing passage, the old general, whom no Cuban had ever dared criticise to his face, became ashen with rage. He listened with every muscle taut, while the interpreter hesitated, mouthed, and stammered over the closing lines. There was a moment of silence; then Gomez rose. He went to where Scovel still sat, put one arm over his shoulder, and patted him, while moisture welled under his spectacles, and one tear slid down his furrowed cheek to the white moustache below.

Next morning, before marching, Gomez ordered the assembly blown, and as publicly as he had reprimanded others he apologized to his officers in the presence of all the forces.

"The Hermita San Jeronimo."

It was on the fifth of June, by a mere coincidence, that we rode over the scene of the first machete charge of the war. It was the Camino Real, from San Jeronimo to Puerto Principe, a broad avenue in the forest, with trees and brush well cleared away on either side of the road. Along it stood the telegraph poles leading to Puerto Principe. Just one year before, three hundred Spanish soldiers were acting as guards to some workmen who were repairing the telegraph wire which had been cut by a small partida on the night before. The advance guard of Maceo's forces came on them suddenly. It was a portion of the road overlooked by an old chapel, the Hermita San Jeronimo (deserted by its priest), a straight-away course for five hundred yards. Maceo's men dashed through there, cutting down everything in sight. The attack was so sudden, that only a few of the soldiers or laborers escaped to the brush. The Spaniards never came back to repair the line or bury their dead. Wild pigs worried and ate the bodies, scattering the bones everywhere, and white fragments of skulls lay on the road like shells on a beach.

NOTE. — At San Jeronimo, one of Gomez' trumpeters brought me a little flower, called "La Libertad" (which I reproduce on page 117), with five green leaves, forming a perfect star, white rose-like petals and a fragrance like the violet. "La Libertad" appears in the forests of eastern Cuba in May, when the soil moistens with the first showers of the rainy season, and for this reason, according to a local superstition, freedom will come to Cuba in the month of May.

Chapter VIII

The Battle of Saratoga

HEADQUARTERS[1] OF GOMEZ' STAFF, NAJAZA, PUERTO PRINCIPE PROVINCE, — THURSDAY, JUNE 11th.

FOR the first time since he has been in Camaguey, Spanish troops have come out to meet Gomez. Two infantry regiments, numbering nearly two thousand men, and two hundred cavalry, marched from the city of Puerto Principe to within three leagues of us three days ago. I send to the Journal my field notes of the three days' fighting which has intervened.

The First Day, June 9th. — At daybreak we had news that General Jimenez Castellanos was marching from Puerto Principe to meet us. Gomez is breaking camp. He has four hundred cavalry and one hundred infantry.[2]

2 P.M. — We have marched in solid column by the high-road towards Puerto Principe to meet the Spaniards; but they have passed in by a roundabout way, and are encamped on the Saratoga estate, near Najaza Mountain, where we camped yesterday. We turn back, taking their trail. The road is cut deep with ruts of field-pieces and caissons.

4 P.M. — Smoke of the Spanish camp-fires in full

---

[1] From the *New York Journal,* July 5, 1896.
[2] Exclusive of one hundred impedimenta.

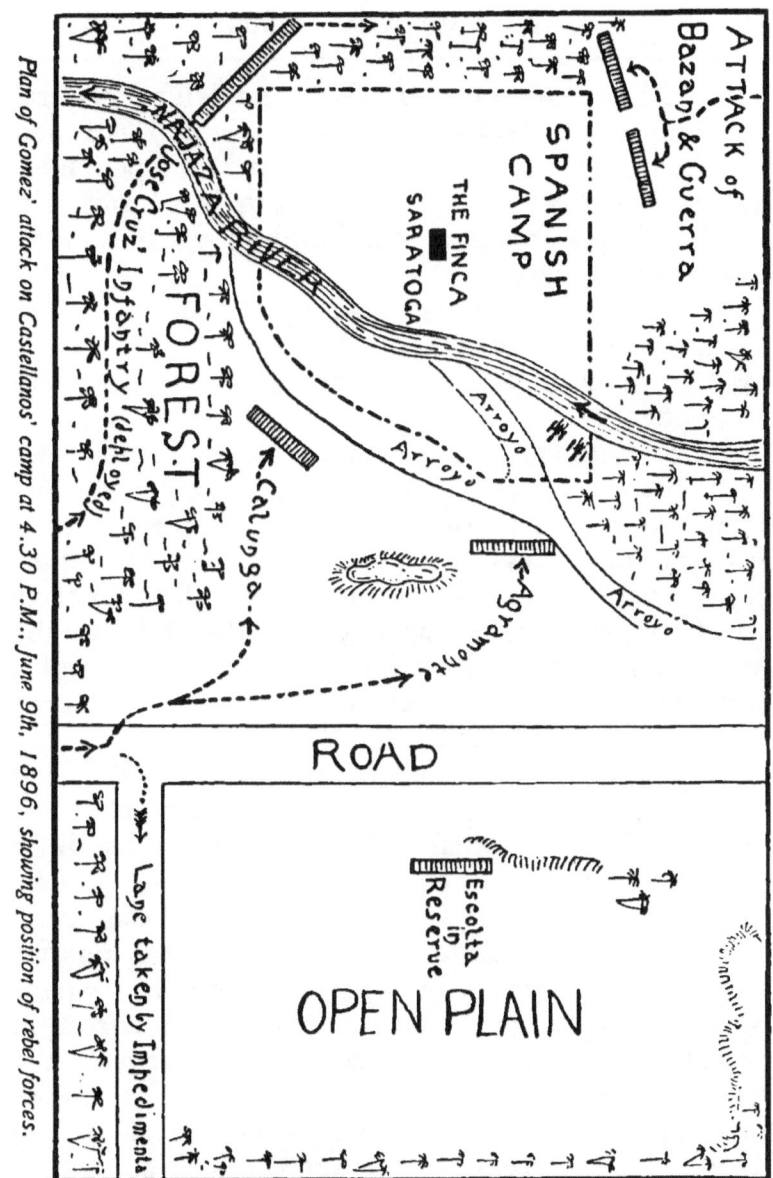

Plan of Gomez' attack on Castellanos' camp at 4.30 P.M., June 9th, 1896, showing position of rebel forces.

sight. They are on a bend of the River Najaza, covering both banks on rolling ground. Thick forests are on their north and west and open hilly country to the east. To the south is a stony hill overlooking a savanna five hundred yards square, ending in a forest.

4.30 P.M.—Gomez is leading the attack. We are approaching the enemy's lines from the south by the main high-road. There is a barbed wire fence between us and the river. The men of Colonel Calunga's squadron are cutting the wires with their machetes. Then they charge on the camp to the left of the hill. Major Sanchez Agramonte follows, charging fiercely to the right of the hill. There is shooting, and the machetes are flashing. Some carry their rifles across the pommel in the bridle hand, machetes in the right. Across the river, Castellanos' staff can be seen running from the house to their horses.

4.45 P.M.—Our men have halted. A deep arroyo prevents a general machete charge. The Spaniards are in plain sight,—dark gray lines splashed with the red of their sashes. Their cavalry are standing in the rear, under the trees.

4.55 P.M.—Calunga's men of the expeditionaries are firing deliberately, sitting in their saddles. Spanish bullets coming thick, but too high. Direction good! Elevation bad! You can feel them in the air. Sometimes they make you wink. The smoke from our Remingtons in the firing line is getting thick. Can scarcely see the Spaniards through it.[1]

---

[1] In fact, we could scarcely see one another. Men banged away behind and on either side of you, so you ran some risk of being "winged" by your friends. An

5.05 P.M. — I ride to the left of the hill where Sanchez is. Our infantry are shooting into the enemy's right flank from the woods. The Peninsulars are getting excited: they shoot higher and faster. Gomez, followed by his staff, is riding placidly up and down, peering at the Spanish lines through the smoke. He has stationed his escolta on the plain back of us as a reserve. He has sent the squadrons of Ramon Guerra and Colonel Bazan by a roundabout way to attack the camp from the north.

The Spanish are opening on us with artillery from the high land just to the right and rear of the hill, on their side of the arroyo: two guns. Elevation all wrong; cannot even hear the sing of their trajectiles.

It is inspiring to see Gomez under gun-fire, his eyes flashing with interest. He looks twenty years younger. His hat is cocked to one side, and he twirls his little machete in his wrist — a trick he has.

5.20 P.M. — They are bringing the wounded from the front. Some are in the arms of comrades, riding double, to be left with the impedimenta. In the firing line some have had their horses shot and are fighting on foot. Gomez trots up on the hill in clear sight of the Spanish line. They are well to this side of the river, but not advancing. Bullets very thick, and we come back.

5.30 P.M. — Enemy won't advance! Signal for our men to retire. Calunga and Sanchez fall back.

---

accident of that kind might easily happen in a smoky firing line, especially when mounted, as I know from experience; for I once came very near shooting a comrade in a troop skirmish, practising on silhouette targets at Fort Bayard, N.M.

Infantry (our "Hundred Heroes") coming one by one out of the woods, firing and retreating, a line of dark-brown figures. They look like Apaches. Some of them crouch and duck — that is odd for soldiers of their experience! We hear the volleys of Bazan and Guerra attacking in the rear.

A solid shot falls in a rain-puddle twenty yards from Gomez, throwing a shaft of water thirty feet into the air. That is the best shot I have seen to-day.

6.30 P.M. — We are going into camp half a league away. Calunga and Guerra are to shoot into the enemy during the night.

8 P.M. — Dr. Hernandez, who was at Gomez' elbow all the afternoon, assists Gustavo Abreu, staff surgeon, in charge of the wounded. He sends word that four have been killed outright and six badly wounded. There are others "winged" who have not gone on the sick report.

The Second Day. — Dawn. — All night long there was shooting from the hill which our men occupied into the Spanish camp, wherever a light showed, to keep the Peninsulars awake. Gomez is preparing to renew the attack.

6 A.M. — In the field. Gomez making every attempt, by dashes to their very lines and hasty retreats, to excite the enemy and draw them out into the open.

8 A.M. — Gomez has just ridden with his staff over the crest of the hill under a hot and noisy fire. Enemy are throwing shells into the woods to the south, where our reserves are stationed.

10.30 A.M. — The shooting continues steadily,

but here and there. Calunga's squadron has made a dash at close range, crossing the arroyo almost into the Spanish camp. A negro's horse was struck in the croup by a cannon-ball and killed,[1] its remains entangling the rider. Lieutenant Tarifa de Armas, with two others, pulled him out under a shower of Mauser bullets. Saddle and bridle saved also.

Col. Calunga, Consuegra, June 10

Noon. — The Spaniards have advanced, the centre of their line covering the hill from behind which we attacked them yesterday and early this morning. That is good. It is what Gomez has all the time been trying to get them to do, — to advance into the open country where a machete charge from both sides would cut them up. We retire now to the shade of some palm trees at a little distance to rest and wait.

Captain Garcia, of Tampa, Florida, General Castillo's aide, and I have been sitting with our backs against a fat palm tree. A moment ago Castillo beckoned, and Garcia jumped up and ran to him. He had just left when a Mauser bullet snapped into the tree, quite low, where he had been sitting. Had Garcia

---

[1] The mangling of a horse and the jolting of a negro were the sole results of the labor of dragging two heavy field-pieces all the way from Puerto Principe, through soft roads, where they left ruts like city coal-wagons. Some of the shells were "cold storage" and burst harmlessly, "scattering bon-bons about," as Tarifa de Armas remarked, showing me an iron ball as big as a marble, which he said plumped into the open pocket of his linen coat. De Armas, by the way, was one of the heirs to the late proprietor of the Socorro de Armas place back in Matanzas.

remained, the bullet would have pierced his abdomen and killed him. As it was, it pierced on its way the instep of a man who was walking by. The man is irritated, but not painfully hurt.

1.50 P.M. — They have brought in a steer and are killing it for breakfast. The men are building parillas — most of them have had nothing much to eat for twenty-four hours. Through our glasses we can see the Spaniards hard at work, as the afternoon sets in, building a breastwork of red stone over the crest of the hill.

3 P.M. — Calunga advances within carbine range, and firing begins again.

4 P.M. — We make a general attack again on both wings of the Spanish line. Guerra and Bazan are still popping away to the rear of the enemy's camp.

Major Guerin, of Gomez' staff, has just been wounded in the hip, the fifth member of the staff hurt in the last five skirmishes we have had, — apparently not dangerous, though. The bullet pierced, on its way, a brass Remington cartridge Guerin carried loose in the pocket of his linen coat.

5.30. — Since noon they have not fired with their cannon.[1] The cavalry we have not seen. Apparently they are afraid of machetes.

Sundown. — Back to camp, leaving Guerra to keep the enemy awake to-night, while Bazan's men take a rest.

Dr. Hernandez reports five killed to-day and thirty-four wounded; almost all from Calunga's force. The enemy are in a pocket. If they stay

---

[1] Castellanos was apparently glad enough to shoot off his heavy ammunition as soon as he could, and drag empty caissons back to Puerto Principe.

there, they will keep getting shot into, and certainly our fire from all sides into such a crowded space must be causing them much loss. If they advance onto the open savanna, it will give us a chance to use the machete.

The last man killed outright this afternoon was Major José Cruz, a Dominican, who commanded the infantry; a very courteous old fellow, with pleasant manners. He was killed a little before sunset. His infantry were not fighting at the time at all; they were taking supper under the palm trees. As Major Cruz was walking up and down looking on, a stray Mauser bullet struck him in the forehead. His knees doubled under him, and he fell on his face without a word, dying instantly.

Third Day. — Heard firing all night. We have saddled our horses. Ammunition has been brought up from a secret store in the forest, on pack-mules, and distributed, — ten rounds per man. Off to the battlefield.

6.30 A.M. — The enemy have thrown out a solid line of infantry beyond the hill as far as the highroad, where they remain. They are firing constantly in our direction. The sun is well up and in their faces. We can see distinctly the flash of their rifles. Their powder is practically smokeless. They probably cannot see us well, for we are in the long grass on the skirts of the forest, but they know our direction. It looks as though they were going to make a general advance. Gomez, with the escolta and infantry, moves to the rising ground to the northeast of their position, where the infantry can stand firm as a reserve; the cavalry can drive through

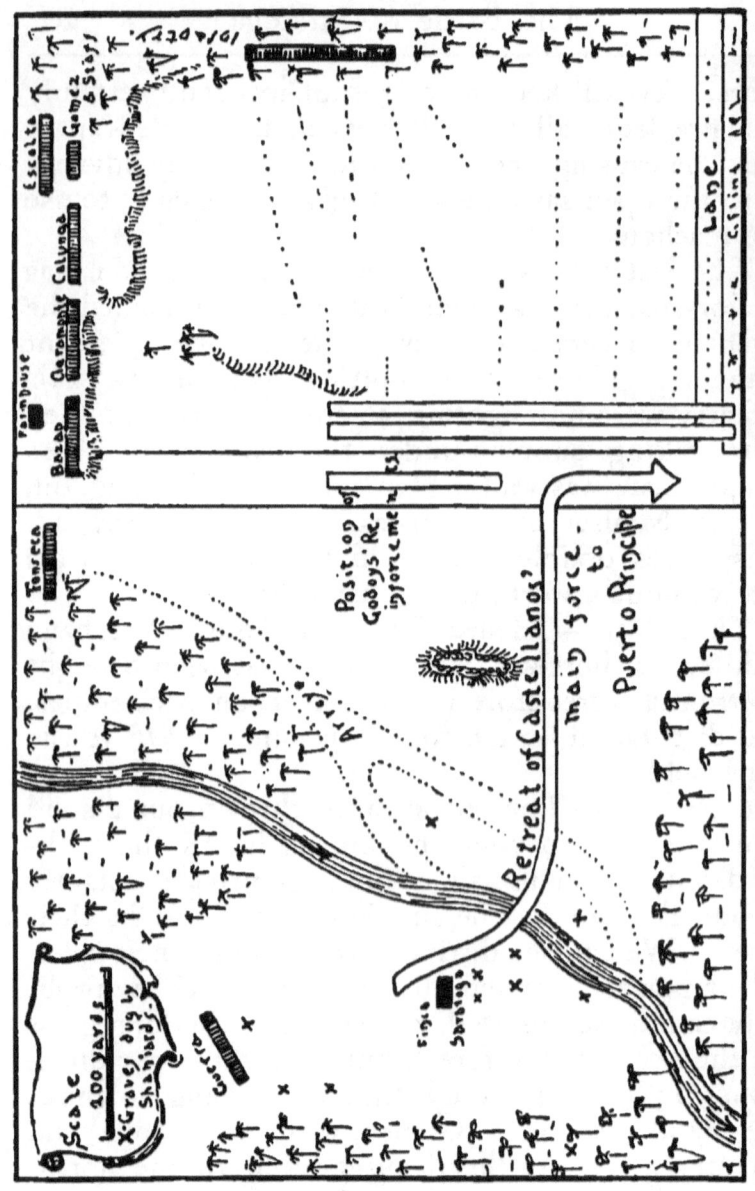

Position of Godoy's column covering Castellanos' retreat at 8 A.M., June 11th, 1896. Gomez' infantry are attempting to draw an advance of the Spaniards, his cavalry, concealed on higher ground, are prepared to charge them.

their left flank on a down grade with the machete as soon as they move onto the savanna.

7 A.M.—Our infantry is deployed into the woods, firing at three hundred yards. It is now time for the staff to take up the march after Agramonte and the escolta, and we pass from the woods to the rear of the infantry, and then out into the open under a rattling fire, and well aimed, for the sun is now high.

Our prize mule has just been shot under Gomez' cook. It was a beautiful mule. I sketched it a few days ago. It stumbled and fell, scattering pots and pans and sweet-potatoes and pieces of cold meat over the rocky path. Moron, the cook, is shifting the saddle to the mule ridden by Grillo, the scullion, who must now walk. Both are angry.

The wounded are hurried past us. I have counted five,—two officers killed outright. One is a Lieutenant Bertrand,[1] shot through the head. His body is swung over a led horse. The other was a young aide of President Cisneros, Diego Ruiz, who was attached to the escolta last night. His uncle is carrying the body in his arms. Ruiz was shot through the heart: his eyes are half-closed and his face is very pale.

At dawn this morning I observed the neatness of Ruiz' costume and the elegance of his equipment. He had just come from the government, where no fighting is done. He had a particularly fine pair of silver spurs. As we formed near headquarters I noticed those spurs especially, and deliberated whether it would be offensive if I offered to buy them at his own price. I was still thinking of the spurs as we

[1] Not the Bertrand whom I met back in Matanzas.

took to the rising land under gunshot. Then I turned, to see their owner past any earthly bargain.

8 o'clock A.M. — We are well placed on high land waiting for them to do something. They can only attack us at a disadvantage, — and then for a charge.

The enemy are retiring. Wonder what they are at!

Noon. — The Spaniards are in full retreat on the Puerto Principe road. It appears that they received a reinforcement of seven hundred men from the city before daybreak, and it was this reinforcement that advanced beyond the road and covered the retreat of the main force.

Gomez has moved into the camp just deserted by the enemy, and has sent Guerra to harass the retreating column. I find my couch of saplings of four nights ago, which saves building a new one.

Cot of saplings, with my canvas hammock doing duty as a shelter tent.

6 P.M. — I rode over the camp this afternoon. There were fully twenty dead horses and mules, and I have counted ten graves, each evidently containing a number of Spanish soldiers. One of these graves they dug at the last moment, and the bodies in it were only partly covered. There were seven bodies thrown in crosswise, any way at all, and pro-

truding hands and feet and faces could be seen between loose clods of earth.

A soldier of the advance guard found a new pair of boots on one of the dead, and pulled him out to remove them. The rest were disinterred in hopes of another stroke of luck. One of the seven was wrapped in a good mackintosh coat and looked like an officer. All were put back, however; but carelessly, as before.

I sketched the grave as I saw it. One face was uncovered,—that of a negro, evidently of the guerilla cavalry. His eyes were wide open, with a dull stare in them, and he must have died suddenly. Those eyes stared from the heap until one of the men, with a "carramba!" tore a double handful of grass up by the roots and slapped it over the face, covering it. At a very conservative estimate, the Spaniards buried sixty men, for some of these graves were larger than the one we opened. Some graves near the house were concealed by boards thrown over them. Possibly there were graves that escaped my notice. The regulars were in too much of a hurry even to fire the house. Bits of bloody clothing, torn rags of blankets, empty cigarette packages, and pasteboard packages such as the Mauser ammunition is served in, were scattered all about. Empty sardine tins everywhere, seemed to be the only traces of quartermaster supplies on the field. Wherever there were stones or logs or mounds, they had been utilized as breastworks for soldiers who had burrowed behind them. Throughout the camp, trees were barked and scarred. Behind the body of one dead horse,

"I sketched the grave as I saw it."

a prop had been placed, and the crushed grass showed that a soldier had taken refuge there.

In the farmhouse where Castellanos and his staff made their headquarters, there were torn papers, documents, and muster-rolls, one of which I preserved, and old bandages strewn about. The general disorder told plainly of the excitement our steady fire caused them night and day.

11 P.M.—Peasants say the Spaniards marched with two hundred wounded. Three died on the way and were buried by the roadside. Guerra and his men followed the column to the outskirts of Puerto Principe, shooting into it whenever an opportunity presented. As an outcome of the fighting, we have eleven killed and sixty wounded. There are also many who have trifling wounds, not entitling them to be put on the sick report.

NOTE.—A few days after Saratoga, I read General Castellanos' official report of the fight, in a Puerto Principe newspaper that found its way to camp.

According to Castellanos' own statement, he expended 50,000 rounds of rifle ammunition. (I quote from memory, having unfortunately lost the newspaper in which the original official report was published.) This allows about 4545 bullets to kill one insurgent, making obsolete the old Franco-Prussian War ratio of 1000 to one man.

The following account, based on Castellanos' report, was cabled to New York from Havana, and published in the Journal on June 15th, before my own account was received of course : —

"'Gomez fights a two days' battle. Incomplete details have been received of an important battle at Najasa. Unofficial reports state that Gomez was in command of the rebels, who numbered 5000 men. He made a manœuvre with the intention of leading the Spanish commander to believe that he intended to surround the troops, who were encamped on the plains of Saratoga. The manœuvre failed of the desired effect, which was to compel the Spanish forces to retreat. The rebels then attacked the troops with machetes, but the latter repulsed the charges.

"The battle is said to have lasted forty-two hours. General Godoy, with a strong Spanish force, arrived on the scene, and with his assistance the troops succeeded in forcing the rebels to retire.

"The battle is said to have been similar to that which took place at Guasimas in the last war.'' (The battle of Las Guasimas, by the way, was a distinct defeat for the Spaniards.)

Nos	Nombres y Apellidos	Clase de Armas de fuego	Parque
1	Ygnacio Osoria	Revolver	..
2	Ygnacio Toledo	"	"
3	Felise Gutierrez	"	"
4	Alonso Toledo	Revolver	..
5	José Escalona	"	"
6	Melicio Avila	Tercerola	50
7	Felis Infante	"	"
8	Saturnino Toledo	"	"
9	Andres Fernandes		
10	Tomás Pina Hidalgo	Tercerola	50
11	Lorenzo Rojas	Tercerola	50
12	Manuel Peres Coica	"	"
13	Miguel Aguilera	"	"
14	Antonio Seyvas	"	"
15	José Agustin Aguilera	"	"
16	Leonardo Palmeres	"	"
17	Valerio Gonzalez	"	"
18	Gabriel Hernandes	"	"
19	Miguel Almaguel	"	"
20	Benito Almaguel	"	"
21	Armelio Almaguel	"	"
22	Juan Vicente Goiez	"	..
23	José Agustin Peña	..	..
24	Rafael Labrada	"	"
25	Flores Mayo	"	"
26	Benito Gonzales	"	"
27	José Agustin Gonzales	"	"
28	José Gonzales	"	"
29	Gustavo Marino	"	"

First page of a Muster-Roll

picked up at Saratoga (one-third actual size).

Chapter IX

Echoes of Saratoga

The youngest soldier.

GOMEZ' sole object in harrying the Spanish troops at Saratoga was to create a moral effect among the insurgents of Camaguey. The skirmish did not further the cause an inch, except indirectly, as can be seen from the wide publication of Castellanos' reports by the Spanish authorities, who would not recognize a defeat in anything short of annihilation of their own forces. At the same time, Castellanos would venture more gingerly from the shelter of the forts in future, and his men must have lost in that confidence without which soldiers of Latin race cannot fight successfully.

That Camaguey sadly needed a freshening example of energy was apparent from the fact that General Suarez, commander of the insurgent forces in that province, lay in his hammock on the foothills of the Sierra Najazes, three leagues away, with two hundred armados, while the fight lasted. In Suarez' camp, as I know from men who were there, the echoes of artillery could be distinctly heard. The aid of those two hundred men would have been of great assistance to Gomez, since it would have enabled him to check and perhaps cut up the reinforcement under Godoy that came to Castellanos' assistance, and to render the Spanish rout more decisive.

Directly after the fight Gomez sent a force to bring Suarez to him, "acting as his escort," and gave the command of the Camaguey forces temporarily to Avellino Rosas, a South American officer of distinction. On appointing Rosas, Gomez made a speech to the soldiers, saying that Camaguey, formerly renowned for courage, was in disgrace. A Spanish general [1] had publicly stated at a banquet that "one could buy the greatest chief in Camaguey [meaning Suarez] for a pound of chocolate." He now trusted that a moral reform had set in, and expected great things from them all in the future.

Suarez' arrival made no commotion of any sort; and while he remained with us, he could only be seen at "bunk fatigue," dozing under his shelter tent just as far from headquarters as possible. Pending his court-martial, Gomez had assigned him to the command of the impedimenta.

An incident of the morning of June 12th was the formal burial of a very gallant mulatto captain, Manuel Ramirez, of the escort. He had led a squad of the escolta in harassing the retreating Spaniards, and fell under a volley with two wounds through his body. He was in advance of his men at the time, who rode up and captured his body. He was brought

[1] Castellanos.

to camp that night, and lay by headquarters covered with a bit of oule. Dr. Hernandez read a service at daybreak in the centre of a square formed by the cavalry troops with us, and the faithful "hundred heroes," who had lost their own commander two days before. Ramirez was buried near the farmhouse called Saratoga, and his grave was marked by a stake — nothing more; some day he will be reinterred, with many who have similarly fallen, under a proper headstone. The wounded were already quartered among the peasants, whose scattered huts on the Sierra Najazes became little hospitals.[1]

Eleven of the wounded found shelter on Polvorin Mountain with the celebrated Rosa, known widely through the district for her skill as a nurse and her knowledge of medicinal herbs. In an acre of forest La Rosa

La Rosa.

---
[1] Effects of the Mauser bullet — see Appendix D.

could find remedies for every ill. From the shoots of a tiny shrub she made a tea equal to quinine in checking a fever; from the bark of a certain tree she made a plaster that would stop any hemorrhage. She had plants at her command that supplied her with antiseptics and sleeping draughts.[1] She was an independent, masterful negress, profoundly confident in her own methods, and scorning "regular practitioners" as quacks.

La Rosa first achieved her reputation in the last war, when she conducted a hospital in her house on the Polvorin. Once the guerrilleros came; but she hid her seventeen patients in the thickets almost within hearing of the enemy, and stole out by night to fill her pails and jugs of water at the spring. The guerrilleros spent a day and a night in her house, and departed after burning it to the ground.

La Rosa knows all the great Cuban chiefs personally, and speaks of them more familiarly than any one else would dare to. She consented to be sketched, and put on her best turban, with a calico gown of riotous color. But her husband, José, a meek colored man about half her size, was timid and suspicious: he would not sit for his picture. He knew a person once who consented to be photographed and fell ill of a fever shortly afterwards. He was old now, and would run no risks.

It is saddening to find men whom you saw yesterday joking and swearing and boasting, lying silent with half-closed eyes, or gasping in spasms of

---

[1] I made a careful list of Rosa's drugs, with the names of the roots and trees from which she compounded them ; unfortunately for the advancement of science it was lost, with some other correspondence.

pain; I did not bother La Rosa much with questions, but retreated,—leaving her to soothe the weak and bully the convalescent.

It was on the first afternoon of the fight at Saratoga that I rode stirrup to stirrup with the youngest patriot of the Cuban army, a soldier just eleven years old, four feet tall, and weighing about eighty-five pounds. Calunga's men with hats and legs and machetes waving in the air were galloping across the savanna, when I found this tiny trooper at my side, full of carnage and flushed with the glory of being a real soldier. When the arroyo checked our charge, he pulled in his horse and sheathed his machete. Then he jerked a Remington carbine that had dangled from a sling at his side, threatening to pull him from the saddle, into the hollow of his left arm, blew in the breech, poked in a cartridge, and carefully aimed and fired through the shifting smoke, with the conscious gravity of Jove hurling a thunderbolt. Several times afterwards I caught sight of him, always in the front, and thoroughly enjoying himself.

On the morning after the Spanish retreat, a delegation of Calunga's men waited on me, bringing their juvenile hero with them. I must sketch him and write his story for my paper, so that Americans should know that a young generation was ready to defend the Republic when the old one should fall. My letter was lost, and I have forgotten the little fellow's name; but here is his history as his camerades told it to me.

We will call him Paco, for somehow that name

comes to me in connection with him. It seems that Paco lived with an uncle who was supposed to be loyal to Spain, on a farm just outside of the city of Puerto Principe. One afternoon some months back, a Spanish convoy had marched by on the road, and a hungry soldier slipped from the ranks to forage on his own account. The soldier spied a fat pullet and laid down his Mauser rifle in the tall grass so as to give chase with greater swiftness.

Little Paco, who was hiding in a tool-house near by, saw the act and made his plan with the promptitude of a veteran. He stole from the shed and hid the rifle under some old lumber, and then got out of the way as fast as his stocky little legs would carry him.

"Paco."

The soldier danced and swore and called on the saints until the rearguard was nearly out of sight; then he remembered that Cuba was not a safe place for soldiers straying by themselves; so he corralled a sucking pig from the sty as a peace-offering for his sergeant, and hurried after the column. Paco said nothing about the affair to his uncle; but as soon as it grew dark he shouldered the rifle and started out to find an insurgent force in the forests that cover the foothills of the Sierra Najazes.

It was a long tramp, and terribly still. When he turned from the high-road into the woods, the darkness became so intense that he lost his way. Boughs of trees struck him in the face, and clinging brambles tripped him and tore his flesh; but he struggled on manfully, still hugging the ten-pound rifle. The moon rose and, tired out, he sank under a tree, where he spent the rest of the night. At dawn he got up stiff and hungry, but he limped along undaunted, still carrying the precious Mauser. The morning wore on, and little Paco continued his search through the woods, breakfasting on berries, for it was not yet the season of mangoes. At noon he heard the beating of hoofs and saw mounted men approaching through an opening in the forest. He didn't know whether they were insurgents or Spanish guerrilleros, so he hid in a thicket of wild pineapple, and, as they rode past, he gave them the Cuban challenge, "Alto! Quien va?" Then he caught a flash of a blue and white cockade, and knew that he was among friends. It was a party of Calunga's scouts who had left camp that morning. Paco was put on a horse before one of them and sent back, rifle and all, to camp, where he became a hero at once. He wanted to be a soldier, and Calunga had not the heart to send him home; so he gave him a carbine that was several pounds lighter than his Mauser, and a horse, a machete, and a pouch of ammunition, and enrolled him as a regular armado of the troop.

Paco was a bright-eyed, cheerful little fellow, and his comrades, although they did not allow him to do guard duty, said he would soon be as good a fighting man as any of them.

But Paco was not the only infant waiting to step into the cavalry boots of the adult generation. That very afternoon Ramon Fonseca, the fighting Camaguey colonel, brought his little son, a shade younger and smaller than Paco, to me, and I struggled to make a portrait of him too. Little Ramon Fonseca rode with his father's force like a grown-up man; and he rode pretty well, as all Camaguey boys do. But his father did not allow him under gun-fire, always leaving him in charge of the camp guard, so little Ramon was only a Cuban soldier *in posse*, after all.

Sketching the smallest soldier.

Chapter X

The Itinerant Government

WE were at supper one evening a few days after the Saratoga fight, when a courier rode up, dismounted, and stood with head uncovered before Gomez' shelter tent. "I come from the President," said he. "The Government is at San Andres, two leagues from here, my general, and will remain there to-morrow."

Firmin, the President's cook.

"Inform the President," said Gomez, looking up, "that I march at daybreak. I will send word by letter where I may be found." The courier, mounting, disappeared in the shadows, and we finished our supper in silence.

In the early dawn Gomez' column turned westward. Then, parting from the commander-in-chief, I took to a forest path with a guide, heading for San Andres, at last to visit the civil head of the

Revolution. Suarez, whom Gomez had not suffered in his presence since he had relieved him of his command, rode with us, silently, by himself, followed by his servant. Two hours later we dismounted before a deserted country house that Salvador Cisneros Betancourt, Marquis of Santa Lucia, with his cabinet, had made a temporary seat of government.

It was a comfortable house, with white stuccoed walls, large windows, caged in handsome iron gratings, and surrounded by broad, shady porches, and above all a pot-tiled roof, with tiny dormer windows showed that there was an attic floor. There were flowers in what had been a garden,—sturdy, high-colored flowers, that held their own against encroaching weeds. To the rear of the main entrance were sheds and stables and a cook-house, indicating that wealthy people had lived there in times of peace.

Through the open front door one could look into a square hall, and out again by an opposite door to the glare of sun and the green of growing plants and hedges beyond. There were long plank tables within, and men in neat white suits were writing busily on sheets of foolscap, or whispering together in groups. There was a soft, cool blowing of a breeze between the open doors, that rustled among the papers, and whisked them about when not weighed down by pistols or drawn machetes or clay ink-bottles.

Alfredo led off my horse, and I walked in without attracting any special attention.

I introduced myself to a young man who looked like an aide or secretary, and requested him to pass my name to the President.

There were two good-sized connecting rooms on either side of the hall. In one of these, to the rear of the house, the Marquis had his hammock swung between an upright beam of the partition wall where lathe and plaster were chipped away, and a bar of the window grating. Cisneros was chatting, when I was ushered in, with the Vice-President, General Maso,[1] who sat opposite in a hammock similarly hitched from the same beam to the bars of the only other window in the apartment.

Cisneros was a large, elderly gentleman, very soft and gracious, with a flowing white beard. He seemed rather relaxed and weary. He had a long

---

[1] General Bartolome Maso, now president of the Cuban Republic, a man of sixty years or more, is a native of Manzanillo, of ancient family, and formerly a man of wealth. At the outbreak of the revolution, Maso organized a rebel force near Santiago de Cuba, and maintained it, in spite of the pressure brought to bear upon him by the Autonomist leaders, and the efforts of Spanish troops to capture him. This force formed the nucleus of the "Liberating Army," and practically put the insurrection on its feet. Maso will go down in history as having done Cuba a great service, and he has sometimes been a little extravagantly called, by his friends, "The Father of the Cuban Revolution." Although not, perhaps, a man of unusual ability, Maso's very name is a synonym for honesty and patriotism.

Neither Roloff, Portuando, nor Mendez Capote, were with the Government at the time of my visit.

Santiago Canizares was Minister of the Interior, and I sketched him as he was writing a despatch at a portable table, with a steaming tin of coffee at his side. Severo Pina, member of a well-known family of Sancti Espiritu, was Minister of Finance, and my friend, Dr. Eusebio Hernandez, was, in Portuando's absence, Acting Minister of Foreign Affairs. Rafael Manduley, a native of Bayamo, held the portfolio of War, in Roloff's absence, and José Clemente Vivanco, a most pleasant and courteous young man, was Chancellor of the Cabinet Council.

Signature of General Maso, now (1898) President of Cuba.

ask Mr. Betancourt
My respects to Dr. Stevens and tell him to give Mr. Primelles all his informations for the building of the hospital.

Yours gratefully
Salvador Cisneros

President Cisneros at San Andres.

life, like Gomez, to look back upon, but he lacked the latter's energy and unyielding will.

He received me pleasantly and kindly, and we discussed shop-worn topics till my special correspondent's note-book was complete.

His views surprised me; they were those one might expect of a New York Cuban. He spoke favorably of annexation, though in a non-committal way, giving the usual reasons,—the danger in a small republic of insufficient external and internal strength, the trade advantage of being part of a great nation, etc.

He speculated on a possible confederation of the Antilles to include Puerto Rico and Santo Domingo, peoples of allied race.

I have stated that no fighting Cuban I ever met favored annexation, nor have I seen a fighting Cuban who distrusted Cuba's ability to govern herself peacefully.

When I asked if he feared a race war when Cuba had gained her independence, his answer was absolutely borne out by my own experience of the Cuban negro.

"No, decidedly no!" he said. "Our negroes are far superior to the colored race of the United States. They are naturally peaceful and orderly, and they desire to be white, and like the whites. In the last war we left our families, our wives, and our daughters in the forests alone with them for weeks at a time, and never suffered outrage or annoyance at their hands. General Maceo has negro blood in him, and is the pride of us all. Our army has scores of gallant officers who are mulattoes. While the dark race of Cuba produces such men we have nothing to fear."

Breakfast was announced in the hall as we talked. Some rice with beef stew and plantains was served in long tin platters, on the deal tables, from which official correspondence and records of secretaries had been removed.

Cisneros found a chair and seated himself first where the board was nearest the door of his own apartment. The Vice-President and Cabinet found themselves chairs or empty boxes, and among them I sat as a guest. The younger aides, the tardy ones, and those who could find no room, having helped themselves from the dishes, leaned in the doorways or against the walls, plate and fork in hand. It was a general, off-hand mess such as I had sat down to with Lacret, and not more formal. There were perhaps twenty of us in all, and through the open door the asistentes and men of the President's escolta could be seen gathered beneath the sheds or messing in groups under trees and hedges.

Firmin, the President's chief cook, a thin little brown man with a straggly brown beard and his hat on, arrived presently with a tin pot of steaming black coffee, and the staff clustered about him. He served Cisneros, and the ministers, and Vivanco the chancellor of the Cabinet Council, and then there was a rush, a pushing and jostling, as each of the juniors tried to thrust his cup or jicara under the nozzle of Firmin's pot. Firmin was hustled this side and that, expostulating mildly, and dealing out dribbles until all was gone. Then those who were crowded out and got none, went off with an air of disgust and rolled cigarettes for themselves, while Firmin sidled back to the kitchen.

After breakfast, forks and spoons and plates were given to the asistentes to be washed, and books and papers were spread once more over the tables.

Cisneros returned to his own room, and the Cabinet divided itself among the remaining chambers, one of which served as the Department of War, another the Department of Finance, and a third the Department of Foreign Affairs. A few busy letter-copiers resumed scribbling in the main hall, and others took to their hammocks on the porches for a morning nap.

The only excitement of the afternoon was the departure of a despatch bearer to one of the smaller towns, where he had means of entering and purchasing things through an arrangement with a corrupt Spanish colonel of the garrison. He could buy encargos and bring them back, and the young officers of the staff wrote their orders on little stray slips of paper. I wrote one that was typical of the rest. It read as follows:—

> *4 pounds coffee.*
> *2 pounds sugar.*
> *4 bundles of cigars.*
> *2 quarts rum.*
> *1 pound chocolate.*

I gave the despatch bearer a gold piece to cover purchases, and proportional expense of corrupting the Spanish colonel, and that was the last I saw of despatch bearer, or encargo, though I learned that they arrived safely two weeks later.

Next morning quite late, after breakfast, the Government bundled up its papers and records and marched to Najaza, some six or eight miles away, where I had camped twice with Gomez.

The order of march was military enough. An advance guard, thirty of the eighty armed men of the

The Government impedimenta on the march.

escolta, the President, Cabinet and staff, the impedimenta and the main body of the escolta. The impedimenta was numerous enough for a far larger force, sixty men or more, and mules laden with chairs, tables, writing-desks, great boxes of plantains, and cheeses, and little bundles of coffee and sugar, and cans of milk, these last items all in the province of Pedro Betancourt,[1] a fat, middle-aged officer, a cousin of Cisneros, who was a sort of commissary general.

The march was slow, and we halted once in a mango grove to rest and gather fruit. Cisneros

[1] Not the Cabecilla Pedro Betancourt operating in Havana Province.

looked well in the saddle; he sat erect; his asistentes kept his bridle, stirrups, and equipments in good condition; he was genial and mild, seeming to absorb the sunshine as old men do.

But on the walls of houses that Spanish columns had passed without burning, on trees where Spanish machete blades had chipped off bark to give room for pencil writing, promises of nameless tortures for "El Marques de Santa Lucia" were mingled with obscene threats of vengeance on Cuban women. The Marquis was the scapegoat whom the troops longed to capture.

Yet somehow no natural anxiety was apparent on the part of those scribblers to make close acquaintance with the great war chief, and Gomez' name did not appear in the legends.

The Government camped among the groves of Ceiba, palm and mango that drape the slopes of the Sierra Najaza to the Najaza river. Trees with abundant foliage to shelter tents and hammocks, good grass, plenty of water, and plenty of cattle roaming at large, made it an ideal camping ground. It was an historic spot, the place where the provincial delegates first met to adopt the present constitution and elect a Government; and long ago, even before the last war, it was the scene of a great battle for Cuban independence.

Here the ministers messed by themselves, and when darkness closed in, flames of many fires gleamed among the trees, lighting the canopy of leaves above.

Five days the Government remained at Najaza,

sometimes moving a mile or less away from camp offal to fresher ground. Then came news that Gomez was at San Andres; and I hastened, with an officer who knew the way, to join him.

All the following day — it was, I think, June twentieth — the Government lingered at Najaza, waiting for Gomez, and Gomez at San Andres waiting for the Government. Cisneros[1] gave in first, and that night word came that he would arrive in the morning.

There was bustle and stir in our camp when day broke on the twenty-first. The house that had served as a Capitol when I joined the Government, a week before, was decorated by Gomez' orders, inside, with palm leaves, branches of flowers, and Cuban flags draped on its bare walls. It was also carefully swept, which it had not been before.

The Acting Minister of War.

It was prepared for guests, and the meeting was made to be a visit from Cisneros to Gomez.

By noon the Government was reported near, and Gomez rode from his headquarters, a stone's throw

---

[1] According to camp gossip, Cisneros was reported to have said, "One cannot oppose Maximo; he must always have his own way."

from the house, on the bend of the Najaza river, followed by his staff, and Gomez and Cisneros met — their first meeting since the invasion — with an embrace, and the officers of both fell in together

The Minister of the Interior.

behind them. The President was escorted to Gomez' camp, where a breakfast was prepared by Moron, in his honor, to which Vice-President Maso, Dr. Hernandez, and the secretaries sat down. Thus the mountain came to Mahomet.

On the following day Gomez moved to a place

five minutes' trot from the Presidency, where a forest bordered the high-road. His command spread by troops along the banks of the river, and all day long the little stream was filled with men, black and white, swimming and splashing and shouting like schoolboys. It was a holiday after the alarms and long marches of the spring campaign.

The two encampments were distinct, and offered a striking contrast. The troopers of the President's escort had the insolence of men untamed by hard fighting, and looked as if some "planazos" all around would do them good — they needed an iron hand sadly. In one of my visits among them my bridle was stolen, and on the same day an expeditionary laid his rifle against a tree near the seat of government, turned his back for a moment, and found it gone. Another expeditionary was slyly relieved of his blanket. Such things did not occur in Gomez' camp.

The Minister of Finance.

There were a number of lusty young aides with the Government, occupying positions one would expect to find filled only by rheumatic veterans. Perhaps it was on that account that, as I mounted once to ride to the Presidency, an aide of Gomez' asked me if I was going to the "Majaceria" (i.e., to visit the majaces).

These incidents, slight as they were, made one wonder where the revolution, then a year old, would have found itself, if, as in the Ten Years' War, the conduct of military affairs had rested in the Civil Government,—if there had been no Gomez.

Gomez' headquarters at La Yaya.

After two days at San Andres, the Government moved with Gomez to La Yaya, where the President made a little "dobe" bungalow his headquarters, and the commander-in-chief pitched his tienda some distance up the road, under a guasima tree.

There was a return of hospitality on the part of the Government. Gomez was invited to dine on the porch, and Firmin prepared a banquet, with the usual bill of fare, and as a luxury, some hard bread brought a long distance from the town of Cascorro.

Cisneros' usual dinner-time arrived, but Gomez did not appear. Firmin grew nervous. The chopped beef and rice and sweet-potatoes and plantains were ready, and Firmin ran to and from the cook-house, looking anxiously up the road for an approaching cavalcade.

An hour or more later, at his usual supper-time, Gomez came from under his bit of canvas and rode to the Presidency with Colete. Then the great banquet took place, and after it there was a conference prolonged far into the night.

So ended a series of trifling circumstances that,

Dr. Eusebio Hernandez, Acting Minister of Foreign Affairs.

when reported abroad, were exaggerated by some to open friction between Gomez and the Government, and flatly denied by others, according to personal interest. I certainly witnessed stretches of prerogative by the Government, as the licensing of the old peddler arrested near Consuegra, and the issuing to personal friends of irregular military commissions. Perhaps the Government had inflated itself in the security that it enjoyed, forgetting that this security was due solely to Gomez' invasion of the Western Provinces, which had diverted Spain's attention from Camaguey; possibly it had put on airs with the old general. At any rate, whatever differences had arisen between the military and civil heads were finally settled by the conferences at San Andres and La Yaya.

> NOTE. — I had the unusual experience at San Andres and La Yaya, of meeting a dozen of my countrymen, useless to a man, filibusters of the Ruiz expedition. Not one of these, to my knowledge, developed any inclination to "rough it" or fight, and two, Quinn and McNally, succeeded in presenting themselves at the town of San Miguel and were forwarded home to "inform" against some members of the Cuban delegation in New York. Besides this bevy of filibusters, I met few Americans in the Cuban field; but constant reports came to me of the gallantry of two men, Mr. Osgood (well known in collegiate circles as a distinguished athlete) and Mr. Choppelot, formerly member of a Massachusetts militia regiment. Both Mr. Osgood and Mr. Choppelot had attracted attention at the siege of Sagua de Guantanamo, by Rabi, where, under hottest gun-fire (at short range) from a Spanish fort, they advanced by themselves from cover, entered the wooden storehouse adjacent to the fort wherein the supplies were kept, set fire to it and returned unscathed. Mr. Osgood received a commission from Gomez as Major of Artillery, and fell later while sighting his field-piece. His last words were, "Well, well!" and he died almost instantly, pierced through the brain.

Chapter XI

Cuba Libre

THE Cuba Libre through which the Civil Government has ramified without hindrance, lies eastward of the Jucaro-Moron trocha. It comprises the provinces of Puerto Principe (Camaguey) and Santiago de Cuba (Oriente); a good half of the Island, where Spanish troops have practically no liberty of movement, but remain cooped up in the larger towns. These outposts of trade, long since commercially defunct, are scattered few and far between, along the coast, and in the virgin forests of the interior. The mountainous, timber-covered country hereabout forms a complete contrast to the flatter provinces of Havana, Matanzas, and Las Villas, where the extreme productivity of the canefields has centred the population. Into this comparative wilderness[1] of Cuba Libre, the soldiers seldom venture,[2] and forays like the move-

---

[1] "The uncleared forests of Cuba comprise 13,000,000 acres abounding in mahogany, ebony, cedar, granadillo, sabicu, and other valuable woods." (Lieutenant A. S. Rowan, U.S.A.)

[2] The only Spanish military operations seem to be the forwarding of weekly convoys, under heavy guards, to Bayamo, Jiguani, Holguin, and Victoria de las Tunas, all interior towns, still garrisoned by Spain. These convoys consist of stores of ammunition, clothing, and "air-tights," as A. H. Lewis' old cattleman terms canned provisions. According to recent accounts, nearly every other convoy is captured, and the supplies thus gained greatly comfort the local insurgent forces.

ment of Castellanos against Gomez at Saratoga are unusual.

The Spaniards did not take the revolution very seriously at first, thinking it would confine itself to its old stamping-ground in the East, where they could crush it out at their convenience; but before they knew it, Gomez and Maceo were at the gates of Havana. Therefore Martinez Campos, and later Weyler, concerned themselves with pacifying the country nearest at hand. The elaborate trocha policy, the guarding of the railroads, the garrisoning of important towns in the middle provinces, and local operations kept busy all the soldiers Spain could spare. The East was left pretty much to itself.

The late José Marti,[1] the agitator and father of this war, said as early as 1884, "If we can sustain the revolution six months, we can count on Spanish mistakes to do the rest."

The inhabitants of Cuba Libre address each other as "Ciudadano (Citizen)." They already feel themselves citizens of a republic, and in addressing strangers and people of consequence, Ciudadano has replaced Señor. In this country many homesteads

---

[1] Marti devoted his life to the cause of Cuban independence and for its sake wore chains as a mere boy, in Spanish prisons. He was a voluminous writer, a fervent orator, and a man with a genius at organization. He gathered the scattered Cuban emigrants into a compact body, by organizing revolutionary clubs, and strove to arouse their patriotism through revolutionary newspapers. Cuban cigarmakers, in Tampa, Key West, and in every large city of the East, paid regular contributions to the juntas organized by Marti with unwavering faithfulness, and in the Island, veterans of the Ten Years' War awaited his call to arms. The call came on February 24th, 1895, and was responded to at once by Maso, Moncado, and others. Antonio Maceo and his brother José landed near Baracoa on March 31, and Gomez, with Marti himself, landed, after danger and delays of voyage, on April 11, near Baracoa also. On May 19th, 1895, Marti fell at Dos Bocas, Oriente, under an unexpected volley from the advance guard of a Spanish column; but his work was accomplished; for the revolution was already under way.

are deserted, for the families who owned them — fearing the lawlessness of Spanish soldiers in the field — fled to the towns at the beginning of the present insurrection: their doors stand open, and tall flowers bloom against the chalk-white walls. Country houses of the rich are vacant too, and their pretentious iron gates are red with rust and half hidden in weeds and grass. Sometimes fire has visited these dwellings, but for the most part they have been spared.

Take it all in all, these two provinces of Camaguey and Oriente are peaceful. The small farms are fruitful and undisturbed. Smoke does not tinge the brilliant blueness of the tropical sky. The peasants live in their clearings on the mountain trails as if there were no such thing as war, making their cheese and honey, — a contrast to the starving, homeless refugees of the Western provinces.

As for travelling, the country is safe as it never was under the old rule; for the insurgents, as I wrote in another chapter, have systematically suppressed outlaws of every description. The prefects are in full sway, each in his district, under surveillance of the civil governors and lieutenant-governors, and in Oriente there are actually schools for the children. To these public schools each citizen is required by law to send his children, despite any notion he may have of his own for their private instruction.

I have before me a little blue-covered pamphlet, the very first primer of Free Cuba. It was written by order of the Government by Daniel F. Ortiz, a brother of the Cuban political writer, M. Desiderio Fajardo Ortiz, of New York City. It reminds one

Cu-ba pa-ra
con-tra a-mo
li-ber-tad E-jér-ci-to

Mi pa-pá es-tá en las fi-las del E-jér-ci-to Li-ber-ta-dor. El pe-lea con-tra Es-pa-ña pa-ra ver á Cu-ba li-bre. Yo a-mo la li ber-tad.

mu-chas es-tán
a-ta-can cu-ba-nos
o-yen-do e-ne-mi-go

Se es-tán o-yen-do mu-chas des-car-gas y ti-ros de ca-ñón. Son los cu-ba-nos que a-ta-can al e-ne-mi-go. La vic-to-ria se-rá nues-tra. ¡Vi-va Cu-ba!

A sample page of Ortiz' first Cuban primer.

of the old New England Primer, and the simplicity of Benjamin Franklin's Almanack.

The little book begins with an alphabet, the vowels, and the simple exercises in the spelling of words of one and two syllables. These are followed by exercises in reading, which tell the story of the Cuban War, and show how the children are educated up to live under a free government. They are simple little exercises, as follows : —

"My pa-pa is in the ranks of the lib-er-at-ing army. He fights against Spain to see Cuba free. I love liberty."

"Many vol-leys and shots of cannon are heard. It is the Cubans, who are at-tack-ing the enemy. *Vic-to-ry* shall be ours. Long live Cuba!"

"The prefect furnishes supplies so that there will never be lack of food for the army. What a lot of corn! Look, there is a fine melon patch."

"Ca-chi-ta is washing the clothes of her cousin, who is a cor-po-ral. She has an uncle, who is a cap-tain. The coun-try must be de-fend-ed. I am going to be a soldier."

The primer provides for the swift intellectual advance of its readers. A few pages bring the pupil to stiffer and more complicated examples of Castilian prose. The child is introduced to the harder words in advance, so that he may get his bearings and sail ahead with confidence. For example : —

Rear-guard	Reg-i-ment
Cav-al-ry	Im-ped-i-ment-a

"What a lot of cavalry! It is a Cuban regiment. Look! there is the general's escort. The impedimenta goes in the centre, and there are forty troopers for the rear-guard. The flag of Cuba is blue, white, and red."

When the pupil is able to read the above exercise, he is prepared to dig deeper into literature, as: —

"Let us go to the camp and you will see how many soldiers there are. There is a sergeant with an advance guard to give warning when the enemy approaches with volleys of shot. Peter is acting as sentinel."

"The people are going to the coast. An expedition has arrived, and they are going to receive the supplies. The Cubans abroad are sending many arms. From Key West they have sent a big cannon. Long live free Cuba!"

"John and Peter are very good friends. They come home together from school and they never quarrel. They are picking mangoes for themselves and their little sisters. How delicious are the mangoes! In Cuba there are many delicious fruits."

To complete the work, there is a study in numerals, an explanation of all the simpler terms of geography, and a topographical study of Cuba, with a list of its principal cities and the provinces into which the Provisional Government has divided it.[1]

[1] Journalism flourishes in Cuba Libre, manifesting itself in little pink or green bi-weekly and monthly newspapers that one finds everywhere in the field.

There are four in all, the largest of which, *El Cubano Libre*, I reproduce (one-third actual size) on page 243. They are struck off in editions of a hundred or so by secret presses in the forests or mountain fastnesses of Camaguey and Oriente, Las Villas and Pinar del Rio. They contain news of successful engagements and Spanish losses, letters of encouragement from New York Cubans, and Government edicts.

It is tardy news brought to the editors by courier, laboriously printed on paper

República de Cuba, 10 de Mayo de 1896.

EL CUBANO LIBRE.

"PATRIA Y LIBERTAD."

PERIODICO POLITICO, ORGANO OFICIAL DEL ESTADO DE ORIENTE.

Año 3º—Número 27.　　Director: Mariano Corona Ferrer.　　Segunda Época.

REDACCIÓN

Federico Pérez Carbó.　Juan Bacques Franco.
Rafael Philip Palacios.　Modesto A. Tirado.
José Miró Argenter.　Ld. Francisco Pérez.
Dr. Joaquín Castillo D.　Mariano Sánchez V.
Ld. Rafael Portuondo.　Dr. Tomás Padró O.
Eugenio Aguilera R.　Pedro Aguilera R.
J. del Carmen.　Álvaro Paté Janliner.
Ld. Fernando Salcedo.　Ld. Andrés Silva Donny.
Dr. Xavier Bertrand.　José F. de Castro.
Dr. G. Pinlen, Moncada.　Carlos Dubois y Castillo.

Secretario de Redacción: Daniel Fajardo Ortiz.

Con el corazón.

La Revolución, que no pudo tener como sudario un pacto infame que no acabará nunca de enlodar á los hombres que supieron defender nuestros derechos, tuvo apóstoles y mártires en los tristes días de paz en los que parecía que los cubanos olvidaban al lado del español la infamia que como sombra degradante y vil cubría el sol hermoso de nuestras libertades.

Entre estos hombres que supieron luchar y supieron conjurar todos los obstáculos y dar la voz de alarma, es el primero y el más grande aquel que supo morir en "Dos Ríos" y desafiar como guerrero las iras de la soldadesca española, después de haber vencido con su propaganda honrada y patriótica los temores de los unos y las ambiciones de los que se llama han cubanos para alargar la vida de esclavitud que les daba honores y riquezas á cambio de la honra vendida.

Pero no estaba solo Martí entre los que con él lucharon ocupan puestos honrosos muchos hombres que fuera y dentro de la Patria continúan su obra redentora.

La guerra tiene su Jefe en el más prestigioso; en el anciano Gómez, que es para todos el primero entre los soldados de Cuba y uno de los magistrados que ha de poner la patria al frente de sus destinos el día ya próximo de nuestra independencia. El es la Revolución y él es el genio de nuestra guerra; por eso el pueblo lo aclama y por eso nuestra constitución le dá el puesto que merece el más alto y también el más difícil. De Oriente ha ido á caballo á Occidente y fuerte y valeroso es el guerrero más digno de los laureles en los combates, y allá está en su puesto erguido sobre los estribos desafiando á los soldados españoles. Viven á su lado los valientes y sólo pueden discutir sus virtudes sus enemigos, españoles que le temen.

De Occidente viene ahora á estas tierras, en donde los hermanos Maceo con sus heroismos han sabido demostrar sus indiscutibles méritos y sus altas virtudes patrióticas, viene á visitarnos, como delegado del ilustre Mayor Gómez, el General Serafín Sánchez á quien ha confiado la organización de nuestro Ejército.

Nacen pocos hombres tan puros y tan nobles como el General Sánchez en su alma sólo hay grandezas y generosidad: por eso puede representar dignamente al General en Jefe.

Modesto pero sincero trabajó Serafín allá en Cayo Hueso por la Revolución y estuvo siempre al lado de Martí, cuando no é l ó quien lo creyera visionario y quien se atreviera á querer lanzar quijotescos veredictos contra el más honrado de nuestros mártires y el más humilde de nuestros hombres valerosos.

Como el apóstol de nuestra honra, como Estrada Palma más merecedor cada día del respeto de todos y cada día más digno del puesto de confianza que le señaló nuestra Asamblea Constituyente,—vé hoy al General Sánchez como crece la obra del genio, como todos vienen á compartir con el soldado de Martí y Gómez y Maceo las glorias y los trabajos y con cuánta rapidez nos acercamos al término de nuestros anhelos.

Martí no ha muerto para Cuba mientras viva el General Sánchez y los que con él supieron romper la tutela degradante y levantar como hombres nuestra bandera libertadora.

Lleve el noble amigo la aclamación más sincera de todos los orientales al General Gómez: con él estamos todos para vencer y á su lado estaremos siempre para honrarlo.

Caerá ante los heroismos de nuestros soldados la dominación que desesperada y maltrecha se revuelve en agonía cruel, pero merecida.

—Y el día de la victoria —Patria, escribirá dos nombres en la bandera de la Revolución, el nombre de Martí el mártir—y el nombre de Gómez el libertador.

Valdés Domínguez.

Oriente, Mayo 3 de 1896.

El Mayor General Daniel E. Sickles.

Entrevista del Sun con el ilustre soldado y Ex-Ministro Plenipotenciario.

"The Sun" de Nueva York, noble y desinteresado campeón de toda causa justa como la de Cuba, no sólo emplea en defenderlas la profunda erudición de su Director, sino que busca para sus columnas las más autorizadas opiniones del país, como son entre otras las palabras del bravo militar é integérrimo político Mayor General Daniel E. Sickles.

La segunda página de su número de 2 de Abril próximo pasado, trae la importante entrevista de uno de sus reporters con el veterano de la guerra de secesión y ex Ministro Plenipotenciario y Enviado Extraordinario de los Estados Unidos en España. Ese documento, tan notable por el fondo como por la forma sencilla y elegante, es la expresión más alta de la opinión política y militar del Ejército americano, acerca de los sucesos

The "talleres," or Government workshops of Cuba Libre, furnish the army to the best of their ability with clothing and equipments; and in some of them firearms and machetes are repaired. For the sake of security, only prefects or sub-prefects of the districts are supposed to know their exact situation. The workmen, however, are prepared for emergencies, and in case of alarm the tools could be carried away at a moment's notice; while the building of new sheds to cover them would be an easy matter. The foremen of these " talleres " are always appointees of the Civil Government, and the workmen are drawn from the insurgents who are physically disqualified for active service.

Hides are plentiful in the Eastern provinces, so the manufacture of leather belts, ammunition pouches, officers' despatch boxes, halters, and shoes, are a specialty. As fast as equipments are made, they are turned over to the prefect of the districts for distribution among the forces.

There are shoe shops in Camaguey, and I visited several of them; in each of which six to a dozen men work together, with their families about them. Hides are sent to them from other "talleres," where

varying in tint and texture according to circumstances, and smuggled from the nearest Spanish town.

Copies are forwarded from one end of the Island to the other by post riders and travelling commissions, passing from hand to hand, from saddle-bag to saddle-bag, until they become crumpled, blurred, and soiled, but never too old to be read and discussed over the camp-fire. Sometimes they stray into the towns, and a family is sent to prison for having one in its possession.

Only editors and compositors are allowed to know exactly where these presses lie hidden, because they could not easily be carried away if an attempt were made to capture them. The presses themselves are ancient affairs. *El Boletin de la Guerra* was for a long time printed with a machine that served as a cheese-press when regular editions of the paper and general orders were not under way.

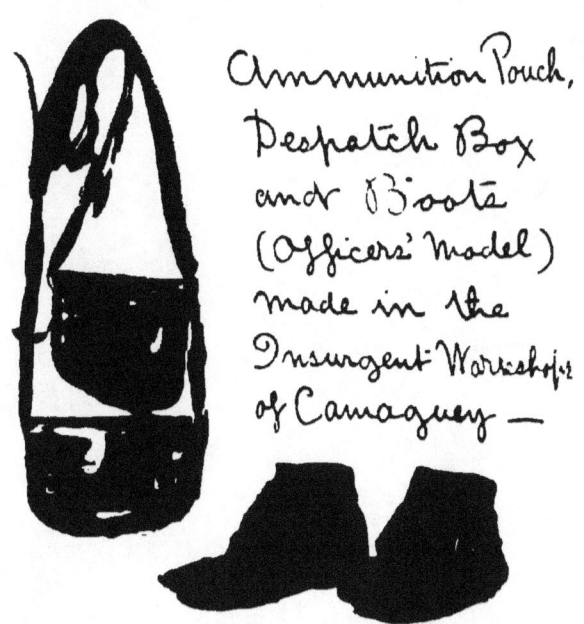

Specimens of Mambi workmanship. Page 244.

The publishing office of El Boletin de la Guerra, in Camaguey.
(See note, pp. 242, 244.)

the tanning is done, and their supplies come regularly to them from the nearest prefectura.

There is an air of secrecy about these little shoe shops, and out of compliment to your hosts you must look profound and mysterious. You hide your horse and tread stealthily through the bushes, by blind, perplexed paths, crossed by fallen trees that you climb over with difficulty. I have suspected that I was being led by "show" paths to

A saddle shop, near Najaza Mountain, Camaguey.

these nooks, "known only to members of the fraternity," and that there were other entrances, "family entrances," smooth, grassy, and above board.

You pardon the little fiction of secrecy when you see the work of these Mambi shoe-makers. They make stout cowhide boots fastening with straps, that will see you through a hard campaign, and are fairly comfortable when once broken in. For the rank and file there are low shoes that fasten with a thong. Grease them well and walk about in the dewy grass for several evenings, and they take the exact form of your feet and fit like a stocking. The material is stout and the sewing an honest, old-fashioned stitch — strong and reliable. The largest shoe shop is said to be Gibara in Oriente, where thirty workmen sit side by side stitching and cutting.

Saddle-making has come to be an art in these forests. The army McClellan tree is taken as a model and perfectly duplicated in light cedar, covered with sheepskin. Brass trimmings and rings are cut in the gun-shops on the pattern of those used in our army. The result is a neat, light McClellan, with no flaps, properly fitted with pommel and cantle rings, lacking only the Mexican cinch and lastigo to be perfect for business or exercise. When you consider that the Mambi carries no other pack than his hammock and a blanket, or waterproof, the lightness of this saddle makes it superior to our own regulation McClellan.

In other " talleres " broad-brimmed straw hats — each one of them two days' work for one man — are turned out, together with thick straw " sudaderos," or saddle packs. A blanket is too precious to put under your saddle, and straw is soft and cool.

Ropes are woven from strips of the inner bark of the " mahagna." They are stout as the best of hemp, and serve to " lariat " horses at night, when they graze on the savannas. The peasants' art of making candles from beeswax, with twisted strips of linen for wicks, comes into requisition, and there are " talleres," too, where balls of beef fat and the ash of the " guasima " wood are rolled by hand into balls of black soap and tied for transportation in strips of palm bark.

These supplies are invaluable to the forces, and it is a day of rejoicing in camp when a convoy comes in from the prefecturas; a great rolling, squeaking two-wheeled cart, drawn by six oxen, loaded high with saddles, sudaderos, halters, belts, shoes, hats tied in dozens together, lariats, stirrups, and bundles of drill clothing. Then the barefooted men, the men without shirts or trousers, the hatless, and those whose horses have the sorest backs, assemble

"*A rolling, squeaking two-wheeled cart.*"

in expectant line and continue to clamor until the last equipments are distributed.

The clothing (coats and trousers) is made from drill bought in the villages by Government agents. The tailoring is done by the peasant women, under direction of the local prefects. It comes ready made to camp, and is portioned out, with other supplies, to the needy rather than to those whom it fits.

There are even regions in Las Villas where the inaccessible nature of the country offers security to Government "talleres." In the safest of these regions, fifteen miles east of Cienfuegos, away up in the Sighuanea Mountains, is the Mayari arsenal, largest of all the Cuban workshops.[1]

From the plain below, the Sighuanea range rises in abrupt steps, peak after peak, until the Mayari is reached; highest of all, and buried morning and night in banks of mist. It is a stiff climb for man or beast, up twisting, rugged paths grown with cactus and wild coffee; down steep declivities with dizzy glimpses of chasms below, then up again almost to the perpendicular, through rifts of clouds, till your head swims and your knees grow weak beneath you.

If you try it on horseback, you must dismount and scramble up most of the way, holding tight to your horse's tail; and you are pretty likely to lame your mount, if it is unused to the ascent, hopelessly.

When you have nearly reached the summit you squeeze through a cleft between two boulders, strongly fortified from above; then by a circular path you wind into a hollow directly under the peak of the mountain.

Once on a level, you find yourself before a turnstile and swinging gate bearing the legend: —

Taller Mayari Fundado Deciembre 20, 1895.

Directly in front of you is the main building; a long, open structure, with a palm-thatched roof supported by light cedar pillars.

About the main building is a neatly terraced little

[1] Near Remedios in Las Villas there is also a large "taller" — a saddle shop. The peculiarity of the last establishment is that the tools used there were carried out by a column of Spanish soldiers and hidden in the woods, where they were promptly gathered by a party of insurgents sent to get them.

garden for onions, sweet-potatoes, radishes, garlic, and lettuce. Horses and mules are not allowed within the gate, but must be unloaded and tied without a long fence that encloses the garden and grounds of the establishment. There is a big furnace near the entrance, where charcoal is made for use in the blacksmith's shop, and a spring of fresh, clear water that gushes into a basin, and runs off through a trench, irrigating the garden.

Within the main building are work-tables and benches in rows, with racks for tools and arms in course of repair. Fifty men are employed in cleaning and repairing carbines, pistols, and machetes. They are well supplied with screws, rivets, and the minute machinery of firearms. There is a furnace with a bellows, and tanks for bronzing long arms and even cannon.

Finishing a machete handle.

An old carbine that has seen hard service may be brought here and fitted with bands, screws, and breech-block, freshly bronzed and stocked, and sent back to the owner nearly as good as new. Gun-stocks are turned out by hand in the wood-carving department, of beautiful red and yellow woods, each stamped with the initials "P. y L.," standing for

"Patria y Libertad (Fatherland and Liberty)." They are as true as if turned by lathe, and finely polished; for everything done at Mayari, so far as it goes, is well done.

The lower end of the hall is devoted to the repairing of machetes. Handles of beautiful design are made and harmoniously fitted to the various styles of machete, from the long, pointed Camaguey blade, to the broad forester's cutlass and Santo Domingo scimitar. The handles are made from layers of ox horn, heated and shaped with brass forms, and pressed over night in a vise. They are then clinched with brass rivets, trimmed with knife and file and polished to their utmost brilliancy.

You may have your machete fitted with a guard of brass or steel if you wish, and may select your design for a handle, or leave it to the taste of the artisan. Care is taken in the selection of horn, and the results are creditable to the taste and patience of the workmen.

Henrique Gomez, a dark, thick-set little man, a saddler by profession and an all-around mechanic, is overseer and foreman of the arsenal. He has brought his wife with him to the mountain, for the Spaniards burned her out of house and home a few months ago. They live in a little rancho on the mountain side. She is the only woman on Mayari.

Industry is the order of the day at Mayari. When work in the armory is slack, the men devote themselves to labor in the garden and to improvements about the grounds. In the wood-carving department extra time goes to the manufacture of boxes, inlaid checker-boards, and card-tables. The pride of the entire shop is a great escutcheon of the Cuban Republic, four feet high, carved from a solid root of the yellow "foutete," in relief. It took Sanchez, the master-carver, a skilful workman who learned his trade in the United States, three months to do it, working at odd moments.

Every arm that comes to the workshop is turned over to a receiving clerk, who sits caged in a little office by the entrance. A ticket with the date and number is given in receipt, and a duplicate is attached to the weapon. Behind the receiving clerk, in a long rack, are the arms waiting to be sent for, and you are reminded of a down-town pawnbroker's shop.

The only outsider who comes to Mayari is the sub-prefect of the district. He makes two trips a week, with beef killed at the base of the mountain. Arms are therefore sent to the prefectura on the plain below, with instructions for their repair, and the owner must wait till they are finished. This is a precaution for the safety of the establishment.

It is always cold at Mayari, especially at night, for the wind is piercing and the mist envelops one with chilling dampness. The officers sleep in a little house on cot beds, but the men have their barracks in a great cavern, like a bandit's lair, under the overhang of the mountain. Here they swing their hammocks from iron rings cemented in the ceiling of solid rock. In the centre of the cave, in a great fireplace where the cooking is done, a caldron of boiling coffee stands night and day; for coffee grows wild on Mayari, and the members of the garrison drink it when the air is chill.

So much for the industries of Cuba Libre. In Matanzas and Havana and western Las Villas the Mambis has no "talleres" to draw from, and he must renovate his costume as best he can. The pacifico was the insurgents' quartermaster in those provinces.

I have often seen a neat, well-fed pacifico, with a good hat, good trousers, a clean shirt and serviceable shoes come out smiling to meet a ragged column of insurgents. The first man of the advance guard claps him on the back and cheerfully changes hats; the second borrows his shirt, while the third negotiates for his shoes or trousers. If he demurs, he is called an unpatriotic, scoundrelly "Gringo," and sent home in the simple gunny sack costume of the militant Mambis. Horses are acquired in the same way; for, like everything useful in the war, they are regarded as Government property. In fact, the best horse I have ridden I exchanged for a jaded ruin of my own with a well-mounted pacifico.

Chapter XII

The Sub-prefectura Yatal

IT was the usual hut of the Camaguey herdsman, rectangular in outline, heavily overtopped by its shaggy brown thatch, as a grenadier's face by his shako. It stood all alone by itself in a mile stretch of flat fallow land and wet meadows, bordered by scrub forests.

A snake fence corral, sectioned off for calves and milch cows by rotting posts and crooked saplings with dry bark still clinging to them, fronted the hut. An arroyo, with a trickling stream at its bottom, finished the landscape, marking its serpentine course by shadowy hollows and an occasional palm or poplar.

The body of the hut, consisting of one large sleeping-room, was walled with planks of palm bark held in place by horizontal poles passed over and

under and corded to the stout uprights with majana
— it was magnified basket work, so thin you could
have kicked a hole in it anywhere. The door was
of stiffened cowskin, the hair worn off where the
hand naturally pushed it, and it swung on hinges of
more pliant leather. There were no windows. The
long roof extended to shelter a table and chairs,
making an open-air living-room for the prefect's
family, and left space above for a loft in the eaves
where the two sons of the prefect and transient
guests slept on a loose flooring of boards. When
any one climbed the home-made ladder to this nest
of bats and moved about in it, dust of rotting wood
and thatch showered the table and people below.

Inside the bark chamber were two four-poster
bedsteads, with gaudy patch quilts, two or three old
hair trunks, an ebony crucifix, a framed print of
the Virgin with the halo done in gilt, and a pair of
broken chairs, retired from public service. This
inventory I made from a furtive glance through the
swinging door; for the bed-chamber in Cuba, of
planter and peasant alike, is sacred to the family.
Sunshine and fresh air filtered under the roof and
through cracks and chinks in the frail partition
walls, drying the earth floor and driving away
impurities. A healthier habitation could not be
imagined.

The cooking at the prefectura was done in a
roomy out-door kitchen, on a bank of hardened
clay, where you could build a wood fire and cook
things in pots and pans without stooping. There
was no chimney, and the smoke followed prevailing
draughts. Bunches of plantains and long strips of

dried beef hung decoratively from the trusses overhead. Two small green parrots with clipped wings made themselves at home, hitching about on the earth floor, or climbing over the chairs and a pile of loose boards that were lying there. The kitchen seemed to be the rallying-point of a "politic convocation" of hens and geese, who acted as scavengers.

Mercedes and Rosalia Perez making hats for the Cuban soldiers.

The main roof and the roof of the kitchen nearly met, and a trough between them shed water into a rain-barrel below. From this barrel one could dip up water to drink or wash in. There was a family basin and a family cake of soap. Rain came pretty regularly every day and night, for it was now the middle of the rainy season. When an unusual quantity of water was expended by cooking or washing, the rain-barrel was replenished by a pailful from the arroyo.

Perez, the sub-prefect, with his wife and daughters and a two-year-old boy, the baby of the family, slept in the chamber on the ground floor. The girls, Mercedes and Rosalia, were verging on womanhood. They had inherited lustrous eyes and neat little features from Moorish and Semitic ancestors in old Spain. On fête days, or to receive visitors, they dressed their hair carefully and appeared in crackling gowns of flowery calico. At other times they were picturesquely slattern.

Mercedes and Rosalia made hats for the Cuban soldiers. One twisted strands of bleached grass into a narrow tape and trimmed the edges with small scissors; the other coiled the long neatly woven braid round and round from a central point in the crown, sewing the overlapped edges together till the brim, wide as you chose, was finished. Each hat was a good two days' work.

Once a week pacificos of the neighborhood came for supplies of meat. Then cattle were rounded up in the meadows and driven into the corral by Perez and his two sons, and a scene of untidy butchery followed. Steers were roped by the horns and dragged to a tree in the centre of the corral, and their throats cut with machetes. Some-

Rosalia Perez (with additions by her own hands).

times if they baulked too much at the blood-soaked soil, a post of the corral fence served instead. Sleek vultures floated lazily up, settled on the highest posts, and gravely watched the spectacle. The meat was hacked into strips, and the pacificos spread it on boards used for the purpose, and rubbed in salt with their hands before the flies had a chance to settle and spoil it. Yatal was close to the shore, and there was plenty of salt, sent from the Government salt works near by.

On killing day, salted meat hung from every available beam and hook about the sub-prefectura, until the pacificos got through with their gossip, and packed off home with their supplies on led horses. Yatal was a secure district, some eight or nine miles from the nearest town, San Miguel, and soldiers had never strayed that far, nor was it likely they

Killing day at the sub-prefectura.

could do so, without alarm spreading through the country long beforehand.

I had left Gomez and the Government at La Yaya, and come to Yatal, with Mario Carrillo and an American doctor to make one of a party about to put off from the coast near Nuevitas. Two boats were said to be concealed along the shore, and we were to escape in the better one. A four days' march, taking our ease by the road, brought us to the sub-prefectura, conveniently near the point where we were to embark. We travelled practically unarmed. I had given my revolver before leaving Gomez to a young officer, d'Etampes, a Louisianian of Cuban family, and like the rest of the party, carried only a machete. So great was the safety of the country, that we slept one night in a farmhouse, with the light of Cascorro blinking at us from the cathedral tower, scarcely a mile away, and a garrison of three hundred men sleeping under it.

Day after day rolled slowly by at Yatal, while we waited for arrangements of every kind to be made. Pilots were to be found who knew the Antillean waters; lines of communication were to be made for tools, sail cloth, etc., from the towns of San Miguel and Nuevitas. The rest of our party, Colonel Céspedes and Lieutenant Eduardo Laborde, brother of Captain Laborde of Competitor fame, were to join us at some time or other.

Meanwhile we made ourselves comfortable, and loafed under the " overhang " of Perez' roof, swore at everybody who went aloft and scattered dust on us, and occasionally quarrelled to pass the time away. I built a cot of saplings for myself, with my canvas hammock stretched above as a shelter tent just outside the kitchen. Carrillo and the doctor hung their hammocks from the upright supports of the "overhang," and my faithful Alfredo slept above in the loft with Carrillo's servant and the Perez boys.

Juanito, the Perez baby, had somehow cut his thumb to the bone a week before our arrival, and the cut had become a gaping, festering wound. Dirt worked into it constantly; for the little fellow ran about perfectly naked, playing with the dogs and hens, and in the mud of recent rains, and there was danger of mortification, with loss of his finger, possibly of his life, by blood-poisoning. The doctor's arrival saved him. Every other day the aseptic preparations, and the holding of the squealing youngster steady while the stitching and re-stitching went on, was a temporary excitement. Juanito was frightened into sitting still in a chair all day, with his hand in a clean sling, by the threat that if he moved the doctor would cut his finger off.

Juanito was a wicked youngster. We had purchased, by encargo from San Miguel, a supply of coffee, sugar, rum, and tobacco, hard bread and chocolate, which we kept in a market basket on the table. Whenever we went to bathe in the arroyo, Juanito would slip from his chair and slyly filch a biscuit, or a bit of chocolate, and he dared not look any one in the eye for an hour afterward. So we slung the basket on a rope and hoisted it up to the flooring of the loft, where it could only be got at by a lowering and hitching and generally complicated process.

Rumors of the doctor's skill spread abroad, and if a family had an anæmic child, one that had fits or strange swellings, or a grandfather with a cataract, a state visit to the sub-prefectura was made, the ladies arriving *de gala* on pillions under big sun-umbrellas. The sufferer was brought, and the conversation turned naturally on his ailments. Then the doctor's opinion was asked, through Carrillo and me, acting as interpreters. They were a kindly, simple lot, these peasants, very pleased and grateful at the doctor's "barn-shed" advice.

Mosquitoes, except after a heavy rain, were numerous and malignant beyond belief. Sometimes swarms of tiny gnats floated upon us from the low-lying shore, mobilizing on our ankles, climbing up under our trousers, prevading the rents in our clothing, stinging with a virulence out of all proportion to their size. Having no other covering, I slept with my feet thrust into the sleeves of an old coat, and a flannel shirt pulled over my head; even then sleeping was an effort. Carrillo and the doctor, though provided with blankets, sometimes gave up sleep and sat up feeding the kitchen fire and talking the night away.

While we waited at Yatal, news came that made our inactivity more irksome. Cascorro was taken by Avellino Rosas' infantry. Garcia had captured a gunboat on the Cauto river and burned the houses of Spanish adherents in the Holguim district. José Maceo had fallen at Lomo del Gato, leaving only Antonio, last of eleven brothers.

At last Céspedes and Laborde arrived, and we accompanied them to Punto del Ganado, where the pilots and some men of the coast-guard were awaiting us.

Rosalia and Mercedes' last wish was that I should bring them when I came back two "Americano legitimo" hats with flowers and birds and artificial fruit, such as they had once seen in a beautiful shop in Nuevitas. In return they would make me a fine Mambis sombero, with a silk escarapela (cockade) of the Republic, — red, white, and blue.

Perez accompanied us to the Punto del Ganado, and went back with the horses. Then we continued along the beach, towards the Boca de Nuevitas, to where the boat lay, leaving a deep trail in the sand. Alfredo tagged along with the coast-guard, for he would not leave till he saw me safely afloat. Alfredo had begged to go to America; but he was inland-born and one glance at the boat and a sweep of his eye over the blue ocean, ruffled with white caps and broken with a spray-dashed line of reefs, changed his mind promptly and firmly.

The path to a land of peace now lay before us; all that detained us was the preparation of our craft.

"No. 5," as she was labelled, was a stout whale-boat, twenty-seven feet of keel and five of beam. She was one of the boats of the Laurada, that landed the Ruz expedition at Punto del Ganado, near Nuevitas, on the 11th of May, 1896. She landed her cargo of men and ammunition successfully, and when the other small boats were burned, "No. 5" was paddled along the shore and hidden among the palms and grape trees, at a point midway between the Punto del Ganado and Maternillos light.

We were eleven in one party — Colonel Céspedes, Captain Mario Carrillo, Lieutenant Eduardo Laborde, the American doctor, three Cuban coast pilots, three negro sailors, and myself. Our "mascot," a gift to the doctor from Perez, — a green and red parrot that would wink intelligently when the word "filibuster" was mentioned, and cry "Al machete! Al machete!" when excited, — completed the make-up of the party.

The labor of refitting "No. 5" for a sea-trip was slow. Sails, oars, masts, kegs for water, a rud-

Salvador Perez, Sub-Prefect of Yatal. — Page 262
[Type of the Cuban Prefecto.]

der, putty, paint, and carpenter's tools, all had to be smuggled by our agents from the towns of San Miguel and Nuevitas.

Days dragged on, and our materials came a little at a time. We lay beneath the palm and wild grape trees, tortured by mosquitoes and sand-flies, half a mile from Maternillos light and the entrance to Nuevitas harbor. In that harbor lay a gunboat, and another was on duty patrolling the coast for a few miles to east and west of us. Stories came from the town that our expedition was the talk of the cafés; that a half-witted negro, called "Viva Dios," had made it the theme of improvised songs, or "decimas," while drunk in the streets of Nuevitas, and the bogy of treachery looked nearer to us than we cared at the time to admit. A Government commission, with State papers and despatches, would be no mean capture, and we felt that our heads would fetch a good price.

By July 20th, after a delay of two long weeks, our tools and supplies had all come to us. At noon on that day the little gunboat *Golondrina*, with a Gatling gun and forty men, steamed between the foam-capped reefs and the shore, and dropped anchor in the channel barely three hundred yards from where we lay concealed.

From between the grape branches we could see the officers and men on her deck, and that was a time for caution. Nails were driven with muffled hammers, fires were small, and the smoke was distributed by a piece of tarpaulin, and we only ventured on the beach at night, while the *Golondrina* lay silent and watchful, with all her lights covered. At times a yellow gleam flashed from a hatchway as some one came on deck.

On the 21st there was an event The *Golondrina* put out a boat; but it only paddled for fifty yards about as if the crew were rowing for exercise and was then hauled on board. We continued to watch and wait under the pitiless sun. We had sent back our horses; we had left our arms with the last insurgent force, and were in no condition to make a fight.

I must own on this day to having refused to take up a ten-dollar bet with Carrillo that we would be captured. Work continued, however, in silence; caulking, painting, and sail-fitting being done by our crew, with the assistance of a small party of the coast-guard. Colonel Céspedes lay in his hammock, slung between two palms, with his shattered leg placed as easily as could be, and superintended the work.

Thursday, July 23d, brought us a second scare. At noon there was a cry from the watchers: "They're coming ashore! They're coming ashore!" The *Golondrina* was steaming silently eastward. We sprawled out on the ground or crouched in the bush. Fifty yards to eastward of us was an opening in the grape trees, through which a lookout with a good glass might have seen us.

The *Golondrina* moved slowly along, very near the shore. Two seamen went aloft to her fore and main tops. With a bound one of our negroes jumped and cut the rope that held a tarpaulin tent over "No. 5"; for from the vessel's mast it would have been discernible.

But the *Golondrina* moved on, skirting the indentations of the shore toward Punta del Ganado. Her officers were certainly suspicious. Had she sent up her lookouts before getting under way, they must have seen us over the low palm tops. But the lookouts looked forward, not backward, and so the *Golondrina* moved on till she became a speck on the blue waters and rounded the Punta del Ganado.

Then all was activity. Nails and cleats were pounded in with reckless clatter, the masts were fitted, and shrouds were fastened in place. Eight kegs were filled with brackish water and rolled down on the beach. A rousing fire was built and a mess of boiled plantains prepared. Some of us bathed in the sea, and then we settled down to wait placidly for nightfall.

At 7.30 all hands were at work, shoving and pulling silently, as became conspirators, to get "No. 5" down to the water. A brisk wind blew in from the northeast, and great black clouds swept over the face of the moon, leaving us alternately in light and darkness. All was done in stillness, broken only by excited shrieks of "Al machete! Al machete!" from our "mascot."

At 7.45 o'clock we launched "No. 5" in the surf, and hurriedly threw aboard our water-kegs, a box of biscuits, a bundle of salted pork, and strips of dried beef. Colonel Céspedes, despite his protests, was picked up bodily by the coast-guards, who waded to their waists in the sea, and placed him tenderly in the stern of our swaying craft. Then it was, "Push off; catch her on the next wave; wade and jump," for the rest of us. A flaw filled our mainsail and jib. "No. 5" answered the helm, and we bore off free to the northwest toward Maternillos light.

We were off at last, after twenty days of toil and anxiety. The strain was too great for the little group of watchers on land. Prudence was thrown to the winds and a "Viva!" rose that a gust caught and carried over the palm trees. "Viva Cuba! Viva la Independencia!" from the shore was answered by a faint "Al machete! Al machete!" from our boat. Then a cloud passed over the moon, and we were fairly started on our voyage.

Our first course lay due northwest toward Maternillos light, in order to make the pass in the reefs that lie in front of the entrance to Nuevitas harbor. We passed in darkness half a mile to seaward off Maternillos light, and then sighted the light of Nuevitas harbor. From this point we struck a north-northwesterly course out through the reefs and past the breakers.

The moon came out from beneath the clouds, and we had fears, as we cut the silver path of its reflection, that we might be seen from the lighthouse and a gunboat sent after us. We pitched along, constantly shipping cold waves over our starboard bow that drenched us to the skin, but making good time. In an hour we had gained the darkness beyond the treachery of the moon's rays, and felt a general sense of relief.

It was a rough, gusty night. Once a squall struck us with a heavy fall of rain and we took in all sail; but the wind settled down again to a northeast blow and we continued on our course. We felt now that odds were no longer against our es-

"We were fairly started on our voyage."

cape, and, though shivering in our scanty rags, wet and cold, and unable to sleep, we were contented. We all of us had seen enough of Spanish methods to know what it meant to be captured, and that the authorities would not be anxious for a repetition of the lingering Competitor trial. If a cruiser or gunboat were to overhaul us, we knew we should be either run down, or quietly shot.[1]

The sun of July 24th rose through banks of purple clouds over a heavy sea, and a head wind was still blowing from the northeast. At noon the heat was blistering. We were off the Columbus Banks in English waters. Below, we could see a sandy bottom, with beds of brown sponges, and the lead told four fathoms.

Night closed at last, and some of us slept, in spite of the waves that still dashed over us, while the others kept themselves awake by bailing out the boat.

At sunrise on the 25th we sighted Green Key. We landed there to stretch our cramped limbs at six o'clock, and were welcomed to English soil by a party of duck-shooters from Nassau.

At Green Key we learned that a quarantine of fourteen days awaited us in Nassau, and that we might wait many days for a steamship to the mainland. I begged that we might continue our trip, regardless of heat, bad water, and lack of provisions, to Jacksonville, or Palm Beach, but the proposition was not acceptable to the " ship's company."

We took to our boat again, after a half-hour's

---

[1] According to newspaper rumors, this was the fate of a small schooner with a party of filibusters, off Pinar del Rio, some months ago.

rest, and continued our course, with a smoother sea but scorching sun. Toward evening we sighted the southern shore of Nassau, a low line of beachless coral, with dwarfed palm trees. Unable to beat against the wind, we took to the oars and rowed half-way about the island, dropping into the harbor silently with the tide.

It was two o'clock on Sunday morning when we floated past the quarantine. It was my intention to "jump" the quarantine if no other escape could be had. We lay alongside a sponge schooner, and I stealthily called to the captain, who awoke and came on deck. He was a negro and suspicious. I offered him large sums to take us to Jacksonville, or into the path of northbound steamers, anywhere: but he scorned all explanations. "Go 'way, white man," was all that could be got from him.

The doctor and I then landed, just in time to be surrounded by a dozen of the Nassau police. Judging from our hard features and clothing, the captain had taken us for pirates and sent one of his men to warn the authorities.

We were then ordered to our boat, and when daylight came were held as an exhibition for the people of Nassau, who flocked, all colors, ages, and sexes, to peer at us from the wharf, until a kind-hearted official ordered us moored in the centre of the stream ; where we remained until towed, at our own expense, to the quarantine station on an island opposite the town, at four o'clock that afternoon.

We broke the Nassau laws in landing, but were courteously dealt with, and our term of quarantine, in spite of the malign efforts of a local Spanish consul, was cut down to four days; after which we were permitted to board the *Antilla*, bound for New York.

At quarantine, we were shut off from the outside world; but received fruits, tobacco, and similar tokens of esteem from the inhabitants, who sailed each day to examine our boat and "admire" us from a distance. Two of our negroes from Jamaica were sponge-fishers, British subjects, and Colonel Céspedes thought best to carry a British flag, relying on the protection Great Britain extends to her own, however lowly.

The sun was low on August 2d when the *Antilla* anchored before quarantine in the narrows of New York harbor. A tug lay alongside, with a number of prominent Cubans, some members of Carrillo's family, and a squad of reporters, whose accounts of our arrival were to glisten in the columns of next morning's papers.

Then, as darkness fell, we steamed to our pier on the East river. A bugle call floated from a long white battleship, moored in midstream, as her colors, the stars and stripes, were lowered for the night. The city before us lay peaceful and misty. A black thread of men and vehicles moved over the Brooklyn bridge. Above us, on imperishable foundations of granite, towered the gigantic bronze figure of LIBERTY, and to those of us who were familiar with it, it seemed noble and impressive as never before.

Appendix A

In the spring of 1896 the "Liberating Army" extended through every district of Cuba, from Cape Maysi to Cape San Antonio. Six Divisions were organized, each under a General of Division, and operating, or campaigning in one of the six provinces. Antonio Maceo, Lieutenant-General of the Liberating Army, was given command of the forces in Pinar del Rio, a division, that, portioned off as it was by the big trocha from the rest of Cuba, conveniently constituted by itself a Department of the West. Aguierre commanded in Havana, Lacret in Matanzas, Carillo in Las Villas, Suarez (who was subsequently cashiered for cowardice) in Camaguey, and José Maceo in Oriente. Garcia landed near Baracoa at this time and a Department of the East, to include Camaguey and Oriente, was established for him, because from position and service in the last war he ranked both Maceo and Suarez. The convenient death of José Maceo, and reduction of Suarez, simplified Garcia's position in the East, and with the death of Antonio Maceo, he became by seniority second to Gomez.

Each division consisted of two or three brigades, commanded by Brigadier-Generals. Each brigade consisted of from three to four regiments, and a regiment comprised from three to four troops, or companies. It was the framework of an army, hastily organized with provision for indefinite extension.

The troops or companies, or fuerzas, as they were generally known, were local, and at that time nearly all cavalry. They operated in districts wherein both officers and men had always lived and were well known, as in the case of Andarje's and Rojas' commands. Two troops constituted a squadron, with a maximum strength (including non-commissioned officers) of one hundred armed men (armados, or bearers of long arms, rifles or shot-guns). Every force was allowed by regulation to muster desarmados to one-fourth of its strength of armed men. These desarmados (the impedimenta) included a servant, or asistente, for every commissioned officer under the rank of Major (two asistentes for Majors and above), and camp followers, roustabouts, ready to fetch water, cook, and do all sorts of work that might absorb the attention of the armados.

Anybody who has travelled with a cavalry troop knows how large a percentage of the force is daily occupied purely in camp duties, and will recognize the economy of arms attendant on this system. Moreover, these desarmados are always ready to take the long arms of the dead, and weapons coming to the force by capture and become available in the skirmish line.

Every squadron was supposed to muster a blacksmith; but in Matanzas and Las Villas there was great difficulty in getting horseshoes, even nails, and in Camaguey, owing to the softness of the forest roads, shoeing, especially in the rainy season, was not absolutely necessary.

In districts where horseflesh is scarce, a force contained a percentage of infantry, as Marto's force in Las Villas.

Besides the local forces, were the expeditionary regiments, recruited generally through the Island, men who had arrived on expeditions from abroad, Spanish deserters; in fact, everything that came along. These men usually were detailed to accompany general officers on their crisscross marches, through their provinces or districts.

The followers of Gomez and Maceo in their invasion of the four Western provinces, including the Orientales (Quintin Bandera's negro infantry), were all expeditionaries, and were termed at the time, "The Invading Army"; for few local forces had then taken the field. When the Western provinces rose, local forces were organized everywhere and kept the country unpacified, while the expeditionary forces marched to and fro, making special demonstrations wherever necessary.

The officers of a squadron, or a full company of infantry, were a Major (in command), a Captain, two Lieutenants and an Alferez, four Sergeants and eight Corporals, the number of officers and non-commissioned officers being large in proportion to the number of enlisted men. A squadron of two local forces acting in co-operation, or an unusually numerous force, was commanded by Colonel or Lieutenant-Colonel.

Every general officer was entitled to an escolta, or bodyguard, to number from 40 to 80 men, usually expeditionaries appointed to this service.

It will be seen that a General of Brigade or Division could speedily mobilize a considerable number of local forces, and travel with as many as need be. I have always found, however, that the Generals were accompanied by small commands, partly because, in the absence of a commissary department, and the impossibility (at least in the Western provinces) of organizing one, there was difficulty in feeding a concentrated body of men.

A small force could live comfortably on the country, roping a steer, or digging up potatoes, as it went along, but the concentration of large forces invariably brought hunger, especially in a country already ravaged by armies. The case was different at the time of the invasion, for the country was new to war, and the "Invading Army" had only to help themselves.

On enlisting in the "Liberating Army" either as an armado or an asistente, a soldier took an oath to support the constitution of the Republic. He was then furnished with a cedula, giving the date of his enlistment, his name and description.

T

A Corporal, Sergeant, or an Alferez was appointed by the General of Brigade, on application of his troop commanders, and received a formal warrant. Commissioned officers were appointed by the Commander-in-Chief, on application of the Generals of Brigade or Division, and received commissions. Naturally, owing to the difficulty of communication, many officers held rank on commissions signed by Generals of Division only; though such commissions were not in accordance with the regulations.

Generals of Brigade and Division held authority through appointment of the Cabinet Council and Minister of War, approved by the Commander-in-Chief.

Both Gomez and his Lieutenant, Antonio Maceo, held authority through the appointment of the same convention that appointed Cisneros President, and panelled the first Cabinet.

The President of the Republic was, by the Law of Military Organization of January 27th, 1896, Commander-in-Chief of all the forces, ranking the General-in-Chief Gomez; but he could only put himself at the head of the army by consent of the Cabinet Council of War (Consejo de Guerra).

In the civil department, Governors and Lieutenant-Governors of Provinces and collectors of taxes held commissions from the Cabinet Council, signed by the Minister of the Interior. Prefects and sub-prefects were appointees of the Provincial Governors, from whom they received commissions, and they in turn might issue cedulas to such armed men as they needed as scouts and to artisans employed in the workshops under their direction.

The legal form of a Prefect's, or Sub-prefect's commission is accurately described by Mr. T. R. Dawley, Jr., in *Leslie's Weekly*, from which I clip the following: —

" The document consists of a sheet of paper about six by nine inches. In the upper left-hand corner is stamped

'Republic of Cuba — Lieutenant-Governor of Trinidad,' with the coat-of-arms of the republic in the centre. It reads thus: 'According to the faculties conceded to me by the law as lieutenant-governor of this district, I have seen fit to name you prefecto of Charco-Azul, trusting that you will know how to comply with the duties which the office imposes upon you in interest of the republic — Patria y Libertad — Cabargancito, December 10th, 1896. El Teniente Gobernador, Enrique Gomez. To the Citizen Juan Bautisto Placé.'"

In the same article, Mr. Dawley, illustrating the difficulties of a Cuban civil officer in Las Villas, continues:—

"The prefecto showed me many of his official documents, which are deposited in the archives carried around his secretary's neck. These were saved from falling into the hands of the Spanish soldiers by the trusty secretary throwing himself into the bush and tumbling over a rocky precipice. He now exhibits himself with his shirt torn into shreds, minus a hat, and body badly scratched. He has shown me the public documents of two marriages officiated by the prefecto, and the proceedings in one case of breach of promise."

Appendix B

Two American Correspondents have lost their lives in Cuba. Mr. Govin, who was murdered by Colonel Ochoa on July 9th, 1896, and Mr. Crosby who was shot while witnessing a skirmish at Santa Teresa, in Las Villas, on March 9th, 1897.

It seems that Mr. Crosby, with Gomez and his staff, was on the outskirts of a forest, watching the Spanish advance across the savanna. The Spanish fire was heavy, and Gomez' horse went down under a well-directed volley. At almost the same moment, Mr. Crosby, who was looking at the enemy through his field-glass, fell from his saddle, between his horse's legs, clutching his head with both hands. He died almost instantly, pierced by a Mauser bullet through the brain, and without a sound.

Mr. Govin was a New Yorker by birth and education, and his father was a member of the Florida bar, for many years Collector of the Port of Key West, and at one time United States Consul at Leghorn. Govin went to Cuba, in an expedition, to join the insurgents, as correspondent of the *Jacksonville Equator-Democrat*, and he bore a correspondent's certificate, endorsed by a Notary Public at Key West, together with a passport signed by Secretary Olney. He carried neither firearms nor machete, and had scarcely been with the insurgents a week, at the time he fell in with Ochoa's command.

Mr. Govin's death, had I been one of the eye-witnesses, would have made a fitting climax to my chapter on atrocities. No statement by an actual eye-witness, to my knowledge, has yet been published; but I know of no more circumstantial and trustworthy account of the affair, than the one furnished me by Major Julio Rodriguez Baz, of Lacret's Division, while he was my guest at the Harvard Club, in New York, in September, 1896. Mr. Baz' statement, as taken down by me, was published in the *Journal* on the 14th of that month, and from it I quote freely.

"Early in July I commanded a small force in the province of Havana, and marched in co-operation with Major Valencia, in whose troop Mr. Govin found himself on his way to join General Maceo.

"On the morning of the 9th of July, Major Valencia's troop of forty men skirmished with the column of Colonel Ochoa, at Correderas, in Jaruco District, near Havana. On retiring from force of numbers, Major Valencia found himself hemmed in by the advance guards of two columns unexpectedly advancing in support of Ochoa. Mr. Govin, as Major Valencia told me, had been requested to remain with the main force; but filled with enthusiasm, he lingered to take a near view of the advancing Spanish infantry.

"On finding his force surrounded, Major Valencia at once gave the order to scatter, 'each man for himself,' and retired with two of his aides under cover of an arroyo, but Govin was nowhere to be found. Time was not to be lost. The little troop, accustomed to tight pinches in a country full of Spanish soldiery, dispersed like the mist."

"We were," said Major Valencia, "in an almost level country, with a small hill to our right; to our left a rolling pasture shut in by a stone-wall, almost hidden in wild pine-apple and brush. The Jaruco high-road lay before us, upon which Ochoa's troops could be seen approaching. Behind the hill at converging angles come the two co-operating Spanish columns.

"Mr. Govin was well mounted, but unaccustomed to

prompt movements of insurgents' forces, he was without a guide. He rode up the little hill only to see Spanish troops advancing from three directions, and an open country about him. His last movements were watched by seven of Major Valencia's soldiers, four white men and three negroes, who had lost their horses in the skirmish early in the day and could not escape with the rest.

"They crouched in the heavy undergrowth of pineapple that skirted the stone-wall of the Jaruco road. These men witnessed his death and reported it to Major Valencia after the columns had retired.

"Mr. Govin, finding himself lost, and trusting to General Weyler's announcement that those who present themselves shall be spared, and being also confident of his rights as a neutral American citizen, rode boldly up to Jaruco high-road to meet the column in command of Ochoa.

"He waved his white handkerchief as he rode. The men in hiding beneath the stone-wall saw him join the advance guard and talk for a moment with the sergeant in command. He was then detained until the main body of infantry and the staff arrived. Then the eye-witnesses, who were only fifty yards away, saw him led before Colonel Ochoa, who dismounted and addressed him with vehemence and gesticulation. His papers were torn from his pockets, and his clothing hurriedly searched. No weapons were found; but the red sealed correspondent's certificate and passport signed by Mr. Olney were handed to Ochoa, who glanced them over and scornfully threw them on the ground.

"At the wave of Ochoa's hand Govin was bound, with his arms back of him, and the rope passed about his waist. An aguacate tree grew near by the high-road, and to this he was led and roughly tied. Colonel Ochoa followed and stood by. Then some non-commissioned officers drew their machetes and stepped up to the tree. In a few moments everything was over.

"The men in hiding under the stone-wall lay there till sunset, when the troops had returned to Jaruco. Then they went to Govin's body, and buried it where it had fallen from its bonds and lay cut in pieces near the aguacate tree. They joined Major Valencia late that night and made a formal report of what they had seen."

"These details," went on Mr. Baz, "I repeat as they were given to me by Major Valencia, . . . and as I wrote them in a deposition before a Notary Public in Key West, at the request of P. L. Govin, brother of the victim, who intended to forward a statement of the facts to the Government at Washington."

Major Baz, who was the first to bring an authentic account of the Govin affair to the United States, returned soon after to Cuba. He was a man of good position, and at the outbreak of the insurrection he was Portuguese Consul in Havana. I have never heard his statement contradicted. If I am to credit the despatch of a Havana correspondent, Ochoa boastfully wore and displayed Govin's watch and sleeve buttons about Havana after the incident, after the manner in which the Duke of Ahumada wore and jested over the wedding-ring found on the finger of Antonio Maceo.

Appendix C

I CANNOT speak from my own experience of Weyler's concentration policy. It was put in force by the Captain-General some months after I left the Island.

Mr. Stephen Bonsal, however, writes that "by the 1st of December, 1896, 400,000 non-combatants and peace-loving peasants, including their aged and infirm parents, their wives and their children, were 'concentrated' in the stations, which, whether they were chosen with this object in view or not, have proven admirably adapted to the realization of a policy of extermination" ("Real Condition of Cuba To-day," p. 99).

These people were driven from their homes, which were burned, and (May, 1897) "from the Jucaro-Moron trocha westward to Cape San Antonio," outside of the towns, of course, "not a single home, however modest and lowly, has been left standing."

Penniless and unable to find work, these peasants were herded within or on the outskirts of the cities and larger towns, and a dead-line was drawn about them by a "blood-thirsty and brutalized soldiery" ready to inflict a speedy death on those who attempted "escape from their pens."

Mr. Bonsal describes a colony of *concentrados*, living, or rather dying, on the Cascorro hill in the city of Matanzas. In the latter part of March, 1897, this colony numbered about 3000 people. The dead-cart daily carried away between 25 and 30 victims of starvation.

Cascorro hill was a healthy residence with perfect natural drainage. "Had the scantiest rations been served out to them or even the most ordinary sanitary laws been enforced, there would have been but little danger of sickness breaking out among them."

"Without exception," Mr. Bonsal continues, "all the other places of residence which have been assigned to the *concentrados*, I found to be uniformly on swampy and low-lying ground, where the most intelligent care and the best of attention could not have prevented the outbreak of the several epidemics by which they are ravaged" (page 120).

Such was the condition of the *concentrados* before the opening of the rainy season, when intense heat and moisture and lack of sanitation make every town a nest of typhus and malarial fever. And these country people, one must remember, "are as unacclimated to fever as though they were Germans and Swedes recently landed. For on the highlands where they have lived a case of fever is quite as rare an occurrence as it is in New York city" (page 127).

Without medicines or medical attendance, it would be interesting to know how many of the original 400,000 are alive to-day.

Appendix D

The Effects of the Modern Mauser Bullet

For two decades military experts, both at home and abroad, have studied to construct a model magazine rifle, with double the range and power of either the Martini-Henry or the Springfield "long-toms," and an ammunition so decreased in weight as to enable a soldier to go into action with a triple allowance of cartridges comfortably packed in his belt. These requirements are fulfilled by three modern rifles,— the Krag-Jorgensen, already adopted by the United States; the Lee-Metford, with which England is arming her forces; and the Mauser, issued by Spain to her regular infantry.

The Mauser Bullet.

The bullets shot by all three are practically of the same pattern. Soft lead will not stand the strain caused by the quick twist in modern rifling; therefore the modern bullet is long, built of hardened lead encased in an envelope of cupro-nickel, turned over at the end to prevent the gas, on explosion of the charge, from getting between the envelope and the leaden core beneath, with a calibre of .305 to .315 inch, no larger than a small lead pencil.

It was thought that the vastly increased range and rapidity of fire of the new weapons would increase the enemy's percentage of disabled, and correspondingly thin his fighting ranks by the number of men required to transport the wounded to the rear,—this on the theory that wounded men hamper an army more than the dead, for whom nothing more has to be done.

On the score of fulfilling their inventors' hopes the Krag-Jorgensen, the Lee-Metford, and the Mauser are eminently successful, the first having, on test, driven its bullet intact into something like seven feet of solid plank; but it remains for the surgical history of the Cuban war to prove that, before the modern bullets can be relied upon to kill or really disable, a further change must be made in their construction.

The clean little Mauser ball, for instance, speeds on its way, sterilizing itself by friction with the atmosphere, and traverses the human anatomy, leaving (at ordinary ranges) a wound scarcely larger at the point of exit than at the point of entrance, and causing only a trifling hemorrhage. Unless it ricochets, or bursts its nickel cap through undue expansion of the lead beneath, it never carries particles of clothing into the flesh, and if it encounters a bone on its route, it drills a small round hole and passes on its way, rarely splintering, shattering, or causing dangerous complications.

Thus, as in several cases that have come under my personal notice, a man may be struck by a Mauser in the thigh or knee-joint, and speedily recover with full use of the joints, while in previous military surgery wounds of the kind have been followed by one of three things, — amputation, death, or permanent lameness.

So slight is the fear of Mauser wounds among the Cuban forces that it has become rather a discredit to a soldier not to have one or more wounds, and for this reason you frequently see men expose themselves needlessly to fire, as a child darts from a doorway into a heavy rain and scampers back again for mere excitement.

At the battle of Saratoga, besides the eleven who were either killed outright or died within a few hours from serious abdominal wounds, sixty-four insurgents were treated in the extemporized hospitals, and forty of them, after one dressing, reported for duty within twenty-four hours. Several others (like Guitierrez at Manajanabo) did not require any especial treatment for wounds through their arms and legs, which scarcely bled and amounted to nothing more than jokes for the parilla fires.

Major Guerin's souvenir of Saratoga.

One extraordinary case was that of Major Paulino Guerin, a bluff and sturdy aide-de-camp, who was struck in the hip (at about 400 yards) late in the afternoon of June 10, while Gomez and his staff were reconnoitring the breastworks thrown up by the enemy on Saratoga hill. The bullet passed through a loose cartridge in the pocket of Guerin's coat, and obliquely through his body, coming out behind and above the hip joint on the right side. It must have cut through some of the intestines; but Major Guerin did not dismount at the time, but had his wound dressed on making camp an hour later. I asked Major Guerin if it did not hurt him; but he replied that it did not "very much," and showed me the pierced cartridge with great pride, assuring me that he felt no fever. I actually saw him in the saddle on the following day, and I never learned that he suffered any evil effects of his injury.

While in Matanzas with Lacret, I saw a man who had recovered perfectly from a remarkable wound. While riding from action, leaning far forward on his saddle to escape fire (at a range of 300 yards), he was struck in the back by a Mauser bullet. The bullet passed (in medical parlance) through the upper portion of the scapula on the right side, through the superficial neck muscles, beneath

Appendix D

the angle of the jaw, and made its exit through the orbital cavity, carrying with it a portion of the right eye. On his back this man bore a tiny white cicatrice, less noticeable than a vaccination mark. Barring the loss of his eye, he offered no other trace of the wound than a deep scarified furrow at the base of his eyebrow, where the Mauser had made its exit.

I had occasion to witness an illustration of the Mauser lack of systemic shock or "stopping power" in Las Villas, where, while retreating from an infantry column, a soldier was struck in

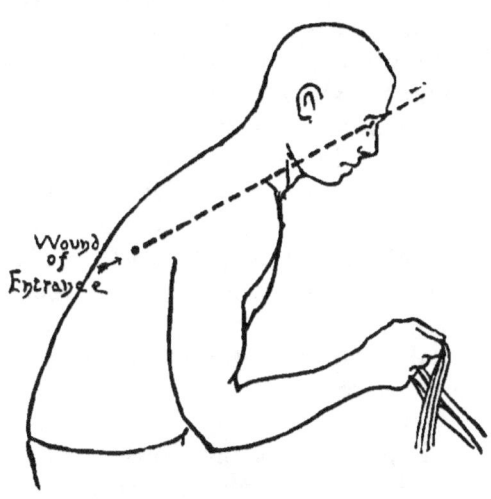

A case of perfect recovery.

the head (at about 500 yards) by a stray shot. He swerved in his saddle for an instant with an "Ay, mi madre!" but promptly straightened up and jogged on. We supposed that the ball had merely passed through his hat; but, after riding perhaps twenty feet, he collapsed on the pommel of his saddle and fell between his horse's feet, dead. The ball had passed directly through his temples, as two small spots of blood in the short hair on either side proved, and it must have caused a hemorrhage of the brain. So far as one could judge, he received less shock than would have been given by an ordinary twenty-two short-calibre bullet shot from a Flaubert rifle.

Excepting abdominal wounds, of which the victims either recovered speedily or died in agony several hours afterwards, the only case of a really painful wound from a Mauser ball, that occurs to me, was received by Brigadier-General Vegas in the leg, on May 10th, near Manajanabo. In this instance the bullet ricochetted from a stony path which Gomez and his staff were ascending at the time, tearing its nickel cover, and carried a piece of Vegas' leather legging into the wound. General Vegas suffered great pain and required almost the daily attendance by Dr. Abreu, the staff-surgeon, for two weeks, and had not ceased to feel the wound when I last saw him a month afterwards. Thus it will be seen that, unless the small-calibre bullet can be clipped or perforated so as to cause it to mushroom, or spread, on striking, it is not sufficient to deter men from advancing or continuing to fight when wounded, unless they happen to be of the fifteen per cent[1] or so of the total wounded who are unlucky enough to be struck in vital places.

I quote from the New York *Sunday Journal* of August 9, 1896, the following extraordinary (perhaps phenomenal) cases, recorded by an American surgeon in the Cuban field; because they are quite in line with my own superficial observations, and I have no doubt that he is scientifically accurate in detail.

"Case * — José H., wounded in the shoulder by a Mauser. The bullet entered the left breast, slightly above the heart, ranged to the left and upward. This bullet passed directly through the upper lobe of the left lung, perforating the scapula on its exit from the body. The wounds of entrance and exit were almost of the same size. There was very little inversion or eversion of tissue, and absolutely no hemorrhage. The man felt slight discomfort, had a slight cough on the second day, but without bloody expectoration. He refused to be confined to his bed or hammock. The wound was first dressed by a

---

[1] I have this percentage, on rough observations, of number of dead and wounded in the several skirmishes mentioned.

peasant, and a soiled sheet was used as a bandage. There were only four dressings, and on the tenth day the patient was performing his regular duties as a private soldier."

"Case ** — Private soldier wounded at 300 yards. Mauser bullet entered the abdomen, ranging upward and to the left. It made its exit considerably to the left of the spinal column. There was very little hemorrhage and no pain. The man received no treatment for four days, other than that of the peasants, who swathed the body in cloths, none too clean. On the fourth day the wound was dressed by a surgeon, and cotton held by rubber adhesive plaster was applied, which was the only dressing available in camp. The temperature did not rise even one degree; the pulse was normal, and recovery splendid. The ball, after going through the abdominal cavity, must have passed through several coils of intestines."

"Case *** — Is similar in character to above. Corporal Alfred G———. Mauser, wounded at 400 yards. The bullet passed first through his right forearm, entered the abdominal cavity, slightly below and in front of the twelfth rib, continued directly through the body, and came out on the left side. The wound of exit was slightly larger than the wound of entrance. There was a slight hemorrhage. No treatment was received for several days, and no operative proceedings were instituted, there being absolutely no chance for same. The patient was cared for by peasants in a hut well ventilated, but filthy beyond description. Recovery was perfect. Wounds of this kind have heretofore always resulted in death."

"Case **** — While not dangerous to life, illustrates the power of the Mauser to penetrate bones without dangerous complications. Lieutenant E———, wounded at Saratoga, just below the middle of his leg. Bullet penetrated the tibia, making a single round hole just the size of the bullet. There was no shattering or splintering of the bone, such as always occurs with a copper-headed or leaden bullet. Hemorrhage was considerable. Lieutenant E—— received no treatment for several days, and the wound healed without suppuration, although recovery was slow."

"Case ***** — J. E., private soldier, was struck by a Mauser bullet, which entered directly in the centre of his knee-cap. The bullet perforated the patella with a range slightly to the right. The wound of exit was one inch to the right of the median line, and the joint cavity was open. There was no splintering of the bone, and a small, round hole was the only visible wound. The wound of exit in this case was considerably larger than that of entrance. The knee was dressed by peasants, who took him into their cabin, which was all the treatment he received for several days. The wound healed perfectly, with the motion as good as ever."[1]

In these cases, the sturdy health and moderate diet of the patients, combined with open-air surroundings, contributed vastly to the speedy recovery. There is, however, a startling contrast, when we turn to the "Surgical History of the Civil War," and read of the effects of the old-fashioned army rifle-bullet from cases directly corresponding to the ones cited above, all of which proved fatal: —

Case (which corresponds to case of the soldier wounded in Matanzas, recorded in diagram above) — Private Wilbur F. Matthews, Twenty-Fourth Indiana, wounded on second day of battle of Shiloh; musket ball entered through scapula, or shoulder, on the right side, the wound entrance being irregular in shape and of the dimensions of a silver quarter, splintered the shoulder and shoulder-blade, causing injuries that would in themselves have proved fatal; then ploughed up through the muscles of

---

[1] At very close range, a few yards from the muzzle, owing to a supposed peculiarity of its rotary motion, the Mauser is said to be far more deadly. Captain Ramirez, who fell at Saratoga at close range, fifty yards or so, had three wounds, all of which appeared larger and showed traces of greater hemorrhage than wounds at longer ranges.

the neck, and actually blew away the jaw-bone and side of the face. The bullet flattened into an irregular shape, finding final lodgment in the socket of the eye, which it dislodged. With these terrible injuries Matthews lingered for two days.

* — Private Henry L. Newman, Eleventh Missouri, Wilson's Creek. Lead rifle bullet entered left breast above the heart, ranged upward and to the left, passing through the upper lobe of the left lung, and, emerging at the shoulder, fractured it and tore a great hole through the shoulder-blade. Newman lingered in great agony for seventy-two hours.

** — Private Wilson, First Ohio Artillery, Chickamauga, musket ball entered abdomen to the left of navel, ranged upward and to the left, passing through the lung, and made its exit to the left of the spinal column. The wound was large enough to pass a handkerchief through.

*** — Sergeant Evan A. Morris, Forty-Third Illinois Cavalry. Minie ball at 400 yards passed through left forearm, with which he was guiding his horse, actually severing both bones so that shreds of muscle alone prevented it from falling away, entered the abdomen, making a most hideous hole, as the ball had been twisted into the shape of an hour glass, and emerged on the left side, below the twelfth rib, the wound of exit being twice as large as the frightful hole by which it entered.

**** — Private Guy, Thirty-Ninth North Carolina, at Stone River. Musket ball entered at the junction of the middle and upper third of the tibia, or large bone of the lower part of the leg, actually carrying away a piece two inches long, while the remainder of the bone above and below was fractured in innumerable places. The bone was fairly shattered, as was the smaller one next to it. Guy died from the shock shortly after.

***** — Private Jonathan Harris, Seventy-Fourth New York. Minie ball of .58 calibre struck the patella, or flat bone of the knee, squarely breaking it into fragments of bone gravel and fracturing every bone of the knee. The diagram of the record, which shows the fractured limb as if reset, shows over 100 fragments of bone. In an observation of 351 cases of gunshot injury to the knee, 27.9 per cent were fatal, and amputation was resorted to in 79 per cent of the cases.

By disposing thus lightly of the effects of the new bullet, it must not be inferred that there is no suffering among the wounded in the Cuban field. In the cases of men injured in the trivial skirmishes, or exchanging of shots that occur so constantly throughout the island between the insurgents and the guerilla bands and cavalry advance guards of marching columns, a different story is told. The guerillas are armed with the Remington carbine, and the "long-tom" of the same pattern is also supplied to some regiments of royal troops. Wounds from these weapons present the same characteristics as those taken from the surgical records of our late Civil War. The surgeon whose Cuban cases I quote above describes a wound by the "yellow ammunition," by far the deadliest known in Cuba. The "yellow" bullets are tipped with a casing of copper alloy, which tears and mushrooms easily on entrance, with such serious effects that a rumor spread that they were explosive. The case in question was that of a soldier struck in the hip, the "yellow" bullet splintering the bones in every direction, carrying away a bundle of tissue, and leaving a hole of exit into which one could have thrust a large orange.

www.ingramcontent.com/pod-product-compliance
Lightning Source LLC
Chambersburg PA
CBHW021207230426
43667CB00006B/591